Other Banalities

Melanie Klein is one of the few analysts whose body of work has inspired sociologists, philosophers, religious scholars, literary critics and political theorists, all attracted to the cross-fertilisation of her ideas. *Other Banalities* represents a long overdue exploration of her legacy, including contributions from acclaimed interdisciplinary scholars and practitioners.

The contributors situate Klein within the history of the psychoanalytic movement, investigate her key theoretical and clinical advances, and look at how her thought has informed contemporary perspectives in the behavioural sciences and humanities. Topics covered range from Klein's major psychological theories to clinical pathology, child development, philosophy, sociology, politics, religion, ethics and aesthetics.

This volume reflects the auspicious future for Kleinian revivalism and demonstrates the broad relevance of Kleinian thought. It will be of great interest to scholars and practitioners of psychology, psychoanalysis and psychotherapy.

Jon Mills is a psychologist, philosopher and psychoanalyst in private practice in Ajax, Ontario, Canada. He is Diplomate in Psychoanalysis and Clinical Psychology with the American Board of Professional Psychology, Director of Curriculum Development, Adler School of Graduate Studies, and President of the Section on Psychoanalysis of the Canadian Psychological Association.

Contributors: C. Fred Alford, Marilyn Charles, Walter A. Davis, Michael Eigen, James S. Grotstein, Keith Haartman, R.D. Hinshelwood, Jon Mills, Michael Rustin, Robert Maxwell Young.

Other Banalities

Melanie Klein Revisited

Edited by Jon Mills

Routledge
Taylor & Francis Group

LONDON AND NEW YORK

First published 2006
by Routledge
27 Church Road, Hove, East Sussex BN3 2FA

Simultaneously published in the USA and Canada
by Routledge
270 Madison Ave, New York, NY 10016

Routledge is an imprint of the Taylor & Francis Group

Typeset in Times by RefineCatch Ltd, Bungay, Suffolk
Printed and bound in Great Britain by
TJ International Ltd, Padstow, Cornwall
Paperback cover design by Jim Wilkie
Cover painting: 60 × 36″, oil on canvas, 'The Blaze Within' (2003)
by Jon Mills

This publication has been produced with paper manufactured to strict environmental standards and with pulp derived from sustainable forests

British Library Cataloguing in Publication Data
A catalogue record for this book is available from the British Library

Library of Congress Cataloging in Publication Data
Other banalities: Melanie Klein revisited/Jon Mills, editor.
    p. cm.
  Includes bibliographical references and index.
  ISBN 1–58391–750–0 (hbk)—ISBN 1–58391–751–9 (pbk)
1. Psychoanalysis.   2. Klein, Melanie.   I. Mills, Jon, 1964–
  BF175.O845 2006
150.19′5′092—dc22

                                        2005022267

ISBN10: 1–58391–750–0 (hbk)
ISBN10: 1–58391–751–9 (pbk)

ISBN13: 978–1–58391–750–3 (hbk)
ISBN13: 978–1–58391–751–0 (pbk)

Contents

About the contributors

C. Fred Alford, Ph.D. is Professor of Government and Distinguished Scholar-Teacher at the University of Maryland, College Park, President of the Political Psychology Section of the American Political Science Association, and on the editorial boards of several journals including the *Journal of Psycho-Social Studies, Journal of Psychoanalysis, Culture and Society, Political Psychology, Psychoanalytic Studies* and *Theory and Society*. He is the author of several books including *Levinas, Psychoanalysis, and the Frankfurt School, Group Psychology and Political Theory, The Psychoanalytic Theory of Greek Tragedy*, and *Melanie Klein and Critical Social Theory*.

Marilyn Charles, Ph.D. is a staff psychologist at the Austin Riggs Center, and in private practice in Stockbridge, Massachusetts. A poet and an artist herself, she has a special interest in the creative process and in facilitating creativity in patients and in clinicians. She is a Training and Supervising Analyst with the Michigan Psychoanalytic Council, Adjunct Professor of Clinical Psychology at Michigan State University, and the author of *Patterns: Building Blocks of Creativity*; *Learning From Experience: A Clinician's Guide*; and *Constructing Realities*.

Walter A. Davis, Ph.D. is Professor Emeritus in the English Department at the Ohio State University, and the author of a number of books on psychoanalytic cultural criticism including *Inwardness and Existence: Subjectivity in/and Hegel, Heidegger, Marx, and Freud; Get the Guests: Psychoanalysis, Modern American Drama, and the Audience; Deracination: Historicity, Hiroshima and the Tragic Imperative*; and *An Evening with JonBenét Ramsey*.

Michael Eigen, Ph.D. is Associative Clinical Professor of Psychology, New York University Postdoctoral Program in Psychotherapy and Psychoanalysis, editor of *The Psychoanalytic Review*, and the author of twelve books including *Rage, Ecstasy, The Sensitive Self, The Psychotic Core*, and *Psychic Deadness*.

James S. Grotstein, M.D. is Clinical Professor of Psychiatry at UCLA School of Medicine and a Training and Supervising Analyst at the Los Angeles Psychoanalytic Institute and at the Psychoanalytic Center of California, Los Angeles. He is past North American Vice-President of the International Psychoanalytic Association. He is the author and/or editor of seven books including *Who Is the Dreamer Who Dreams The Dream? A Study of Psychic Presences*.

Keith Haartman, Ph.D. is a psychoanalyst in private practice in Toronto. He completed his graduate degree in Religious Studies from the University of Toronto and is a graduate of the Toronto Institute for Contemporary Psychoanalysis. He teaches in the Department of Religion and the Creative Writing Program at the University of Toronto and is author of *Watching and Praying: Personality Transformation in 18th Century Methodism*.

R.D. Hinshelwood, M.D. is a Member of the British Psychoanalytic Society, and a Fellow of the Royal College of Psychiatrists. He was previously Clinical Director of The Cassel Hospital and is currently Professor at the Centre for Psychoanalytic Studies, University of Essex. He has authored many books including *A Dictionary of Kleinian Thought*; *Clinical Klein*; *Thinking about Institutions*; and *Therapy or Coercion*.

Jon Mills, Psy.D., Ph.D., ABPP is a psychologist, philosopher, and psychoanalyst in private practice in Ajax, Ontario, Canada. He is a Diplomate in Psychoanalysis and Clinical Psychology with the American Board of Professional Psychology, President of the Section on Psychoanalysis of the Canadian Psychological Association, Director of Curriculum Development, Adler School of Graduate Studies, editor of an international book series, *Contemporary Psychoanalytic Studies*, and on the editorial board of *Psychoanalytic Psychology*. He is the author and/or editor of nine books including *Treating Attachment Pathology*; *The Unconscious Abyss: Hegel's Anticipation of Psychoanalysis*; and an existential novel, *When God Wept*.

Michael Rustin, MA, AcSS is Professor of Sociology at the University of East London, and a Visiting Professor at the Tavistock Clinic in London. He is the author of *The Good Society and the Inner World: Psychoanalysis, Culture, Politics*; *Reason and Unreason: Psychoanalysis, Science and Politics*; *Narratives of Love and Loss: Studies in Modern Children's Fiction*; and *Mirror to Nature: Drama, Psychoanalysis and Society*. *Reason and Unreason* received a Gradiva Award from the National Association for the Advancement of Psychoanalysis in 2002.

Robert Maxwell Young, Ph.D., was for many years Director of the Wellcome Unit for the History of Medicine and a Fellow of King's College, Cambridge. He was later and until his retirement Professor of Psychotherapy and Psychoanalytic Studies at the University of Sheffield. He is also Honoured Professor and Co-Director of the Institute of Human Relations at the New Bulgarian University. He is a Full Member of the Lincoln Clinic and Institute of Psychotherapy and the Forum for Independent Psychotherapists and registered with the British Confederation of Psychotherapists and the United Kingdom Council for Psychotherapy. Among his many books are *Mind, Brain and Adaptation*; *Darwin's Metaphor, Mental Space*; and *Whatever Happened to Human Nature?* He founded Free Association Books, edits the journal *Free Associations*, is associate editor of the ejournal *Kleinian Studies* and is on the board of a number of journals concerned with psychoanalysis, science, and culture.

Introduction

Jon Mills

Perhaps no one since Freud has offered psychoanalysis such a robust and profound paradigm of mind as Melanie Klein. In the words of Hanna Segal, "The vitality and importance of her work cannot be doubted,"[1] leading Julia Kristeva to declare that she "has become a major figure of indisputable worth."[2] In fact, her theories are so penetrating and controversial, that she is readily misinterpreted or rendered too opaque to be properly appreciated. Whether loved or hated, during her lifetime she was both unsettling and monumental – to the point of revolution. Many tried to discredit her unjustly, culminating in the contentious "controversial discussions" of the British Psycho-Analytical Society where she went head-to-head with Anna Freud and her followers, what antagonist Edward Glover later referred to as the "Klein imbroglio," despite the fact that he had previously referred to her work as "a landmark in analytical literature."[3]

Klein has been "sniffled at,"[4] labeled a "heretic,"[5] "branded, vilified, and mocked,"[6] and even called an "inspired gut butcher."[7] In a letter to Jones, Freud writes that despite his "opinion" that the British Society had followed Klein down "a wrong path," he nevertheless conceded that since her observations of children were "foreign" to him, he had "no right to any fixed conviction."[8] Let the ladies battle it out for themselves! And so after the debates solidified, the society arrived at a "gentlemen's agreement": the two factions diplomatically resigned themselves to a mutual, amicable co-habitation within the society, and as an offshoot, an independent, "middle group" was formed. But Freud held a grudge that Jones did not back his daughter. Jones himself waffled in his support of Klein while attempting to ingratiate himself to the master. After inviting her to England and paving the way for her reception in the British Society – where Klein was inducted as the first female member – he proved to be an indecisive sycophant. In a letter to Anna Freud, although acknowledging Klein's contributions, Jones writes that she "has neither a scientific nor an orderly mind and her presentations are lamentable."[9] But in another letter, Jones is equally unflattering of Anna Freud who he said had "no pioneering originality."[10] For Jones, Melanie was trail-blazing yet rueful, while Anna was simply banal.[11]

Klein's work is another kind of banality, one based on the ordinary nature of unconscious revelation: anxiety and desire, love and hate, envy and guilt – we know them all too well. Klein's vision of the psyche is a radicalization of projectively re-internalized oppression, a discourse on the aggressively internalized *Other* – both destructive and appetitive, horrific yet sublime – a brilliant simplicity of repetition sustained through a cacophony of opposing forces. What is banal is what is most basic, most essential – namely, the internalization of objects subjected to our own desires. And just as objects are abject, thus dominated by anxiety, persecution, and dread, desires are base, sadistic, gluttonous – evoking and sustaining an antediluvian pattern of projection and introjection – a brilliant simplicity – the foundations of mind.

No one can read Klein without experiencing some form of ambivalence. The "positions" attribute advanced psychological processes to an infant's mind derived from the most primitive forms of anxiety and sadism to the refined expressions of love and reparation based upon the labor of self-reflective conscience. Is this fantastic or merely fantasy? And her direct inter-pretation of children's fantasies in the consulting room evokes an ethical concern of traumatization.[12] But here Klein offers her most incredible obser-vations and theoretical musings on the ontology of unconscious life. From her early extensions and departures from classical theory that generated both disapproval from Freud as well as rupture within the British Psycho-Analytical Society, to her remarkable ability to forge a new movement in theory and practice, she became, in the words of Phyllis Grosskurth, "the stuff of which myths are made."[13]

But Klein's evolving theories were born out of a return to Freud. She reified the death drive (*Todestrieb*) and canonized the subterranean dominion of fantasy and internalization, thus becoming the edifice and fulcrum of her own system. Paradoxically orthodox and indebted to Freud, her texts are peppered with quotes from the founder despite her revisionistic project. No genius is content in deferring to others, so it is merely natural that her work would lead to theoretical supplements, clinical modifications, and redirecting shifts in emphasis. And with this came the charges of subversive-ness that threatened group loyalties uncritically pledged to Freud's original formulations. Yet Klein's clinical observations carried their own inferential conclusions: death and anxiety became the cornerstone of psychic economy dominated by unconscious "phantasy" instantiated originally as an aggres-sive object relation, only later to become converted into our capacity to love. As a result, the Oedipus complex logically emerged much earlier than was professed by Freud, along with the notion that the superego was present at birth. This explained, among other things, why the transference was rapidly conspicuous in children, particularly its negative valences, and how this impacted on the explanatory and technical nature of interpretation and cure. By introducing her theoretical model of the positions and the notion of projective identification, developmental theory and clinical technique were both advanced at once. Recall that Klein practically single-handedly built the institution of child therapy. From these noteworthy achievements, we can truly appreciate how Klein's revolutionary innovations have influenced generations of analysts since her time.

Neo-Kleinians have attracted a great deal of attention for their clinical work and theoretical refinements, thus finding worldwide recognition, particularly in the United Kingdom and South America. In his exposition and critique of the contemporary Kleinians of London, Roy Schafer noted their propensity to be "loyal Freudians" who ground their conceptualizations in clinical material, repeatedly focus on transference and countertransference manifestations, emphasize interpretation, and remain devout to uncovering unconscious phantasy.[14] From this standpoint, the "Kleinian-Freudians," as Schafer calls them, are stubbornly devoted to 'analyzing' in the truest sense of the word, viz. the excavation and explication of unconscious process. This retention of classical technique steadfastly sets Kleinians apart from the interpersonal, self-psychological, and relational schools that emphasize inter-subjectivity, dialogical meaning construction, and the phenomenology of conscious experience. Despite this contemporary shift in psychoanalytic theory and technique that dominates much of the work of American training institutes under the influence of postmodern politics, we are nevertheless witnessing a firm allegiance to preserving the insights of the old school by revisiting Freud's and Klein's indelible mark on our discipline.[15]

And yet there are other banalities, such as the politics of Kleinianism. It may be said that group loyalties surrounding a particular identification with any school of thought often mirror, perhaps unconsciously, an element of theory exemplified within that school. Contemporary Kleinians are no exception. In fact, there was controversy with regard to this volume from its inception. I had originally envisioned this project as a comprehensive overview of Klein's collective body of work from the standpoint of her historical, theoretical, psychobiographical, clinical, and philosophical contributions to the behavioral sciences. Several recognized contemporary Kleinians were invited to participate in this venture, yet many declined, including all invited board members from the Melanie Klein Trust. More specifically, most of them did not even respond to my invitation. In response to this lack of interest, this project was reformulated and now focuses on revisionist Kleinian perspectives that explore topics ranging from Klein's major psychological theories to clinical pathology, child development, philosophy, sociology, politics, religion, ethics, and aesthetics. As a result, this book is one of the first interdisciplinary texts on post-Kleinian thought.

We approach any text with prejudice due to preferred identifications that inform our apprehension of any subject matter. This is only natural. And when we anticipate or fear that others will not align with our cause or promote our side, we may become suspicious, guarded, and protective – even hostile. Following Klein herself, most Kleinian writers pride themselves on offering theoretical contributions that are heavily focused on clinical material; and deviations from this format are often frowned upon. Perhaps Hanna Segal had this in mind when she declined to participate in this volume. Or perhaps it was because she does not know me. In her words, the project was "misguided." I can understand why she may take a mistrustful, deterrent attitude given that she and others from the Klein Trust in all likelihood felt ambushed and betrayed by Phyllis Grosskurth after they turned over Melanie's diaries, only to bemoan their generosity when she was unseemly portrayed. Perhaps Segal did not want to take this chance again. The need to defend our heroes and safeguard them against future exploitation reflects the need to remain attached to our idealizations, to the point that any indication that potentially threatens them, whether in reality or fantasy, is seen as an unforgivable act of dissension. One author was so offended by the title of this book that he pulled his essay at the last minute because I refused to change it. These attitudes nicely echo the splitting and paranoia that Klein herself illuminated as being elemental to human nature. Regardless of some contemporary Kleinians who are content only with pursuing clinical work, there is a value in realizing how Klein's testament extends far beyond the consulting room. And no amount of blind loyalty, narcissistic arrogance, or felt resistance can impede the pursuit of furthering our knowledge. I believe Klein herself would be elated with the extent to which her ideas have commanded such respect and influence among so many disciplines.

The contributions in this volume represent an atypical yet long overdue compilation of original essays by acclaimed interdisciplinary scholars and practitioners who explore the legacy of Melanie Klein. They range in scope from expository and exegetical attempts to situate Klein within the history of the psychoanalytic movement, to expatiating her key theoretical novelties and clinical advances, as well as how she has informed contemporary perspectives in the behavioral sciences and humanities. The contributors here are from variegated scholarly and clinical backgrounds including practicing psychoanalysts, psychologists, and psychotherapists, including those in formal psychoanalytic training environments, and academics in philosophy, sociology, literature, religion, social criticism, and political science. There is no other book of its kind that examines Kleinian thought through such extensionist and revisionist lenses.

What is further unique about this book is that the contributors are not 'Kleinians' in the sense that they are strict adherents of the British school, but are post-Kleinians coming to her work from the behavioral and social sciences and the humanities. Many authors write from within the frameworks of psychology and psychiatry, and hence their contributions are not merely a collection written by psychoanalysts from the British Psycho-Analytical Society as is typically the case among Klein books. Furthermore, the philosophers and contributors from the humanities and social sciences tend to write from phenomenological, existential, and humanistic perspectives, which differentiates them from other traditions that mainly rely on clinical case material, literary cultural theory, or postmodern sentiments. As a result, this volume brings together some of the most significant and authoritative thinkers in the field of Klein studies today.

One of the most perspicacious expositors of and commentators on Klein is R.D. Hinshelwood. His contribution situates Klein's thinking at the beginning of her career and lays the historical and biographical context for the shaping of her ideas. Several other chapters are devoted to a precise elucidation of Klein's theories as they evolved over her lifetime, including how they developed in relation to other prominent analysts and theoreticians. Known for his aesthetic prose, Michael Eigen illuminates the destructive element of Klein's theory and shows how the death drive is the fountainhead of her theories of splitting, projective identification, the developmental positions, guilt and reparation, envy and gratitude, and the striving for creativity and fulfillment. A similar aesthetic is advanced in Marilyn Charles' chapter, which, after successfully articulating several key Kleinian insights, brings them to bear on the applied conceptualization and clinical treatment of an extended case study of trauma, a subject matter Charles treats with great sensitivity, empathy, and technical skill. Robert Maxwell Young, a long-time advocate of Klein, meticulously chronicles what he considers to be her most pivotal concept, that is, projective identification. His chapter is a very thoughtful overview of how this construct has been interpreted and advanced in the psychoanalytic literature.

Klein is one of the few analysts whose body of work has inspired sociologists, philosophers, religious scholars, literary critics, and political theorists attracted to the cross-fertilization of her ideas. Michael Rustin persuasively argues how Klein's theories are one of the most important contributions to the understanding of human nature in the social sciences, including showing how relatedness is the essential aspect defining human motivation. The significance of Klein's humanistic implications can be seen in the revisionist projects of James S. Grotstein and Keith Haartman who advocate a spiritual function through psychic transcendence and the symbolic production of meaning, as well as expand on the moral and aesthetic dimension implicit in her thought. They, in particular, draw on the role of attachment and metaphor in the mediation of affect and offer extensionist perspectives on Klein's paranoid-schizoid and depressive positions. Grotstein specifically questions the developmental epigenesis of the positions and offers his amendments through scholarly rigor, while Haartman brilliantly shows how meaning is ultimately mediated by unconscious semiotics.

Klein has been rarely examined within philosophy. In my chapter, I offer an ontological systematization of Hegel's dialectical logic in relation to Klein's and Bion's notion of projective identification; and through Hegel's philosophical psychology, I argue that he anticipates and supports many of the key theoretical tenets underlying Kleinian thought. Through Hegel, Klein is philosophically legitimized, which points toward further implications dialect-ical psychoanalysis has to offer the field as a whole. Walter A. Davis also advances the philosophical, moral, and aesthetic principles of Klein's thought by examining how childhood play is an intimate engagement with the tragic. Drawing on his own moving experiences, Davis beautifully depicts how suffering is both memorialized and surpassed through the innocence of childhood fantasy. Finally, in a highly evocative and astute application of Kleinian theory, C. Fred Alford cogently shows how Klein's theoretical cor-pus is none other than an application of natural law theory. Here Alford admirably engages the question of the ethical.

If there is a theoretical thread that yokes this project together, then perhaps it may be said to broadly engage the construct of projective identification, the sum and substance of Klein's original contribution to psychoanalysis. Since Klein's introduction of this technical principle, projective identification remains the essence of psychic reality, the motional flux behind the generation of otherness, an otherness reincorporated. At once an exteriorized internal-ization, mental life becomes the reorganization of what is both familiar and alien, a generative recapitalization of previously experienced experience, the return of the same – an-*Other* banality. The contemporary revisionist theories exemplified in this volume collectively point toward an auspicious future for Kleinian revivalism that has the promise of reaching far greater audiences than those wed to clinical practice. This is what I believe Klein herself intended. In one of her last written entries of her autobiography, preoccupied with her impending death, she nicely conveys her life sentiment: "It is a mix-ture of resignation and some hope that my work will perhaps after all survive and be a great help to mankind."[16] Taken together, these essays show how Klein's psychoanalytic vision is none other than a treatise on the ontology of human experience and a harbinger for our advancement.

Notes

1 New Introduction to Klein's *Envy and Gratitude* (London: Virago Press, 1988), p. xi.
2 Julia Kristeva, *Melanie Klein*. Trans. R. Guberman (New York: Columbia University Press, 2001), p. 6.
3 Edward Glover, review of Klein's *The Psychoanalysis of Children*, in *The Inter-national Journal of Psycho-Analysis*, 14 (1933), p. 119.
4 Alix to James Strachey, January 12, 1924, *Bloomsbury/Freud: The Letters of James and Alix Strachey 1924–1925*. Eds. P. Meisel and W. Kendrick (New York: Basic Books, 1985), p. 182.
5 Judith Hughes, *Reshaping the Psychoanalytic Domain* (Berkeley: University of California Press, 1989), p. 44.
6 Phyllis Grosskurth, *Melanie Klein: Her World and her Work* (Cambridge, Mass.: Harvard University Press, 1986), p. 3.
7 This quote is attributed to Lacan by Julia Kristeva who had attended his seminars. See Kristeva, *Melanie Klein*, p. 229.

8 Letter dated May 26, 1935. In Ernest Jones, *The Life and Work of Sigmund Freud: Vol. 3* (New York: Basic Books, 1957), p. 197.

9 Letter to Anna Freud, January 21, 1942, cited in P. King and R. Steiner (eds.), *The Freud–Klein Controversies* (London and New York: Tavistock/Routledge, 1991), p. 235.

10 See King and Steiner, *The Freud–Klein Controversies*, p. 229.

11 It is interesting to note that at one time Jones had romantic inclinations for Anna Freud when she was young, and that later in life Jones had his children analyzed by Klein herself. See P. Grosskurth, *The Secret Ring* (Toronto: MacFarlane, Walter & Ross, 1991).

12 In Klein's *Narrative of a Child Analysis* (London: Hogarth Press, 1961), she interprets a 5-year-old boy's desire to have intercourse with her by the fifth therapy session, upon which he becomes palpably anxious.

13 Grosskurth, *Melanie Klein*, p. 3.

14 Roy Schafer (ed.), *The Contemporary Kleinians of London* (New York: International Universities Press, 1997), p. xii.

15 See Jon Mills (ed.), *Rereading Freud: Psychoanalysis through Philosophy* (Albany, NY: SUNY Press, 2004); and *Psychoanalysis at the Limit: Epistemology, Mind, and the Question of Science* (Albany, NY: SUNY Press, 2004).

16 Care of the Melanie Klein Trust; cited in Grosskurth, *Melanie Klein*, p. 435.

Chapter I

Who wants to be a scientist?

The historical and psychoanalytic context at the start of Klein's career: circa 1918–1921

R.D. Hinshelwood

The aim of this chapter is to try to reconstruct the points of interest in the development of psychoanalysis around the time when Melanie Klein became an analyst. She was in analysis with Ferenczi on and off during the First World War, and began to take a professional interest in using psychoanalysis herself around 1918. Her first paper was given in 1919 to the Hungarian Psychoanalytical Society and the second in 1921 to the Berlin Psychoanalytic Society. I shall therefore be looking at the development of Freud's ideas around 1918–1921, a time of radically new departures for him, and following the defection of Jung. Not surprisingly at this time, the psychoanalytic movement suffered a considerable tension between new ideas and constraining conformity. This climate of suspicion and the actual issues under discussion were, I shall argue, important factors influencing Klein's initiation into her own career as a psychoanalyst.

The First World War was immediately followed by a time of social and political turmoil, and this included the psychoanalytic movement. Freud signalled new developments in 1917 at the IPA Congress in Budapest (Freud 1918), the first occasion when Melanie Klein would have seen Freud. His paper was inspirational for the future of psychoanalysis, which had done well in the war, as it was accepted by the military on both sides as having the only coherent theoretical and practical approach to war neurosis (PTSD as we now know it). However, all was not well within psychoanalysis. The dispute with Jung had ruptured Freud's alliance with him in 1913 and though Jung was still President of the IPA in 1918, he was soon replaced.

Following the war, women's suffrage developed rapidly, and women were looking for ways to advance themselves socially. The older professions remained conservative, but the newer professions, including psychoanalysis, welcomed women as recruits.

Melanie Klein suffered from bouts of depression after the birth of all her children. The last one, after the birth of Erich in 1914, led her to seek treatment. It is not clear how she found Ferenczi. Peters (1985) noted that Klein's husband Arthur Klein worked shortly before the war at a paper factory where Ferenczi's brother also worked, but we do not know if this was the route her initial contact with Ferenczi took. It is clear that Ferenczi encouraged Klein to take a psychoanalytic interest in children, which she did, at first observing her own children. She developed her form of child analysis with Abraham's encouragement after she arrived in Berlin, in 1921.

What was happening in psychoanalysis at that time?

I shall review a number of issues that seem to me to have been important for Klein as she began to read, probably Freud being her main source of understanding, whilst also guided by Ferenczi (Likierman 2000) and after 1921 by Abraham in Berlin. The issues most pertinent seem to be the understanding of child development, the economic model, the place of object relations and subjectivity in a deterministic science, love and tenderness, and finally the nature of aggression. These topics formed a backdrop to her early formation as a psychoanalyst.

Child development

In his *Three Essays on Sexuality* (Freud 1905b), Freud turned from symptom relief, to developmental psychology and the understanding of fixation points in the course of the development of the libido in childhood. His ideas drew on his work with adults. To check his ideas he was interested in a direct understanding of children. So, in 1905, he called for people in his acquaintance to observe children in close detail. Little Hans was the most productive of the results. Max Graf engaged his son in 'conversations', reported to Freud who told Graf what interpretations to make to the 5-year-old boy. The Little Hans 'case' was published in 1909. Ferenczi (1913; English translation 1916) eventually contributed a formal paper on his 'Little Chanticleer', which replicated the Little Hans case. In turn, he encouraged Melanie Klein in this direction, and she made her first observations on her own children around 1918. It must have been natural for Klein to refer to Freud's work. From Little Hans she picked up the inhibition he had in understanding the Oedipal issues underlying his phobia.

Klein in her earliest work followed the same lines. She started with the observation that children's phantasies have a compulsive and repetitive quality. They had particular difficulty in facing the question of origins – origins of siblings and babies (Klein 1921, 1923). When she answered children's questions about brothers and sisters and so forth with frank answers, she found them inhibited in listening to the answers. They repeated their questions despite having received answers based on reality (instead of explanations based on the mystifying children's myths that were usually used in the culture at the time). Intellectual comprehension of the explanations was clearly blocked. The compulsiveness, the inhibition of questions, and the restriction of intellectual activity seemed to be connected with states of tension, or anxiety, in the children. This led Klein to believe that the Oedipus complex was at play. She extended her understanding to intellectual development at school, and the problems a child might have for instance in putting letters together as they learned to write – the combining of letters representing the coupling of the parents. Therefore intellectual development was beset at all turns by primitive emotional anxieties deriving from the Oedipus complex.

In those early years, her observations of children already had distinguishing features. First of all, she emphasised intellectual development and inhibition. The second feature of her work was the central focus she gave to anxiety, which she always thought was the emotional cause of inhibition. She elaborated her own theory of anxiety on the basis of this clinical work and observation, and became increasingly confident that children's anxiety arose from their anxieties about their own aggression. Only in hindsight did she elaborate metapsychological explanations.

Her earliest work was largely observation. It is believed her subjects were her own children (Grosskurth 1986), just as Graf had had similar conversations with his son. It was not until later, when she was in Berlin and under Karl Abraham's tutelage, that she really turned her mind to consider how one might apply a truly psychoanalytic technique to treating children who suffered from neurosis. Klein was approaching the problem in the way that Hermine Hug-Hellmuth had done. Hug-Hellmuth, a Viennese analyst, had considered the use of psychoanalysis with children. She believed that it was best as a form of psychoanalytically oriented upbringing, rather than a specific treatment (Hug-Hellmuth 1921). Hug-Hellmuth's experience, like Graf's, was largely with a child of her own – in fact, she was the adopted mother of her sister's illegitimate child.

This approach strongly influenced August Aichhorn (1925) when he established an institution for delinquent boys in Vienna and thought in terms of a psychoanalytically informed education. Anna Freud, too, when she became interested in understanding children psychoanalytically a little after Klein, some time around 1922, based her view on her experience as a teacher. Consequently, she at first thought of the psychoanalyst as a cross between a parent and a moral educator.

Klein moved beyond Hug-Hellmuth who decided that analytic interventions were impossible before the age of 6. Her observations of Fritz (probably her son Erich), reported in 1919, were made when he was 4½ years and onwards. She criticised Hug-Hellmuth's hesitancy before the age of 6:

> it is well known that analyses of the neuroses reveal traumata and sources of injury in events, impressions or developments that occurred at a very early age, that is before the sixth year. What does this information yield for prophylaxis? What can we *do* just at the age that analysis has taught us is so exceedingly important not only for illness but also for the permanent formation of character and of intellectual development.
>
> (Klein 1921, pp. 15–16)

A little later, in 1924, Hug-Hellmuth was murdered by the son she had subjected to a psychoanalytic upbringing. This set going a good deal of hesitation about the advisability of psychoanalytic interventions in children. Klein's response was to reinforce her view that psychoanalysis should be restricted to a formal treatment setting and not used as an adjunct or even contaminant in upbringing by parents, or in education by teachers. By this time she had already worked out a formal treatment setting. She called it the play technique. Play is for children what free association is for adults. The analysis of resistance, as psychoanalysis largely was then, became the analysis of the inhibition in children's play.

The economic model

Significant as psychoanalytic child development was for Klein's development, probably in the long run it was the ambiguity in Freud's scientific approach which influenced her own professional development. A great deal has been written about Freud as a scientist (Popper 1954, Sulloway 1979, Clark 1980, Grunbaum 1984, Webster 1995, Forrester 1997). He was avowedly a nineteenth-century natural scientist, and had been committed to a natural science explanation of psychology for twenty-five years – since his 'Project' in 1895. His economic theory consisted of quasi-quantifiable explanations of the location and flow of mental energy, and these were his credentials for claiming a scientific, objective natural-science-like theory. Freud had always proceeded as a scientist. However, from early on, he was meeting actual patients who were intent on being regarded as subjective human beings engaging in relationships. Scientific determinism, and Freud's version of that, 'psychic determinism', sit poorly with the imploring neediness of suffering people. Mental energy and mental suffering can only clumsily be equated.

So, Freud's scientific mission was in fact distinct from his practice. Freud's research methods evolved from his training as a neurophysiologist with Helmholtz and Brucke. He used the 'law of conservation of energy' to derive the hypothetical notion of psychic energy. He tried to work in the same way as a physicist might deal with electrical currents in experiments in a laboratory. He saw the role of the analyst as controlling the play of psychic forces. Freud continued with this view as late as 1913, the analyst's role being to handle these forces almost like a military general. We can see him emphasising a meta-level here. The analyst's primary focus was on the play of forces in the mind, and *less* on the actual meaning in the suffering. Once revealed to consciousness, those meanings would no longer be problematic. If the play of forces between conscious and unconscious were readjusted then the mental content (whatever it was in each individual) could flow and function normally again. For Freud, the analyst could stand above the meaning of the suffering, as a surgeon poised to operate. The anguish of the meanings tended to be a matter for the patient to work through.

This tension between scientific determinism, and listening to the suffering of another human being, caused further distress sometimes. A crisis over this tension occurred early on, with the Dora case in late 1900 (Freud 1905a). At that time, Freud was publishing his *Interpretation of Dreams* (1900), and in Dora's analysis he had focused on her two dreams. He intended it as an exemplary analysis to supplement the *Interpretation of Dreams*, one useful for demonstrating his new science of psychoanalysis (Jones 1953). His role was to act as the manager (or even manipulator) of the forces in Dora which resisted and concealed the meanings in the dreams.

However, Dora posed a challenge to this. For her the analyst was not just a distant observing researcher enquiring dispassionately into the play of forces in her mind. The message Dora gave Freud was, 'This is personal; this is personal between you and me.' Belatedly, long after the analysis had been interrupted, Freud realised that there was something about him that reminded Dora of some specific other person; in fact, a certain Herr K. The story was nasty. Herr K was a friend of Dora's father, who in turn was having an affair with Frau K. In order to appease Herr K, Dora's father was willing to collude in the seduction of Dora by Herr K. In fact, Dora refused the seduction. It would seem that Dora felt the analysis was a version of this same outrageous seduction. She felt that she was given to Freud in the same outrageous way her father offered her to Herr K. The story is so nasty, and the part allotted to Freud, as seducer, so outrageous that it may be under-standable that for Freud it took a long time for the penny to drop – from Dora's point of view he really *was* an outrageous seducer.

For Dora this very specific meaning identified Freud as a repeat occurrence of her previous trauma. It became directly experienced in the here-and-now of Freud's experimenting. His single-minded pursuit of the dreams to the exclusion of her experiences felt to Dora like the sexual needs of her father and Herr K excluding her own experience. Freud eventually realised, too late of course, that he represented this previous (sexual) exploitation by Herr K. It is not surprising that she rejected analysis exactly as she had fled from Herr K. Perhaps it is not too surprising that Freud was slow to recognise these unconscious undercurrents that expressed themselves directly within the analytic relationship. However much this could be interpreted in terms of the economy of psychic energy discharged in dreams, it was the personal relational experience which really counted at the crucial moment.

Of course Freud learned from this. He, as the analyst, was not simply the commander of the 'good' forces. He was a significant representative of the forces that made Dora resist as well. He was confronted with 'negative trans-ference', and the full versatility of repetition in the analytic relationship. This case was extremely significant in the historical development of psycho-analysis. Its implications took a long time to take full effect, but by the time Klein came to psychoanalysis, relational repetition was a powerful force to be reckoned with (Freud 1914). The difficulty that Dora's affront to Freud caused for his theories based on psychic energy and psychic topography was that Dora's experience in analysis enacted a human narrative with Freud. Human narrative does not easily conform to natural science. He never really did reconcile his two explanatory conceptions of the person – the natural science of energy, topography and dynamics, or experiential, narrative empathy. As his practice continued he was increasingly pushed towards recognising the subjectivity of his discipline, and the core feature in his practice became the transference – that is to say the dramatic representation of relations with others. His 'metapsychology' was an attempt to rise above the conceptual conflict by separating the levels of explanation. One level was the patient's experiences of relations and of others (objects), and the other level that of the scientific analyst interpreting those experiences in abstract terms.

However, the trend towards Freud's experiential narrative goal, which has gained force over the years, cannot so easily be confined to a separate level of abstraction. Klein's work implicitly demonstrated that. There is an important sense in which from the beginning she allowed her children to speak for themselves. For instance, Rita (aged 2¾ years) needed her toy elephant as a boundary keeper at night-time, to express for her the super-ego function of protecting the parents who excluded her, from 'doing something to them or taking something away from them' (Klein 1923, p. 6). Later, when she was embarking on theory building herself, patients' phantasies became metapsychological theory, for instance the fear of aggression towards the loved object became the depressive position arising from the confluence of opposing instincts. The disjunction between patients' phantasies and analysts' theories was thereby partially collapsed.

In Freud's scientific theorising, psychic energy arises from an instinct which has a source, an aim and an object of its aim. The nature of the 'object' on whom an aim is carried out was of secondary importance scientifically. Its own subjectivity did not connect with the psychoanalytic examination of how psychic energy is deployed. Freud's theory of psychic energy gave rise to a whole field of 'economics'. That is, the energy is deployed as are the forces in an actual economy, to turn the cogs of the psychic world.

Why did Klein not pay more attention to these scientific theories? They were at their height during the period of the metapsychology papers (Freud 1915) just before Klein became an analyst. One might have expected her to start with a study of those papers. But it is as if she never mastered them.

In fact even at this time, as Freud was writing his great metapsychological treatise, the economic theory was not a complete answer and had never been so. It leaves out of account the personal responding subject, who engages with other subjects. Patients feel those things. If the analyst removes personal suffering, constructed narratives, and enactment of those narratives to a different level, a level of data not of explanation, then a patient can, like Dora, feel unheard. Although Freud was sensitive to the importance of narrative and always prioritised the fundamental narrative of human beings, the

Oedipal story, these subjective meanings were important only insofar as they attracted energy. The lack of explanation at the level of the patient's experience moved Freud away from his patients' experience; or rather, as in Dora's case, patients could dramatically demonstrate the distance by moving themselves away.

When Dora attributed intentions to her analyst she was alive to *his* subjectivity as well as her own. Her object (Freud in this case) was not simply an object which her libido could cathect. Her object had a subjectivity, intentions (good or bad), an agency to realise those intentions, and so on. In terms used today, Dora 'mentalised' her objects.

This kind of debate about the importance of the object as another subject with whom meaning is transacted, was also in the psychoanalytic culture at the crucial time for Klein. In her crucial formative years the narrative approach to psychoanalytic treatment was deeply and implicitly embedded in certain ideas that Freud was introducing, without a full explicit awareness in the analytic world that subjective experience and psychic economy are parallel universes. Freud's theory of narcissism in 1914 was an attempt to understand self-interest and self-consciousness in terms of libidinal cathexis, but when he developed this a year later to explain melancholia, he was on the track to developing a point of view which prioritised the 'object' over the energy. In that theory of loss, Freud recognised that the mind of a person is extraordinarily occupied with objects, the need for objects, and the consequences when the subject hates his object. And in 1921, Freud came close to asserting that social psychology is primary rather than individual psychology – 'individual psychology . . . is at the same time social psychology' (Freud 1921, p. 69). By this he meant that all psychology is in the context of relations with parents, siblings and others.

However, Freud retreated from that direction when, in 1923, he reassessed the importance of his economic model and delineated the internal relations within the mind, as the notions of id, ego and super-ego. The mind once again in his metapsychology became a sealed system for managing perceptions and instincts.

All this created a to-and-fro motion in Freud's conceptual development, as he continued to focus on the expression of one side or another of his ambiguity. Melanie Klein began her professional career in this context. That tension in psychoanalysis was at its height, whilst being equally understated. Klein was not trained as a scientist, nor as a doctor; in fact she had no university education at all. Perhaps, she never really understood Freud's work in the sense that he wanted to claim psychology as a natural science. Instead, her initial approach to children immediately confronted her with their anxiety, their questions they repetitively asked, their urgent experiences. First she encountered anxiety, not energy or theory or science. Greenberg and Mitchell came to similar conclusions about her mature work:

Klein's treatment of energic concepts also reflects the innovative shift in her usage of the concept of drive. The drives for Freud are finite amounts of energy; they are treated as physical substances, having specific quantities . . . . [T]he more expended in direct gratification, the less available for sublimation or aim-inhibited activities; the more directed towards one person, the less available for others . . . . Not so with Klein. Without explicitly announcing that she is doing so, she changes all of Freud's basic economic principles. In Klein's system, the energy of the drives is not finite or preset . . . . Love for one object does not limit, but increases love for others.

(Greenberg and Mitchell 1983, pp. 143–144)

There is no attempt in Klein at estimating quantities of libido. She was interested in ego-strategies to increase love over hate. This configuration – conflict between love and hate – is the basis of Klein's theory of anxiety. It does have a kind of quantitative aspect to it, but it is not the quantitative theory of Freud. It is not a deterministic theory since the accentuation of love is an ego-strategy, an act of agency it would seem. For instance in her theorising of eroticisation much depends on the ego's deployment of a premature genital eroticism as if it is a strategy rather than a quantity of energy. These are later features of Klein's conclusions, but my argument is that they are possible because at the outset of her formation as an analyst these issues were in the air, and she could implicitly pick her own preferences, on the basis of her observational experience. It may not have been a conscious choice, simply a choice to address her children's experience, and neglect the metapsychology interests which Freud and his close colleagues were otherwise engaged upon. This choice was perhaps to do with her temperament and how it expressed itself in her work and her response to her child patients, but it was also in key with the changing times.

Object relations and subjectivity

At the time she was beginning her work, and no doubt reading Freud, Klein was also influenced by Ferenczi. He was Freud's most important and gifted supporter in the early days of psychoanalysis, but he had differences with Freud, and these would soon come out into the open (Ferenczi and Rank 1925). Like many others, some of whom became dissidents – Jung is an example – he was not keen on the extreme scientism that Freud proclaimed. Ferenczi freed himself to follow his own interests in the human side of the analytic relationship, as he later demonstrated in his remarkable *Clinical Diary* of 1932 (Ferenczi 1988). He was interested in human subjectivity, and the problems of equality in the analytic setting. He wanted to pioneer developments in technique in that more 'democratic' direction (see Haynal 1988). This too may have influenced the young Melanie Klein to concern herself primarily with the person rather than the psychology.

So, her work stressed the unconscious subterranean world of object representations inside the person, and how they came to be fluidly exchanged with the external world – that is, expressed in the toys children played with. She stressed more and more the process observable within the analytic setting, the narratives and relations which the children's toys were made to enact. Her intention was to understand the processes by which her patients (children) struggled with their anxieties, and not primarily to create abstract knowledge about the human mind.

Despite that, after Freud's *Papers on Metapsychology* in 1914–15, the psychoanalytic vernacular turned towards generalisation and abstraction in the scientific manner, i.e. metapsychology. In that context she was obliged as everyone else to formulate her contributions in that mode, acceptable to the practitioners of psychoanalysis of the time. Since that meant the terms and concepts of metapsychology, from early on she did raise general questions of metapsychology – the timing of the Oedipus complex, the origin of the superego, the discreteness of the libidinal phases. She certainly thought of herself as contributing scientifically; however, her basic intentions and motivation seemed to remain fundamentally therapeutic and curative. Klein's focus on the patients' own theories of how their minds worked approached them as subjective persons in their own right. We are thus all psychologists, since we all try continually to understand ourselves, and to understand the other persons with whom we come in contact. Patients, in fact, trouble themselves a great deal about their minds and others' minds.

To clarify this, if a patient says they are angry right now, then the analyst will want to understand how that impulse and feeling-state arose – was it some figure in the family, in the street outside, in the session itself? There is a psychology of that person's anger that the analyst primarily wants to understand. Then, taking a step back from this clinical experience, an analyst begins to place his patient's psychology within a broader spectrum of ideas about anger in general. That super-ordinate form of understanding is 'metapsychology'. However, the situation becomes more complex when we consider that the patient himself will have his own theories about why he is angry. And the analyst has the opportunity to take a step back from this clinical material as well, and to work on the patient's understanding as an instance of the patient's own agency and subjectivity. It was Klein's genius to be able to take this approach from Abraham and develop it into a specific form of psychoanalytic practice.

Since Freud's classical work on this subject (*Three Essays on Sexuality*) we are accustomed to distinguish the sexual *aims* of the individual from those processes which concern his relations to his sexual *object*. What we have said so far about the ontogenesis of object-love does not sufficiently cover the field of facts .... In analysing [the 'narcissistic neuroses'] we meet with a number of psychosexual phenomena which our theory must take account of. And I propose . . . tracing separately the development of the relation of the individual to his love-object.

(Abraham 1924, p. 480)

This statement of Abraham's is in effect the manifesto for the object-relations project which Klein took over and which through her entered the British psychoanalytic tradition with such force.

So, Klein listened to the patient's account of his own psychology, but she listened in as well to what she could interpret of the patient's unspoken aspect of his psychologising, his unconscious knowledge of how he and others think. As we know, what she heard as she listened was the patient's accounts in terms of his object relations. So, Klein's metapsychology has this particular core characteristic. The patient's own account of his psychology is paramount, and should rise above the analyst's metapsychology as the theoretical structure of psychoanalysis. When she came to trying to generalise her discoveries it was an attempt to generalise the patients' accounts of themselves at the unconscious level.

These developments in Klein's method of listening to the patient's psychologising (in effect listening to the patients' own metapsychology) stamped a style on her work, her writing and her later development. Her approach can be seen to come from one strand of Freud's thinking (the narrative, 'unscientific' strand) plus the influence of Ferenczi and of Abraham together with her lack of university training and academic naivety. I suggest Klein's characteristic development could not have occurred outside this context of the time, with Ferenczi's initiating encouragement to explore her little patients' experience as openly as she could, and Abraham's incipient object-relations approach. Her academic naivety was also a result of the opportunity at the time for women, hitherto disadvantaged, to enter a profession.

In this account, Ferenczi, and also Abraham, were responsible for a radical departure from Freud's scientism, which led, it seems to me, to characteristic views on love and aggression, views which are still not as openly debated as they might be.

Love

Ferenczi's influence probably did not extend far into the development of Klein's technical method, for that was developed after she left Budapest in 1921 and settled in Berlin. There she sought and gained encouragement from Abraham. However, Ferenczi's somewhat divergent view from Freud on the nature of love may have steered the new analyst. Abraham's views on whole object love then continued that influence.

Freud's view of non-erotic love was narcissistic. It derived from sexual libido that had been withdrawn from a sexual object and directed towards the ego. In the process the sexual energy was desexualised (Freud 1914b). He called this ego-libido (as opposed to object-libido). Such ego-directed libido was then manifested as the self-preservative instincts, needed by the infant for satisfying its hunger, thirst, etc.

Ferenczi however wanted to go in a different direction, and postulated a primary love, one that sought devotion and tenderness from others from the beginning. Primary tenderness was not libidinal in Ferenczi's ideas, and he did not have to derive tenderness from erotism and instinctual organ-satisfaction in the way that Freud was compelled to. Klein in many writings from the earliest to the latest (e.g. Klein 1957) talks of love in this same sense of tenderness, both needed and given. As her views developed, she became more interested in how impulses of hate and destructiveness frighten the infant in case they overcome loving feelings. This kind of 'interference' by the aggressive impulses in the free play of loving feelings took over from her interest in how the violence of the Oedipus complex interfered with curiosity and intellectual activity. Eventually she formulated this innate conflict as the depressive position (Klein 1935).

This revision of the nature of love was not just a concern of Ferenczi, Jung too parted from Freud partly on those grounds. And indeed, Abraham (1924) also had a concept of love for the whole object. He identified it with the genital libido but it has a much wider reference than just sexuality in his writing. The contrast he made was with a 'partial love' which was purely genital and nothing else. This very likely enhanced what Klein must have experienced with Ferenczi. It seems likely that when Klein went to Berlin she found in Abraham something of this unspoken debate about the nature of non-erotic love.

Klein never discussed these points. However, it is clear her notion of drives (or instincts) was not in accord with the economic model, but instead referred to innate potentialities for good feelings and relationships and for bad ones. Her development of the depressive position relied on a concerned feeling *for* the object, not necessarily sexual desire at all. And this is so fundamental it cannot be desexualised libido. For instance, her discussion of envy (Klein 1957) counterpoises it with gratitude as primary opposites. The gratitude to an object for satisfying the baby's needs is not sexual love, nor is the 'pining' she postulates as the central anguish of the depressive position. Klein appears oblivious to her usage of these ideas from Ferenczi and Abraham, and their contrast with Freud's. Her apparent naïve ignorance may of course be a calculated strategy to deny her deviance, but in her private notes, never published, she never directly addressed this discrepancy with Freud.

Her unusual view of the erotic comes through not uncommonly in her earlier writing when she talks of erotisation. An erotic relationship, or erotic impulses in a relationship, are described as a strategy for enhancing positive feelings, and imply an agency in 'cultivating' the erotic. For instance, 'the sexual act serves to restore the mother's injured body and thus to master anxiety and guilt' (Klein 1932, p. 248). Thus the erotic impulse is devoted to a strategy aimed at dealing with the anxious belief that negative feelings are interfering in a relationship, and that the positive ones need to be enhanced. The implication is that the person (or ego) is in a position to struggle with their own impulses in a way which is not deterministic. Love is a state to be struggled for, and sex a strategy in that struggle. Erotisation is not simply a mechanical discharge of libido. Sex is not simply an energic release. In this view, erotomania and perversions are a cover-up strategy when the struggle appears to be lost.

Anxiety and aggression

When Klein first tried to listen to her little children, it was their worries and anxieties that came immediately to the fore. Children are more open than adults, who cloak their anxiety behind symptoms that have become entrenched. Being more transparent, they made it easier for Klein to relate to their troubled experience. She did not have the intellectual luxury of working out complex and disguised meanings to put to dreams and symptoms. Instead she was confronted with children suffering night terrors, naked fear, or temper tantrums in which fury only transparently covered fear. The object they attacked so violently was attacking them too with equal violence.

Klein's observations pointed out to her how anxious the child gets when its aggressive feelings are stirred. She could see from play how the child tried to protect the good figures of the parents, and at the same time tried to inhibit the aggression. The child had various strategies, including the erotisation which I have just mentioned. In addition one of the commonest strategies the child uses is to visualise the aggression as a retaliation against something that is attacking it. This is the mechanism of projection which attributes the aggression to an object, felt then to be bad, and deserving of the child's aggression directed as a retaliation. Klein found this as a regular occurrence in temper tantrums and night terrors, as well as gross inhibitions and a disturbance to symbol formation and intellectual development.

This was the experiential material she had before her eyes, and ears, as she started. Theorising the death instinct was not her priority, or at that stage not within her capabilities anyway perhaps. Insofar as she conceptualised aggression at all, she at first simply lifted Abraham's views which he himself adopted straight from Freud. Aggression is derived from the sado-masochistic component of the libido. Although Freud elaborated this with his discoveries from working with manic-depressive patients, it was standard psychoanalytic theory going back to *Three Essays on Sexuality*. Klein in her initial period saw this as a libidinal expression within the Oedipus complex. She relied wholly on the more conservative view of aggression being derived from sadism as a component of the libido. This was central to the views of Abraham under whose influence Klein came from 1921 until his death in

December 1925, when she lived in Berlin. He described sadistic sub-phases to the oral, anal and genital libidinal phases (Abraham 1924). Hence he saw sadism as part of the component instincts of the libido, as had been standard in Freud's metapsychology prior to 1920 (Freud 1905b, and subsequent editions). Abraham never absorbed the implications of a separate source of aggression in another instinct. In fact, he never made comment on the death instinct (before he died in 1925), and he may have been unable to relate Freud's new idea to his own descriptions of the inherent sadism in the libidinal phases – the death instinct was in any case a perplexing idea for most of Freud's colleagues. Klein relied heavily on Abraham's ideas on sadism as inherent in the development of the libido. Even after she moved to London, in 1926, she frequently made reference to Abraham's views on sadism.

Klein started her work by using the Oedipus complex as her explanation of children's anxiety and inhibition, but it was the affect that she concentrated on, particularly the anxiety. For her, it was an anxiety that arose from the aggression towards the parents, or in retaliation against the child, or towards a sibling, or the violence supposed to occur between the parents and so on. At this stage, in the 1920s, aggression remained more or less untheorised by Klein even though it was an important part of her observations. As the major factor in causing inhibition in her children, she merely assumed that aggression was somehow at the root of resistance and repression.

Though Klein is likely to have read Freud's *Beyond the Pleasure Principle*, when it was published in 1920, the notion of the death instinct does not appear in her work until much later. As Klein probably never understood the economic model, and did not use the theory correctly, she used the notion of an instinct in a way which was imprecise and became increasingly anachronistic as ego-psychology developed the idea into drive-theory. Klein referred to 'instinct' as a specific potentiality for one or another kind of object-relating, loving or hating an object (or the self). Klein saw both loving and hating as subjected to ego manipulations in order to minimise anxiety.

Klein later did adopt Freud's concept of the death instinct, in her book *The Psychoanalysis of Children* in 1932. She conceived it in her own way, moulded by her early experience of children's struggles to find ways to minimise the effects of aggression on loved ones. She saw the death instinct as a particular kind of attitude (rather than impulse) towards the self, and by projection towards others. The concept was a support for belief in the innateness of aggression in her child patient. So, it was the innateness she drew upon, and not the scientific determinism, nor drive-reduction theory. Her first interest was the problem posed to the child by its awareness of its own destructive impulses. It was the child's struggles to cope with it, however unconscious, which absorbed her, as it did the child. Any real interest in the abstract notions of instinct, energy and mechanism continued to pass her by.

British psychoanalysis had by then developed its own character, and so the theory was absorbed into a different conceptual framework, one that would question the innateness of aggression and prefer to see it as the result of privation.

Conclusions

Klein's burning ambition as a child to train to be a doctor may have been diverted as an adult into being a psychoanalyst. However, despite being brought up in Vienna, one of the major centres for medical research at the time, she was not trained in medicine or as a scientific observer. Nor did it appear that she was aware of the characteristics of science which might be applied to psychoanalytic work, as Freud had assiduously done. In particular, she was impressed by the agency of young children in relation to their state of mind, and their anxious need to express their preoccupations with other human persons. She was, I think, hardly aware of what Freud really meant by psychic energy. Her sacrifice of the scientific economic model was no great hardship, as it opened her way to a more consistent attention to the experiential, as opposed to the scientific – an approach which was not original since others, including her two analysts, were also edging in the same direction. Having by chance slipped away from Freud's conflict, it opened up a number of new conceptions.

Klein's entry as a psychoanalyst was in the wake of Jung's departure, and so it would not have been wise to proclaim the newness of the approach she was taking even if she had been able to articulate it. What she did was to make innocent observations and put the innovations into the mouths of children. Many of these innovations stem from Klein's induction into the profession and movement at a particular moment in psychoanalytic history. Freud himself, after the First World War, was engaged on a new beginning for many of his established theories. New beginnings were part of the ethos of the time. It suited Melanie Klein's adventurous character, and though dangerous she seems fearless in following what her observations told her. Some of those characteristic aspects of Kleinian thought have not been much discussed. They failed to be openly reflected upon, and she fudged some issues, partly because she was not primarily a theoretician and partly because of the threat of exclusion following Jung's dissension. Another reason that silence has hung over some innovations is that, lacking a university education, she was hardly aware of how radical her innovations were, and was not in a position to articulate the necessary debate. However it is never too late to undo neglect, and the implicit assumptions behind Klein's development have steadily surfaced, to which process the points raised in this chapter have tried to contribute.

References

Abraham, Karl (1924) A short study of the development of the libido, viewed in the light of mental disorders. In Karl Abraham (1927) *Selected Papers of Karl Abraham*. London: Hogarth.

Aichhorn, August (1925) *Wayward Youth*. New York: Viking Press.

Balint, Michael (1949) Early developmental states of the ego: primary object love. *International Journal of Psychoanalysis* 30: 265–273.

Bruner, Jerome (1986) *Actual Minds, Possible Worlds*. Cambridge, Mass.: Harvard University Press.

Clark, Ronald (1980) *Freud: The Man and the Cause*. London: Jonathan Cape.

Fairbairn, Ronald (1952) *Psychoanalytic Studies of the Personality*. London: Tavistock.

Ferenczi, Sandor (1916) A little chanticleer. In Sandor Ferenczi (1957) *First Contributions to Psychoanalysis*. London: Hogarth.

Ferenczi, Sandor (1949) Confusion of the tongues between the adults and the child (the language of tenderness and of passion). *International Journal of Psychoanalysis* 30: 225–230.

Ferenczi, Sandor (1988) *The Clinical Diary of Sandor Ferenczi*. Cambridge, Mass.: Harvard University Press.

Ferenczi, Sandor and Rank, Otto (1925) *The Development of Psychoanalysis* (*Entwicklungsziele der Psychoanalyse*). New York: Nervous and Mental Disease Publishing.

Forrester, John (1997) *Dispatches from the Freud Wars*. Cambridge, Mass.: Harvard University Press.

Freud, Sigmund (1895) The project for a scientific psychology. *Standard Edition of the Complete Psychological Works of Sigmund Freud, Volume 1*. London: Hogarth.

Freud, Sigmund (1900) *Interpretation of Dreams. Standard Edition of the Complete Psychological Works of Sigmund Freud, Volume 4*. London: Hogarth.

Freud, Sigmund (1905a) A case of hysteria. *Standard Edition of the Complete Psychological Works of Sigmund Freud, Volume 7*. London: Hogarth.

Freud, Sigmund (1905b) *Three Essays on Sexuality. Standard Edition of the Complete Psychological Works of Sigmund Freud, Volume 7*. London: Hogarth.

Freud, Sigmund (1909) Analysis of a phobia in a five-year-old boy. *Standard Edition of the Complete Psychological Works of Sigmund Freud, Volume 10*. London: Hogarth.

Freud, Sigmund (1914a) Remembering, repeating and working through. *Standard Edition of the Complete Psychological Works of Sigmund Freud, Volume 12*. London: Hogarth.

Freud, Sigmund (1914b) On narcissism. *Standard Edition of the Complete Psychological Works of Sigmund Freud, Volume 14*. London: Hogarth.

Freud, Sigmund (1915) *Papers on Metapsychology. Standard Edition of the Complete Psychological Works of Sigmund Freud, Volume 14*. London: Hogarth.

Freud, Sigmund (1918) Lines of advance in psychoanalytic therapy. *Standard Edition of the Complete Psychological Works of Sigmund Freud, Volume 17*. London: Hogarth.

Freud, Sigmund (1920) *Beyond the Pleasure Principle. Standard Edition of the Complete Psychological Works of Sigmund Freud, Volume 18*. London: Hogarth.

Freud, Sigmund (1921) *Group Psychology and the Analysis of the Ego. Standard Edition of the Complete Psychological Works of Sigmund Freud, Volume 18.* London: Hogarth.

Freud, Sigmund (1923) *The Ego and the Id. Standard Edition of the Complete Psychological Works of Sigmund Freud, Volume 19.* London: Hogarth.

Greenberg, Jay and Mitchell, Stephen (1983) *Object Relations in Psychoanalytic Theory.* Cambridge, Mass.: Harvard University Press.

Grosskurth, Phyllis (1986) *Melanie Klein: Her World and her Work.* London: Hodder and Stoughton.

Grunbaum, Adolph (1984) *The Foundations of Psychoanalysis: A Philosophical Critique.* Berkeley: University of California Press.

Hacking, Ian (1999) *The Social Construction of What?* Cambridge, Mass.: Harvard University Press.

Haynal, Andre (1988) *The Technique in Question.* London: Karnac.

Hug-Hellmuth, Hermine (1921) On the technique of child analysis. *International Journal of Psychoanalysis* 2: 287–305.

Isaacs, Susan (1930) *Intellectual Growth in Young Children.* London: George Routledge.

Isaacs, Susan (1933) *Social Development of Young Children.* London: George Routledge.

Isaacs, Susan (1948) The nature and function of phantasy. *International Journal of Psychoanalysis* 29: 73–97. Republished in Melanie Klein, Paula Heimann, Susan Isaacs and Joan Riviere (1952) *Developments in Psychoanalysis.* London: Hogarth.

Jones, Ernest (1926) The origin and structure of the super-ego. *International Journal of Psychoanalysis* 7: 303–311.

Jones, Ernest (1953) *Sigmund Freud: Life and Work, Volume 1.* London: Hogarth.

Klein, Melanie (1921) The development of a child. *The Writings of Melanie Klein, Volume 1.* London: Hogarth.

Klein, Melanie (1923) The role of the school in the libidinal development of the child. *The Writings of Melanie Klein, Volume 1.* London: Hogarth.

Klein, Melanie (1929) Personification in the play of children. *The Writings of Melanie Klein, Volume 1.* London: Hogarth.

Klein, Melanie (1932) *The Psychoanalysis of Children. The Writings of Melanie Klein, Volume 2.* London: Hogarth.

Klein, Melanie (1935) A contribution to the psychogenesis of manic-depressive states. *The Writings of Melanie Klein, Volume I.* London: Hogarth.

Klein, Melanie (1957) Envy and gratitude. *The Writings of Melanie Klein, Volume 4.* London: Hogarth.

Kleinman, A. (1988) *The Illness Narratives.* New York: Basic Books.

Kohut, H. (1982) Introspection, empathy, and the semi-circle of mental health. *International Journal of Psychoanalysis* 63: 395–407.

Likierman, Meira (2000) *Melanie Klein: Her Work in Context.* London: Continuum.

MacLean, George and Reppen, Ulrich (1991) *Hermine Hug-Hellmuth: Her Life and Work.* London: Routledge.

Martínez-Hernáez, Angel (2000) *What's Behind the Symptom.* Amsterdam: Harwood Academic Publishers.

Peters, Uwe Henryk (1985) *Anna Freud: A Life Dedicated to Children.* London: Weidenfeld and Nicolson.

Popper, Karl (1954) *Poverty of Historicism.* London: Routledge.

Sandler, Joseph and Joffe, Walter (1969) Toward a basic psychoanalytic model.

International Journal of Psychoanalysis 50: 79–90. Revised version in Joseph Sandler (1987) *From Safety to Super-Ego*. London: Karnac.

Sarbin, Theodore (ed.) (1986) *Narrative Psychology: The Storied Nature of Human Contact*. New York: Praeger.

Sontag, Susan (1983) *Illness as Metaphor*. London: Penguin.

Sulloway, Frank (1979) *Freud: Biologist of the Mind*. London: Burnett Books,

Webster, Richard (1995) *Why Freud was Wrong: Sin, Science and Psychoanalysis*. London: Fontana.

Will, David (1964) *Homer Lane: A Biography*. London: Allen and Unwin.

Chapter 2

Klein on human nature

Michael Rustin

Melanie Klein's work was located almost exclusively in clinical practice and writing, and she engaged little in broader social, philosophical, cultural or political reflections. She did not follow Freud in trying to extend or apply her psychoanalytic teaching to other fields of knowledge, such as, in Freud's case, anthropology, the history of art, literature, religion, or politics. She attempted few applications of her ideas, in her writing, outside the domains of clinical practice and psychoanalytic theory. The main exceptions are three essays: 'Infantile Situations Reflected in a Work of Art and in the Creative Impulse' (1929), which discusses Ravel's opera *Les Enfants et les Sortilèges* and a painter, Ruth Kjar; 'On Identification' (1955) which after a brief introduction discusses a novel, *If I Were You*, which was published in 1950 by a French author, Julian Green; and the late paper, 'Reflections on the Oresteia' (1963). The most substantial of these, the Oresteia paper, is a powerful application of Klein's ideas to a canonical dramatic work, which she sees as a symbolisation of unconscious processes and conflicts in human development. But these pieces are mainly intended to exemplify her psychoanalytical ideas, for once outside the clinical context, and were probably in any case intended for readers already familiar with her thinking. They do not claim to say much that is new (unlike Freud's writings) about culture itself. There are few references in Klein's published books and articles to writings outside the field of psychoanalysis,[1] though she is reported by those who knew her to have been a keen theatregoer and reader of literature (Segal 1999). It was in the highly specialised field of the clinical practice of psychoanalysis that she set out to make her contribution, and she did not stray far from this choice throughout her forty years of working life.[2]

Klein was one of the most original and influential of Freud's successors in the psychoanalytic movement – the other most salient figure, so far as influence is concerned, being Lacan. The development of psychoanalytic theory and practice since Freud owes more to Klein's contribution, and those successors, like W.R. Bion, whom she taught and influenced, than to any other psychoanalyst. Obviously assertions of this kind are in part evaluations, not only factual descriptions, and they are no doubt shaped in this case by the

English psychoanalytic location from which they are made – seen from elsewhere in the world, Freud's heritage may look somewhat different, certainly more contested. But few within psychoanalysis seem to doubt Klein's importance in developing one of the most influential strands of post-Freudian thought, what is generally referred to as 'object-relations theory'.

My argument in this chapter is that Klein's writings on psychoanalytic theory and practice were one of the most important contributions to the understanding of human nature that were achieved in any of the human sciences in her lifetime. She addresses, in her psychoanalytic writing, fundamental questions about human beings' relatedness to each other, about differences of gender, about developmental needs, about good and evil, about the essence of morality, and, in a tentative way, about the origins and functions of thought. She thus addresses many of the questions that have to be addressed if one seeks to develop an understanding of what it is to be a human being living in association with others, and to consider what norms and beliefs might be relevant in this situation. Like Freud, she was wholly post-religious and secular in her approach to these fundamental questions. Whereas Freud, who was born in 1858, found it necessary to attack religious beliefs, by explaining their psychic origins and functions by reference to his own theories, Klein, born twenty-six years later, made little reference to religious ideas, perhaps assuming that for serious intellectual purposes they had already been supplanted. Thus it seemed self-evident to her that descriptions of the human situation now needed to start from another place. Not from the 'other world', but, she thought, from this world, and from the first human experiences that take place within it, that is, from the earliest weeks of life. This starting-point now seems such an obvious one, from the standpoint of contemporary psychoanalysis and developmental psychology, than one scarcely recognises what a radical step it actually was, both for Freud and for Klein, to seek a new understanding of human beings' place in the world by attending to what happens to them from the moment they enter it.

It is a common feature of fundamental recastings of beliefs about human beings' place in the world that they construct narratives which describe and explain origins. For example, secular theories of human experience written two centuries before Freud – for example those of the political philosophers of the Enlightenment of the seventeenth and eighteenth centuries – also described beginnings, notably in different versions of the social contract, by which sovereignty and political order were supposed to have been instituted. These various theories also sought to make a fresh (or as we might now say a 'modern') start to human understanding, assuming that the traditional teachings of medieval philosophy, the church, and hereditary monarchy were no longer sufficient or relevant to answer fundamental questions. Different conceptions of the individual – including, in the philosophical work of Berkeley, Locke, Hume and others the nature of the mind and feelings – were among the building blocks of these theories. These philosophers started from another kind of *tabula rasa*, namely the idea of an individual and his (it usually was his) primary attributes. Their dominant concern however was more with political society and the different forms – more or less authoritarian, consensual or democratic – that sovereignty could take, than with the inner subjectivity of individuals themselves. A conception of the pleasure-seeking, pain-avoiding individual which derived ultimately from English empiricist philosophy (Freud translated four works by John Stuart Mill) was a core element of Freud's thought, though of course his achievement was to elaborate and deepen this conception in terms whose emotional and imaginative complexity derived from other cultural sources. (Carl Schorske (1998) refers to Freud's dual attachments to the 'passion' of French and the 'reason' of British culture.) We could say that Klein's revision of Freud's theory of infancy, and her postulation of a state of initial, innate relatedness of infant to parents, is an indirect riposte to the atomistic theory of liberal individualism[3] first formulated by the English empiricist philosophers.[4]

The origins of human nature were reconsidered from a different perspective in the nineteenth century by Charles Darwin, who investigated the emergence of the human species from its earlier evolutionary beginnings. His writing on the origins of human emotions (Darwin 1872/1998) is a significant forerunner of psychoanalytic and other modern psychological research, though it has so far had a more direct influence on attachment theory than on psychoanalysis itself.

Klein was more single-minded than Freud in her focus on the earliest months and years of life as a primary source of understanding of human nature. Freud had been a medical doctor, and a neurologist, before he developed his psychoanalytic perspective. As a clinician, he worked more with adults than with children, and he was as interested in the different forms of adult psychopathology he encountered as in the narrative of early development which he believed could illuminate their origins and psychic functions. Freud was of course an immensely widely-read and cultivated individual, interested in English philosophy and French culture even in the early part of his adult life when his psychoanalytic discoveries were being made, and which subsequently reflect these influences. The psychoanalytic world-view that he formulated thus rested on many investigative pillars, the experiences of infants and children being only one of them, and by no means the most important.

Klein's case is somewhat different. There seem to be important differences of experience, of both generation and gender, in how Freud and Klein came to formulate their ideas. Klein was an analyst of the second generation, and already had available to her, from her own analysis and from teaching, the theoretical system developed by Freud and his colleagues, notably Ferenczi and Abraham.[5] This was both a powerful resource for her, no doubt helping to develop her extraordinary powers of self-reflection and her understanding of extreme states of mind, but it was also a corpus of ideas available to her to develop and sometimes to challenge. It seems also vitally important to Klein's contribution to psychoanalysis that she was a woman and also herself a mother.[6] She was thus close to, and immersed in, the intense early emotional experiences of mother and infant in a way that Freud himself was not. Just as Freud developed psychoanalysis in part by means of his own self-analysis, so Klein, we have learned, pioneered the psychoanalysis of children, and the understanding of the emotional relationships between mothers and babies, through her psychoanalytic treatment of her own son Erich,[7] and, no doubt, through her reflections on her own maternal experience.[8] In the gendered world in which Klein lived, it would be unlikely that any male analyst would have had the intense contact with the world of infancy or young children that Klein did. Even now, responsibility for the care and development of children under the age of 11 is largely devolved to women. The child psychotherapy profession which has now largely taken over the practice of child analysis in Britain from the psychoanalysts, and is in the majority Kleinian or post-Kleinian in its orientation, is largely composed of women. One of its core elements of pre-clinical training consists of two years of naturalistic observation of infants in their family setting. (Miller *et al.* 1989).

Relatedness as the essence of human nature

Klein's account of human nature derived from her investigations of infancy, and began with a significant challenge to one of Freud's early ideas. Freud's theory of primary narcissism asserted that individuals began life alone, without a conception of others or relationships with them, but then became engaged in relationships as a consequence of their state of dependency.[9] The most fundamental proposition of Kleinian psychoanalysis was the idea that human beings were inherently and from the beginning related to others. In infancy, of course, this was to those who cared or failed to care for them. Narcissism, if and when it developed (for example, as was later investigated in the form of autistic or psychotic states in children), was not a primordial infantile state of mind, but a response to subjectively perceived failures in the caring environment. As Klein wrote:

> The analysis of very young children has taught me that there is no instinctual urge, no anxiety situation, no mental process, which does not involve objects, external or internal; in other words, object-relations are at the *centre* of emotional life. Furthermore, love and hatred, phantasies, anxieties, and defences are also operative from the beginning and are *ab initio* indivisibly linked with object relations. This insight showed me many phenomena in a new light.
>
> (Klein 1952, p. 53, original emphases)

This idea is the foundation-stone not only of Kleinian theory, but of psychoanalytic object-relations theory more broadly. (Other object-relations theorists like Winnicott accepted this idea of Klein's (and similar ideas developed contemporaneously by other writers such as Fairbairn and to a degree in anticipation of her work) but rejected other theoretical commitments of hers, notably the idea of primary destructiveness and envy.) Although it challenged Freud's view of the infant's development, it was consistent with and indeed developed from what Freud said in his later work, for example in *Mourning and Melancholia* (1917), about relatedness as the precondition of psychic well-being. The development of Freud's own ideas during his lifetime, and the writings of some of his colleagues such as Abraham, were a precondition of the development of Kleinian ideas. Nevertheless, around the theory of primary narcissism, the difference between Freud and Klein is stark.

What is challenged in Klein's assertion, and in the 'psychoanalytic research programme' which followed from it, is the preconception of atomistic individualism which had uncritically underpinned Freud's early theory. Gendered perceptions seem to have been important in bringing about this realignment. The idea that human beings might start from a state of primary interdependency and relatedness, albeit one full of conflict and tension, perhaps made particular sense in the context of the experience of giving birth, and holding a newborn baby at the breast. Most importantly, in the light of the later development of Kleinian ideas, this gendered situation makes sense of the mother's as well as the baby's preoccupations, of her temporary state of near-fusion with her baby, the state of 'reverie' and 'primary maternal preoccupation' described respectively by Bion and Winnicott. Klein's imaginative brilliance was to extrapolate from her understanding of the core experience of mothers and infants theoretical conjectures which were radically to change the understanding of human nature.

The exceptional quality of Klein's insights has been confirmed by subsequent developments not only in psychoanalysis, but in empirical studies of infant development. The first few months of life, once thought of as a blank period so far as mental life is concerned, have been shown to have a remarkable complexity. Infants once thought to be indifferent to the particular identity of the adults who looked after them, but having needs only to be cared for physically, are now known to be able to recognise their mothers by sound and smell minutes after birth. The organic development of the infant's brain and its neural system, which continues for two years or so after birth, appears to be responsive to the baby's emotional well-being, measured by indicators of stress and anxiety. Ethologists have demonstrated many parallels between mammalian and human attachment patterns. Evolutionary biologists have been able to show that a variety of patterns of attachment behaviour in infants – the repertory of characteristics and behaviours which makes them attractive to their mothers in particular, and to adults in general, their innate suspicion of strangers, their innate rivalry with siblings – was functional for survival in the hunter-gatherer societies in which the human genetic endowment became more or less fixed, and these remain as templates of mental life today. Sarah Hrdy's remarkable book on this topic (Hrdy 2000) convincingly suggests that mother and baby – even mother and placenta – are in certain circumstances competitors for scarce 'survival resources', notably food, and she provides thereby an evolutionary explanation for the conflictful and ambivalent nature of mother–infant mental life which Klein formulated psychoanalytically. Many of Klein's conjectures about infant mental life, made in some cases in the 1920s, have been supported by empirical researches conducted many decades later.[10] A fully relational theory of human development, which connects neurological conditions, states of mind, and social interactions, is in process of emerging, as a rival to a variety of one-dimensional theories of atomistic individualism, whether these be based on materialist, organicist, information-processing, or hedonistic building-blocks.[11] Although Melanie Klein was only one of the significant contributors to this evolving multi-disciplinary paradigm-shift, she was one of the earliest and most influential. How striking it is that this revolution in the understanding of human nature and its relational basis should have depended on a gendered, female perspective, in a world of ideas previously almost wholly dominated by men.

Childhood

Klein's most influential innovation of clinical technique was her discovery that it was possible to undertake psychoanalytic treatment with small children, even under 3 years old. She saw that to provide simple materials with which children could play and draw, while their therapist talked with them about what the meaning was of what they were doing, was an effective substitute for techniques of adult analysis relying on the couch, free association and the interpretation of dreams, as set out by Freud (Klein 1932, part 1). In the 'Controversial Discussions' in the British Psychoanalytic Society between 1943 and 1945 (King and Steiner 1991), Klein and her supporters gave papers which reported this work, and sought to justify significant revisions to Freud's theory of development, against doctrinal opposition from Anna Freud and her associates, newly arrived in London as refugees from Nazi-occupied Vienna. The empirical evidence of the clinical sessions she reported proved decisive in that debate. British analysts who took part in these discussions, who were not as interested in theoretical differences as either the Anna Freudians or the Kleinians, were impressed by Klein and her colleagues' clinical evidence, and were persuaded by their findings. These were that complex inner life clearly commenced in children rather earlier than Freud had supposed, and that it was accessible to psychoanalytic observation, investigation and understanding. It was this which prepared the way for the acceptance of Klein's major theoretical developments among sections of the Society, notably her concept of the paranoid-schizoid position (Klein 1946) and depressive position (Klein 1935, 1940) and her idea of the much earlier onset of the Oedipus complex than Freud had supposed.

Empiricism

Just as Klein's new formulations about human relatedness were founded on the particular experience of mothers (including herself) and their babies, so her theories of psychic development also drew on her clinical knowledge of the experience of children, just as radical a departure in terms of the legitimation of fundamental ideas about human life. One element of the English cultural tradition with which this conception did have some resonance was that of literary romanticism, which had also privileged childhood as a source of insight into human potential, and the damage that could be inflicted on it by inappropriate and oppressive environments. The poetry of Wordsworth and Blake, and the novels of Dickens, for example, take up this child-centred perspective, and make use of it to formulate both critiques of existing social arrangements, and conceptions of the kinds of relationships which would enable emotional growth to take place. But although such conceptions had long been represented in literature, and in other classical art forms such as painting, they were less commonly deployed in the human sciences as decisive evidence of what human beings needed for their development. Thus Klein introduced two new kinds of 'evidence' into the field of the human science, the one derived from the experience of women, and the other derived from the experience, albeit accessed through adults, of children. This may now seem commonplace, with all the subsequent developments of educational and psychological theory,[12] and of the feminist movement itself. But Klein began her published output as early as 1921.

It might seem surprising in some respects that such a theoretically radical system of ideas as Klein's should have been so fully accepted in Britain, where Klein after all only arrived at Ernest Jones's invitation in 1925. One reason for this was their groundedness in a particular variety of empiricism. This was the empiricism of the clinical case study, and of naturalistic observation, rather than of experiment and measurement, but nevertheless it assigned priority to firsthand experience. Although some have considered Freud to have been mistaken in representing psychoanalysis as founded on a scientific method, the clinical case study was central to Freud's work, and is a major element in the continuity of the psychoanalytic tradition, especially in Britain.

The importance of this empirical dimension to Klein's reception can be seen in the 'Controversial Discussions' between the followers of Anna Freud and those of Melanie Klein which took place in the British Psychoanalytical Society in 1944 (King and Steiner 1991). These were a series of meetings held in effect to decide on the place which Klein and her followers were to be accorded in the Society, Freud having recently died, and Anna Freud his daughter having come to England with him. Klein and her colleagues presented papers to members of the Society in London, which were strongly criticised by Anna Freud and her colleagues. A group of British psycho-analysts seem to have been the chorus in this drama. They were most impressed, as I have noted, by the clinical material from the psychoanalysis of children which was presented by the Kleinians, which provided evidence that mental life in children developed earlier, and to a different timetable, than had been proposed by Sigmund Freud. They were less sympathetic to Klein's theoretical departures from Freud's ideas, which the Kleinians therefore chose tactically to downplay. But the group were also unpersuaded by Anna Freud's demand for doctrinal fidelity to her father's teachings, holding that these disputes should be decided by reference to clinical evidence. The out-come of the debates was a kind of treaty, and the institution of a state of 'peaceful coexistence' in the British Psychoanalytical Society between three psychoanalytic factions (the Freudians, the Kleinians, and the Independents or 'Middle Group'), which has persisted to the present day, though not with-out strain. This consensual solution to psychoanalytic differences, rather unlike what has happened elsewhere, was consistent with English societal norms. The psychoanalytic incomers from Germany and Austria restrained their theoretical passions, not without continuing difficulty, and achieved acceptance and integration in Britain.

Although Kleinian psychoanalysis is theoretically bold and ambitious, introducing many new concepts to map unconscious mental life, it has always maintained a strong commitment to its own version of the empirical, that is to the kinds of facts ('clinical facts', some have called them)[13] generated by consulting room interactions and, some would add, naturalistic obser-vational studies.[14] Its acceptance in Britain, and its staying power, owes as much to its commitment to clinical practice and to the citing of clinical material in most of its writing, as it does to its theoretical brilliance.[15] This 'empiricism of the consulting room' involves close attention to the particulars of emotional experience, and is the strongest unifying feature of the British psychoanalytic tradition.[16] The theoretical (and woman-centred) radicalism of Klein's thinking thus was able to find links with two more conservative aspects of British intellectual tradition, its empiricism on the one hand, and its endorsement of family norms marked by innate differences of gender and generation on the other.

Love and hate

Klein's theory of human nature, developing Freud's later thought in particu-lar, is firmly dualistic, holding that both life and death instincts, impulses and feelings of both love and hate, are central to the self and its development. One could suggest that Klein, like Freud, was merely attending sensitively to the realities of the twentieth century, and its terrible outbursts of violence and destructiveness, in formulating this position, though this context only figures obliquely in her work. (For example, her patient in her *Narrative of a Child Analysis* (Klein 1961) is much preoccupied with news from the Second World War which is taking place during his analysis. Bombs fell on London during the 'Controversial Discussions' in London in 1944–1945, and of course Sigmund and Anna Freud had fled from Nazi Vienna only a few years before.[17]) At any rate, Klein was as unsympathetic as Freud had been to utopianism or to unduly optimistic views of the human condition and its improvement. The facts of life with which understanding needed to start were those of the extremes of love and hate, beginning with the infant's passionate, possessive, violent and devouring relationship to its objects, and its feelings of persecution by them.[18] Klein seemed particularly sensitive to the negative and destructive aspects of this primary relationship with mother's breast, others such as Winnicott, and some later Kleinians such as Meltzer (Meltzer and Harris Williams 1988), giving more emphasis to its more passionately loving and admiring qualities. But in whatever tonal register one might choose to describe the infant's state of mind, there is no doubt that for Klein it invariably held both positive and negative aspects. The infant's objects appeared to it as both loved and, in their depriving and frustrating aspects, hated. In early mental life, these aspects were split, in what Klein later came to term the paranoid-schizoid position which characterised the early months of life. There was a good mother and a bad mother, or in her terms a 'good breast' and a 'bad breast', and the infant's state of mind oscillated between them.

As development proceeded, and as mother's care and understanding of the baby's feelings led it to mitigate its frustrations, and sustain its experiences of satisfaction and comfort, so feelings of love would come to predominate. Both the infant's objects, and its ego, became more unified. The onset of the 'depressive position', in the latter half of the first year of life, signified that the infant was able to recognise an object which had both good and bad aspects, not two different objects. Subsequently, psychoanalysts have come to believe, following Bion (1963), that the paranoid-schizoid and depressive positions are modes of mental functioning that persist as potentials or templates throughout life. They are not simply chronological stages of an irreversible development. Klein's model was one in which a favourable balance between loving and hating impulses can be incorporated into the self if the caring environment is sufficiently benign. Klein's view always acknowledged the significance of primary dispositions – it was the infant's subjective experience of its maternal environment that was decisive, not the objective differences between one environment and another, however important these might also be. One might now interpret such differences in terms of genetic endowments leading to more or less contentment or intolerance of frustration on the part of the infant, and the impact this disposition might have on parents. Nevertheless, for all these necessary qualifications, Klein's view that excessive frustration of infantile needs for love and understanding would have negative implications for the formation of identity has been amply borne out by both psychoanalytic practice and other developmental psychological findings, for example those within the field of attachment research.

Klein's view was that infants internalised a model of primary object-relations, a kind of internal family constellation, by a process of introjective identification. This 'internal world' of phantasy was, she believed, a shaping influence on the child's (and later adult's) perception of the external world. If the internal world imagos of parental and child figures were dominated by violence, hatred, or deprivation, this would profoundly influence expectations of experience in the real world. Since this phantasy world was in Klein's view unconscious, but nevertheless potent in shaping conscious perceptions and adaptations, it could have a part in bringing about serious difficulties in character and behaviour. Once psychic damage had been done, mere alleviation of external circumstances might well not suffice to bring about improvements. In any case, the 'external world' of the child – its family, school, or friendship network – was likely to be influenced and perturbed by unconscious projections from the child and others. Disturbance, in other words, was liable to be reciprocal, as in pathological patterns of family relationship, or in the difficulties of schools or other institutions in resisting provocation by members carrying disturbances or vulnerable to the projected disturbances of others. Families, schools and other institutions can sometimes respond in harsh ways to such projections.

The later development of the Kleinian model, by Bion and others, gave increasing weight to the mental functions involved in the early mother–infant relationship. The modulation of anxiety in the infant through the attention and understanding of caring figures, in a process termed 'containment', was held to be necessary to maintain a state of emotional equilibrium in the infant – indeed in the infant–mother couple. This equilibrium provides the 'growing medium' for the development of the mind of the infant, in particular its capacity to attend to reality. Klein had pointed the way to this development of her ideas in her postulation of an 'epistemophilic instinct' in the infant (Klein 1928, 1931), an innate desire to explore reality. From this insight followed the interest by Bion in particular in the development of the mind, or 'mental apparatus', and in the emotional conditions which sustained this. Although this mentalistic perspective elaborated and developed Klein's ideas in new ways, there is an essential continuity between these ideas and Klein's own conception of the conditions necessary for the psychic development of the infant. Essentially, this model proposes that the hatred and destructiveness which is an inescapable element of the human psychic endowment can usually be mitigated by nurturing environments in which love and understanding are sufficient.

Kleinian therapeutic technique gave particular attention to negativity and envy and its unconscious manifestations, for example in profound therapeutic resistance. Kleinians have been notable for their commitment to extend the frontier of 'treatable' pathologies. Psychoanalytic work with children and families in Britain has given increasing attention in the last thirty years to the treatment of 'severely deprived children', often located as 'looked after children' in the public child care system, whose extreme states of mind and feeling other psychological specialists find it more difficult to manage (Boston and Szur 1983). Thus despite some scepticism about psychoanalytic ideas among other mental health professions, psychoanalytic psychotherapists have found a niche because of their capacities to work with exceptionally difficult cases.

The moral sense

Throughout her work, Klein is deeply preoccupied with the development of moral capacities in human beings. Indeed one of the main implications of her theory of object-relations is the different description and explanation it gives, compared with Freud's, of what moral capacities are. Freud explained the emergence of guilt, the conscience, and moral awareness as expressions of the power of the superego, as an internalisation of prohibitions of desires in the Oedipal situation. Klein accepted this view, and further explored its implications. Since in her view the onset of the Oedipus complex was much earlier than Freud had supposed, emerging in the first year of life, the superego was liable to be even more violent and persecuting than Freud had supposed, since it involved anxieties arising from oral and anal sadism felt towards the infant's primary objects. Klein agreed with Freud that the consequences of a persecuting superego and the excessive sense of guilt it produced were harmful, as likely as not leading to the projection of persecutory impulses into others, who became the unfortunate bearers of the unwanted and unloved parts of the self.

But Klein added a new dimension to ethical understanding, scarcely present in Freud's account of the superego and the conscience. The depressive position was defined not only by the recognition of the other as a whole person, but also by concern for its well-being, by identification with it, and by anxiety about the harm which the self was liable to inflict on it, through its enactments of greed or hatred. The depressive position is defined by the presence of love for the object. It is the balance between the impulses of love and hate which is decisive in Klein's view in defining the development of character, the nature of the superego, and thus the moral sense. Where relations with objects are dominated by hatred, the superego is inclined to be persecuting and violent, since it is having to punish and inhibit destructive states of mind in the self. Where relations with objects involve a more favourable balance between love and hate, persecution is less, because both self and object are felt to be less imbued with destructiveness. Klein writes with great eloquence in 'Love, Guilt and Reparation'[19] (1937) about the emergence of the capacity for love in the infant, and its role in later life, and it is worth quoting her at some length:

> I said before that feelings of love and gratitude arise directly and spontaneously in the baby in response to the love and care of his mother. The power of love – which is the manifestation of the forces which tend to preserve life – is there in the baby as well as the destructive forces, and finds its first fundamental expression in the baby's attachment to his mother's breast, which develops into love for her as a person. My psychoanalytic work has convinced me that when in the baby's mind the conflicts between love and hate arise, and the fears of losing the loved one become active, a very important step is made in development. These feelings of guilt and distress now enter as a new element into the emotion of love. They become an inherent part of love, and influence it profoundly both in quality and quantity.
>
> Even in the small child we can observe a concern for the loved one which is not, as one might think, merely a sign of dependence upon a helpful and friendly person. Side by side with the destructive impulses in the unconscious mind both of the child and the adult, there exists a profound urge to make sacrifices, in order to help and put right loved people who in fantasy have been harmed or destroyed. In the depths of the mind the urge to make people happy is linked up with a strong feeling of responsibility and concern for them, which manifests itself as a genuine sympathy for other people and in the ability to understand them, as they are and as they feel.

She goes on to discuss identification and making reparation:

> To be genuinely considerate implies that we can put ourselves in the place of other people: we 'identify' ourselves with them. Now this capacity for identification with another person is a most important element in human relationships in general, and is also a condition for real and strong feelings of love. We are only able to disregard or to some extent sacrifice our own feelings and desires, and thus for a time to put the other person's interests and feelings first, if we have the capacity to identify ourselves with the loved person.
>
> (Klein 1937, p. 311)

Identification and affection have a larger place in Klein's view of the personality than in Freud's, no doubt because of her focus on the infant–mother relationship as one of the templates of identity. Whereas Freud's subjects have to struggle to balance desires and their prohibition, unconscious phantasy and reality, Klein's subjects struggle rather with the impulses of love and hate, sexuality and its perceived objects being formed within an emotional climate which can be dominated by different balances between them. Klein by no means minimises the power of destructive forces – indeed her theories have been widely criticised and rejected for the emphasis which they give to innate hatred and envy. But her theory also sets out more positively than Freud's the nature of the positive emotional bonds which make social relatedness possible, though this aspect of her thought is often disregarded. From her conception of human nature, one can infer that a good society is possible, if always liable to be precarious.

Klein was interested in criminal personalities – it is one of the areas in which she sought to apply her psychoanalytic thinking to an issue of social concern. She thought a moral sense was innate in human beings, even though sometimes in ways which might do little good, or worse. Where object-relations were dominated by destructiveness, in infancy, the superego and the sense of guilt would be correspondingly persecuting and severe. Criminals and delinquents, she believed, suffered from an excess of unbearable guilt, not from its lack. They could deal with this only by projecting it into other victims, or by seeking punishment for themselves. Many criminal careers involve repeated enactments of both kinds. She thought that in children at least, some element of love for objects was nearly always to be found, even if hidden and denied in the recesses of the personality. For this reason she was hopeful about the psychotherapeutic treatment of delinquency in children, though she acknowledged that criminal states in adults could be far more intractable.[20] Klein's ideas about criminality and the sense of guilt have a potentially large but neglected application to the issues of crime and punishment,[21] though the increasing interest now in ideas of restorative and reparative justice indicates that they may be being put to some use.

Klein's psychoanalytic writing is in fact saturated with terms which embody moral discriminations, that is categorisations of dispositions and states of feeling which have ethical significance. The prominence of terms such as love, hatred, envy, gratitude, jealousy, reparation, and guilt in her work – all of them explored in their psychoanalytic meanings, but nevertheless retaining their everyday resonance – indicates how profoundly ethical in their thinking Klein (and her associates) were. Klein's approach to ethical questions is however somewhat distant from the dominant traditions of English moral philosophy, which has been committed to rationalist models of moral judgement rather than to the description and clarification of the states of feeling and disposition which give rise to ethical behaviour. Klein's approach to these issues, and that of the psychoanalytic tradition which she has influenced, is much closer to the descriptive and exploratory methods of literature than to philosophical prescription.[22] Psychoanalysts in this tradition have generally given more attention to literature as a source of insight and inspiration than to philosophy. While the Kleinians acknowledge the necessity of the superego and its functions,[23] albeit in a modulated form, and thus acknowledge the significance of prescription and obligation in maintaining ethical norms, they are concerned also with the balance of love and hate in the formation of desires themselves. Good is done not merely when people act according to principles, but also, and perhaps to a greater degree, when their desires and impulses are dominated by love rather than hate. It was held that the formation of desires and dispositions could be affected for the better by the social environment – in the nurture of children, for example – and a number of psychoanalysts became involved in social interventions in the 1940s and 1950s – in nurseries, schools, in developing child and family mental health services – aimed to improve this.[24] Thus the conceptions of human nature and development influenced by Klein and her colleagues became one strand in the programme of post-war reconstruction and in the creation of the welfare state.

Klein formulated her theory of the origins and nature of moral dispositions primarily from her investigations of the relationships between infants and their objects of love and hate. Her definitions and explanations of moral sensibilities arise as deductions from the first principles of her theories of attachment and development, and from the combinations of loving and hating dispositions which motivate them. It is not obvious why, biographically or culturally speaking, Klein gave such emphasis to moral issues, unless one assumes that they are such innate aspects of human nature that anyone who starts as Klein did from its earliest developmental moments would be bound to give them this priority. But it is clear that she was centrally interested in what a good life might be, for whatever reason. Kleinian psychoanalysts were criticised later on for being too morally focused, for being too morally prescriptive towards their patients, seeking to bring them therapeutically towards a morally desirable 'depressive' state of mind, rather than helping them to come to their own choices and decisions about their lives. The influence of Bion and other post-Kleinians has somewhat alleviated this tendency, though without departing from its fundamental insights or evaluations. Perhaps there is a connection between the threat to social cohesion and continuity experienced in Klein's lifetime, with two world wars and the rise of Nazism and the Jewish genocide, and the centrality of moral concerns to her theory. A close parallel was the development of the Leavisite tradition in English literary criticism over almost the identical period, in which value in literary works was to a great extent equated with the moral discriminations which they realised in imaginative form. This critical tradition was much preoccupied with the development of a cultural idea of Englishness which would sustain a democratic kind of social order against aristocratic, materialist and fascistic challenges. Kleinian psychoanalysis and its various allies seemed to be attempting to restore and develop a compassionate social order at the level of the primary family, and one which assigned greater recognition to the role of women.[25]

In the post-Second World War period in particular, explorations and assertions of primary values felt recently to have been in grave peril seem to have had great cultural resonance. Writers such as Orwell, Camus, Sartre, D.H. Lawrence and T.S. Eliot became iconic figures after the war because they seemed to be addressing the need for the reassertion of fundamental moral values and convictions, different as of course all these were. Other writers, such as Samuel Beckett, were regarded as profound witnesses to the collapse of values and settled existence. With the weakening of religious authority, publics turned to literary and cultural figures for moral example. Where Freud had been part of a modern movement whose main impetus had been to attack and overthrow traditional conventions and verities (though like other modernists he was also the pioneer of a new and revolutionary way of thinking), the generation of intellectuals formed in liberal societies like Britain after the pre-First World War *ancien régime* (Mayer 1981) by the experiences of two world wars, revolution and fascism, was more reparative, constructivist and restorative in its perspectives, aspiring to different kinds of moral affirmation, or social reconstruction.[26] Melanie Klein seems to belong in this cultural context, setting out as she does to formulate a morally informed understanding of human nature from her particular sphere of experience.[27]

Klein's significance

Why is Melanie Klein such a significant figure? Her own writings are so confined to the theory and practice of psychoanalysis itself, and often so difficult for lay readers, such is her uncompromising engagement with abstract psychoanalytic concepts, that one might wonder about such high claims for her standing. Can she really be said to have made one of the greatest contributions to the understanding of human nature in the twentieth century?

The evidence that she should be regarded in this way is to be found in the influence which her work has had in the field of psychoanalysis. The psychoanalysis of children became established following her example and method. The 'object-relations' school of psychoanalysis, though it has drawn on many contributions other than Klein's, was principally inspired by her work. An extensive development in psychoanalytic theory and practice, both within and influenced by the Kleinian school, has elaborated and developed her ideas.[28] Although Klein herself did not in her writings stray far from the consulting room, her associates and successors have explored the implications of her ideas in many other contexts of application – in work in social services, hospitals, nurseries and schools, and in a variety of other organisational settings. Hanna Segal did much to develop Kleinian psychoanalytic thinking in the literary and cultural sphere, through her papers on symbol-formation and art (Segal 1952, 1957), and has had many successors in this work. Through the Tavistock Clinic in London, Kleinian approaches have found a significant embodiment in clinical practice and training in a public sector setting, in contrast to the more usual dependence of psychoanalysis on private practice for its support. 'Infant observation', invented as a form of training by Esther Bick on the basis of a Kleinian interest in infancy and in mother–infant relationships, has been adopted worldwide as an emotionally rich form of pre-clinical education in psychoanalysis and for other mental health workers. With its contemporary evolution into 'post-Kleinian' psychoanalysis, the tradition founded by Klein shows every sign of continuing strength and vitality. It is this broad influence of her ideas that confirms the great significance of Klein's contribution both to psychoanalysis, and to the understanding of human nature itself.

Notes

1   Though she refers to Nietzsche's idea of the 'pale criminal' (Klein 1927), and she quotes Keats (Klein 1937).
2   However, others influenced by Klein have made many fruitful applications of her ideas to cultural and social fields, beginning perhaps with the papers edited by Klein, Heimann and Money-Kyrle (1955).
3   Schorske (1998, p. 1996) writes: 'Though he does not speak of a debt to Bentham, Freud's early theory of instincts, with its duality of pleasure principle and reality principle, resonates with echoes of Bentham's hedonistic system.'
4   There is now a substantial literature developing a feminist critique of liberal social contract theory, e.g. Pateman (1988).
5   Meira Likierman's *Melanie Klein: Her Work in Context* (2001) is illuminating on these connections, and on Klein's theoretical development more generally.
6   Janet Sayers in *Mothering Psychoanalysis* (1991) persuasively describes the contribution of four major women psychoanalysts – Helen Deutsch, Karen Horney, Anna Freud and Melanie Klein – in making the experience of mothering and the relationships of mother and infant central to modern psychoanalysis, in contradistinction to Freud's patriarchal perspective. Lisa Appignanesi and John Forrester (1992) in *Freud's Women* put forward a similar argument: 'Most importantly, Klein's work pioneered a slow and subtle shift, one, perhaps, that transformed psychoanalysis more than any other single factor: the reorientation of the understanding of the child's inner world around its relation to its mother. Mothers became models for the profession of psychoanalysis, mothering provided descriptions of what psychoanalysts were supposed to be doing; via the mother, the normative life-story was introduced' (p. 454). See also Julia Kristeva's *Melanie Klein* (2001).
7   Her son Erich is the 'Fritz' of Klein's 'The Development of a Child' (1921).
8   Phyllis Grosskurth (1985) develops this view in her biography of Klein. Although some Kleinian analysts were offended by this book, possibly objecting to some of its disclosures, it seems to me that the connections it proposes between Klein's personal experience and her contributions to psychoanalysis are both convincing and relevant to our understanding. It is not unreasonable to suggest that major psychoanalytic discoveries may sometimes emerge from courageous introspective reflections on experience. Freud said as much in relation to his own work, and in proposing Sophocles' Oedipus as an exemplar of self-discovery.
9   Freud wrote: 'Recent investigations have directed our attention to a stage in the development of the libido which it passes through on the way from auto-erotism to object-love. This stage has been given the name of narcissism. What happens is this. There comes a time in the development of the individual at which he unifies

his sexual instincts (which have hitherto been engaged in auto-erotic activities) in order to obtain a love-object; and he begins by taking himself, his own body, as a love-object and only subsequently proceeds from this to the choice of some person other than himself as his object' (Freud 1911, pp. 60–61). And earlier, 'Narcissistic or ego-libido seems to be the great reservoir from which the object-cathexes are sent out and into which they are withdrawn once more; the narcissistic libidinal cathexis of the ego is the original state of things, realised in earliest childhood, and is merely covered by the later extrusions of libido, but in essentials persists behind them' (Freud 1905, p. 219). The argument is restated in Freud 1913, pp. 88–89.

10 Peter Fonagy and Mary Target (2003, ch. 6) review the recent empirical research bearing on Klein's theoretical conjectures. They conclude: 'it has to be said that some of Melanie Klein's ideas no longer seem as far-fetched as they did at first, None of this is proof of her ideas, but they cannot be dismissed as implausible given the direction in which developmental science is progressing' (p. 134).

11 Alan Shuttleworth (2002) has referred to this as 'a bio-psycho-social model'.

12 Vygotsky (1896–1934) and Piaget (1896–1980) undertook their very different investigations of the development of the child in a period more or less contemporary with Klein.

13 See the symposium 'The Conceptualisation and Communication of Clinical Facts in Psychoanalysis', *International Journal of Psychoanalysis*, 1994, 75, part 5/6, edited by David Tuckett.

14 On psychoanalytic infant observation, see Miller *et al.* (1989).

15 A parallel can be drawn with the influence of F.R. Leavis and his journal *Scrutiny* over English literary criticism in the 1940s and 1950s, which was based on a practice of 'close reading', and an affirmation of values of the moral imagination which (unlike Kleinian psychoanalysis) remained largely untheorised (Mulhern 1979). Both Leavisites and Kleinians drew inspiration from the English Romantic poets, e.g. Coleridge and Keats.

16 Richard Wollheim, the leading philosophical advocate of psychoanalysis in Britain in recent years, defended psychoanalysis for its affinities with the psychological understandings embedded in everyday language, drawing on Wittgensteinian ideas in doing so. He argued that Freud 'extended', 'deepened' and 'elaborated' the language of commonsense psychology, but did not seek to replace it with an alien conceptual system (Wollheim 1991). But the achievement of British psychoanalysis has been to combine what are at times very abstract forms of thinking, with giving close attention to the facts of patients' experience. Klein was outstanding in both these capacities, and Kleinian child analysis had a particular influence since child analysts had to learn how to communicate with child patients in necessarily direct and simple ways.

17 We might note also that many of those whom Klein analysed, or with whom she was in close professional contact (Bion, Rickman, Money-Kyrle, Bowlby, for example), were members of the armed forces. Their involvement in the issues of war and post-war reconstruction is evident in their writing. Klein must have been fully immersed in the worldly preoccupations of the time, even though her writing is almost exclusively concerned with psychoanalytic issues, and the development of children.

18 Klein formulates her concept of the depressive position in Klein 1935 and Klein 1940. While she writes of paranoic anxieties and a 'paranoic position' in these papers, full formulation of the paranoid-schizoid position followed only in Klein 1946.

19 'Love, Guilt and Reparation' (1937) is one of only three essays that Klein wrote

for wider audiences, the others being 'On Weaning' (1936) and *Our Adult World and its Roots in Infancy* (1959).

20   'Just as with perversions and psychoses, it may be impossible to find ways of approaching adult criminals. But as regards analyses in childhood the position is different. A child does not need special motives for analysis; it is a question of technical measures to establish the transference and keep the analysis going. *I do not believe in the existence of a child in whom it is impossible to obtain this transference, or in whom the capacity for love cannot be brought out.* In the case of my little criminal, he was apparently devoid of any capacity for love, but analysis proved that this was not so' (Klein 1927, pp. 184–185, original emphasis).

21   Arthur Hyatt Williams (1998) is one psychoanalyst who has made impressive use of Klein's ideas in his work with long-term prisoners convicted of violent crimes.

22   An exception in post-war British moral philosophy was the position taken by Philippa Foot (1978, 2000, 2001), who argued against abstract prescriptivism and utilitarianism, and for attention to the complex moral discriminations embodied in ordinary language, in terms influenced by the later Wittgenstein. Kleinian psychoanalytic thinking has relevance to a 'naturalistic ethics' to which characterisations of human nature are plainly relevant.

23   Bion (1959), O'Shaugnessy (1999) and Britton (1998, 2003) are among Kleinian analysts who have devoted much effort to describing the distortions of the superego.

24   Winnicott, who gave radio broadcasts on child care, and Bowlby, who made important interventions in social policy debates concerned with families, were prominent examples.

25   One can argue that the priority accorded to the construction of the welfare state in post-war Britain (at the expense of the productive economy, some critics have argued) represented a 'feminisation' of the political agenda, even though it was not defended on feminist grounds and indeed later provoked feminist attack.

26   One can contrast the different temper of a later generation of 'post-modern' cultural figures. By these, the ideas of 'nature', 'human nature' or absolute cultural value are criticised as essentialist or provincial. Instead there is a celebration of difference, choice, the pleasurable, the cosmopolitan and the diverse. An aesthetic register takes precedence over an ethical one. Clearly the critique of Marxism and Communism has been one important dimension in this widespread rejection of absolutist positions, but it is by no means its only motive. This post-modern critique of foundationalism in its various forms has no doubt been liberating and enlivening in many respects, certainly in its cultural inventiveness. But Melanie Klein's severe commitment to understanding what she thought of as the realities of psychic life, and its troubles, and to investigate the emotional realities of human development, reveal her work to have been formed in a quite different intellectual and moral climate.

27   Roger Money-Kyrle, the Kleinian analyst most engaged in exploring the ethical and political implications of Kleinian ideas during Klein's lifetime, described himself as a 'humanist', a description which Klein would probably also have accepted of herself.

28   The collection *Melanie Klein Today*, Vols 1 and 2, edited by Elizabeth Bott Spillius (1988), provides the best introduction to this tradition of work.

References

Appignanesi, L. and Forrester, J. (1992) *Freud's Women*. London: Weidenfeld and Nicolson.

Bion, W.R. (1959) 'Attacks on Linking', *International Journal of Psychoanalysis*, 40, part 5/6. Reprinted in Bion (1962).

Bion, W.R. (1962) *Second Thoughts*. London: Heinemann.

Bion, W.R. (1963) *Elements of Psychoanalysis*. London: Heinemann.

Boston, M. and Szur, R. (eds) (1983) *Psychotherapy with Severely Deprived Children*. London: Routledge and Kegan Paul (reprinted London: Karnac, 1990).

Britton, R. (1998) *Belief and Imagination*. London: Routledge.

Britton, R. (2003) *Sex, Death and the Superego*. London: Karnac.

Darwin, C. (1998) *The Expression of the Emotions in Man and Animals*. London: HarperCollins (First edition published in 1872).

Fonagy, P. and Target, M. (2003) *Psychoanalytic Theories: Perspectives from Developmental Psychology*. London: Whurr.

Foot, P. (1978) *Virtues and Vices*. Oxford: Oxford University Press.

Foot, P. (2000) *Moral Dilemmas – and Other Topics in Moral Philosophy*. Oxford: Oxford University Press.

Foot, P. (2001) *Natural Goodness*. Oxford: Oxford University Press.

Freud, S. (1905) *The Case of Schreber: Psychoanalytic Notes on an Autobiographical Account of a Case of Paranoia*. Standard Edition, Vol. XII.

Freud, S. (1911) *Three Essays on Sexuality*. Standard Edition, Vol. VII.

Freud, S. (1913) *Totem and Taboo*. Standard Edition, Vol. XIII.

Freud, S. (1917) *Mourning and Melancholia*. Standard Edition, Vol XIV.

Grosskurth, P. (1985) *Melanie Klein*. New York: Basic Books.

Hrdy, Sarah Blaffer (1999) *Mother Nature: A History of Mothers, Infants and Natural Selection*. London: Pantheon.

Hyatt Williams, A. (1998) *Cruelty, Violence and Murder: Understanding the Criminal Mind*. London: Karnac.

King, P. and Steiner, R. (eds) (1991) *The Freud–Klein Controversies 1941–45*. London: Routledge.

Klein, M. (1921) 'The Development of a Child', reprinted in Klein 1975a.

Klein, M. (1927) 'Criminal Tendencies in Normal Children', reprinted in Klein 1975a.

Klein, M. (1928) 'Early Stages of the Oedipus Complex', reprinted in Klein 1975a.

Klein, M. (1929) 'Infantile Situations Reflected in a Work of Art and in the Creative Impulse', reprinted in Klein 1975a.

Klein, M. (1931) 'A Contribution to the Theory of Intellectual Inhibition', reprinted in Klein 1975a.

Klein, M. (1932) *The Psychoanalysis of Children*. London: Hogarth Press.

Klein, M. (1935) 'A Contribution to the Psychogenesis of Manic-Depressive States', reprinted in Klein 1975a.

Klein, M. (1936) 'On Weaning', reprinted in Klein 1975a.

Klein, M. (1937) 'Love, Guilt and Reparation', reprinted in Klein 1975a.

Klein, M. (1940) 'Mourning and its Relation to Manic-Depressive States', reprinted in Klein 1975a.

Klein, M. (1946) 'Notes on Some Schizoid Mechanisms', reprinted in Klein 1975a.

Klein, M. (1952) 'The Origins of Transference', reprinted in Klein 1975b.

Klein, M. (1955) 'On Identification', reprinted in Klein 1975b.

Klein, M. (1959) *Our Adult World and its Roots in Infancy*. Reprinted in Klein 1975b.

Klein, M. (1961) *Narrative of a Child Analysis*. London: Hogarth Press.

Klein, M. (1963) 'Reflections on the Oresteia', reprinted in Klein 1975b.

Klein, M. (1975a) *Love, Guilt and Reparation and Other Works 1921–1945*. London: Hogarth Press.

Klein, M. (1975b) *Envy and Gratitude and Other Works 1946–1963*. London: Hogarth Press.

Klein, M., Heimann, P. and Money-Kyrle, R. (eds) (1955) *New Directions in Psychoanalysis*. London: Tavistock Publications.

Kristeva, J. (2001) *Melanie Klein*. New York: Columbia University Press.

Likierman, M. (2001) *Melanie Klein: Her Work in Context*. London: Continuum.

Mayer, A.J. (1981) *The Persistence of the Old Regime: Europe to the Great War*. New York: Pantheon.

Meltzer, D. and Harris Williams, M. (1988) *The Apprehension of Beauty*. Strath Tay, Perthshire: Clunie Press.

Miller, L., Rustin M.E., Rustin M.J. and Shuttleworth J. (eds) (1989) *Closely Observed Infants: Case-Studies in Infant Observation*. London: Duckworth.

Money-Kyrle, R. (1978) *The Collected Papers of Roger Money-Kyrle* (edited by D. Meltzer). Strath Tay, Perthshire: Clunie Press.

Mulhern, F. (1979) *The Moment of Scrutiny*. London: New Left Books.

O'Shaugnessy, E. (1999) 'Relating to the Superego', *International Journal of Psycho-analysis*, Vol. 80, Part 5, pp 861–870.

Pateman, C. (1988). *The Sexual Contract*. Cambridge: Polity Press.

Sayers, J. (1991) *Mothering Psychoanalysis*. London: Hamish Hamilton.

Schorske, C.E. (1998) 'To the Egyptian Dig: Explorations in the Passage to Modernism', in *Thinking with History: Explorations in the Passage to Modernism*. Princeton: Princeton University Press.

Segal, H. (1952) 'A Psychoanalytical Approach to Aesthetics', *International Journal of Psychoanalysis*, 33: 196–207. Reprinted in Segal 1986.

Segal, H. (1957) 'Notes on Symbol Formation', *International Journal of Psychoanalysis*, 38: 291–7. Reprinted in Segal 1986.

Segal, H. (1986) *Delusion and Artistic Creativity and other Psycho-analytic Essays*. London: Free Association Books.

Segal, H. (1999) 'Psychoanalysis, Dreams, History: An Interview with Hanna Segal', by Daniel Pick and Lyndal Roper. *History Workshop Journal*, 49, Spring.

Shuttleworth, A. (2002) 'Turning Towards a Bio-Psycho-Social Way of Thinking', *European Journal of Psychotherapy, Counselling and Health*, 5(3): 205–223.

Spillius, E.B. (ed.) (1988). *Melanie Klein Today: Vol. 1: Mainly Theory; Vol. 2: Mainly Practice*. London: Routledge.

Tuckett, D. (ed.) (1994) 'The Conceptualisation and Communication of Clinical Facts in Psychoanalysis', Symposium, *International Journal of Psychoanalysis*, 75, part 5/6.

Wollheim, R. (1991) 'Desire, Belief and Dr Grunbaum's Freud', in *The Mind and its Depths*. Cambridge, Mass.: Harvard University Press.

Chapter 3

Destruction and madness

Michael Eigen

There are many threads in psychoanalysis and madness is a privileged one. Freud's structural concepts are imbued with portrayals of madness. Id as seething cauldron of excitations, no no in the unconscious, opposites meld, reverse, are indistinguishable, the law of contradiction and common sense do not hold. Ego as hallucinatory organ, idealizing–denigrating (over–underestimating), projecting, identifying, denying, splitting, disintegrating; a double agent, developing anti-hallucinogenic properties and perceptual, reflective sanity. A sanity often soaked with madness that seeps through personal and world events. A superego concerned with morals, turning moralistic, overly self-critical, punishing, cancerously destructive, devouring reality with hate-filled ideals. Freud takes us to places where madness stains psyche. Capacities that try to set things right are not exempt. Psychoanalysis can lay no special claim on sanity but joins the struggle, replacing obsession with sin by analysis of madness, opening possibility for further ethical development (Eigen 1986).

It took time for psychoanalysis to come out of the closet and trace psychotic processes masked by neurotic organizations. "Behind every neurosis is a hidden psychosis," a remark I heard Henry Elkin make in the late 1950s, if not a rallying cry or psychoanalytic koan, expresses a current that gathered momentum. A current that fit a thread in cultural life concerned with meaninglessness, disintegration, destruction, emptiness, warp. Disaster that hit not only individual personalities, but the social fabric.

Many voices bearing witness to psychotic dynamics arose, Melanie Klein's one of the strongest. She does not say every human infant is mad, but she does say all have psychotic anxieties. Some felt anxiety too weak a word and spoke of agony (Elkin 1972; Winnicott 1989), catastrophe and nameless dread (Bion 1970). Still, Klein put madness on London's psychoanalytic map and changed the direction of British psychoanalysis. Her sail caught a wind already blowing, but few went as far with it.

Her background includes Karl Abraham in Germany and Sandor Ferenczi in Hungary, rich envisioners of early states of mind. Both were concerned with the fate of destructive urges. Abraham (1973) emphasized oral sadism and Ferenczi (1955) the importance of the mother in modifying an infant's death drive. Association of psychosis and destruction was part of the air Klein breathed and she gave it significant turns.

She picked up on Freud's depiction of infantile hate in relation to externality, together with the infant's attempt to expel disturbance. In her vision (1946), the infant tries to rid itself of disturbance by splitting it off and projecting it outwards. This assumes some good feeling nucleus that attempts to go on maintaining good feeling. One positively identifies with a good feeling current, negatively identifies with bad feeling. This is an extremely important emphasis, a movement that informs her thinking. The infant tries to rid itself of pain and disturbance without knowing the source of the irritant or how to relieve it. It gets rid of bad feeling by changing its place, displacing, hallucinating or imagining it elsewhere. It gets rid of bad feeling by placing it into an outside object.

An object outside of what? An object caused by bad feeling to begin with? Bad feeling attributed to an object, bound as an object? Her work abounds with inside objects placed outside, outside objects absorbed inside, a kind of psychic breathing. Doubleness permeates her work. Split drives, affects, ego, objects. Almost a psychic gnosticism: good and bad warring throughout the psyche.

One of the greatest war zones is the mother's body, good and bad breasts outside, good and bad babies, wombs, penises, rivals inside. The infant's psyche swims through maternal insides encountering rivals, father's penises (good and bad), golden milk babies and spoiled fecal ones, good and bad mothering moments solidifying as objects locked in strife. The confused, agonized baby god attempts to split regions of being, separate good from bad, inside from outside, triumph over rivals, control mother's insides (body, mind), access and own the greater god's creativity (to generate babies, milk, thoughts, feelings). To feel good and keep feeling good: an activity confused with winning.

The Kleinian baby is very busy controlling bad things, keeping the good going. Where is the good located? In body sensations, affect sensations, attitudes? Mixtures that keep shifting? How does one shift with it, keep up with it, as good–bad conditions change? Mother's body, an hallucinated heaven based on heavenly moments, turns out to be an arena of threat, conflict, challenge and terror as well.

Psychic breathing is more complicated than physical breathing. It is not just a matter of expelling bad, taking in good. Good and bad are inside and outside, fused and split. The Kleinian psyche is a kind of fantasy pump, circulating good and bad affects/ego elements/objects inside and out in order to keep a modicum of good feeling going in face of the ever pressing bad.

A pass Klein brings us to, of crucial importance, is use of good feelings, a part of psychic reality, to blot out, substitute for, displace bad ones. Good blots out bad with variable success, bad returning, even blotting out good for a time. Good and bad feelings in tension, struggling, magnified through the prism of fantasy. The good trying to offset the bad, the bad threatening to overwhelm the good.

An inherently stressed, pressured psyche trying to maintain good feeling in face of bad. Great tension, great struggle. A war psyche. Every capacity potentially defending against and attacking every other. A psyche constantly trying to keep up with its own destructiveness.

Death and life drives: Freud

A turn occurred in psychoanalysis, shifting emphasis from sex to death (Eigen 1993, ch. 9; 1996, chs 1–2). Freud associated anxiety with sexual excitement, which had to be modulated for the sake of individual, social and cultural development. A depressive-anxious tendency attended sexual desire as part of the latter's cultural formation. Anger was part of passional energy, as index of frustration, as force to overcome obstacles, as part of energic vigor, as part of self-affirmation, as response to threat. Social and professional injury (blows to the ego, blending injury with anger) important in themselves, tapped infantile sexuality, impossible wishes, re-routing of desire. Repressed sexuality, its symbolic spread through culture, together with an angry mix of depressive anxiety, formed a grouping that, after thirty years of intellectual and clinical labor, Freud (1920, 1940) associated with life drive, libido, a tendency to weave drives, affects, objects into more complex unities, a tendency to build.

After thirty years of labor, Freud also posited a destructive force that was more or other than the anger of the life drive. A force that worked against growth, a kind of entropy, inertia, catabolic tendency breaking down unities. As if psychic life, too much for itself, tore itself down and/or collapsed under its own weight, unable to take its own pain, its sensitivity, the challenge of its own development. To be something and suffer and grow or to be stress free nothing, that is, not to be.

One sees this shift in the change of meaning of death wish, which earlier meant our angry wish for others to die, and now expressed a force aimed against ourselves (Freud 1920, 1937; Eigen 1986, 1996). Freud analogizes life and death drives to anabolic–catabolic processes, a quasi-biological substratum for psychic forces: to build up, to tear down, parallel to symbolic–diabolic, to tie together and break apart.

Some call Freud's death drive a cancer psychology, a war psychology, a death psychology growing up as it did after the First World War, the death of a daughter, his own cancer. Whatever the fate of the death drive as a scientific concept, it ripples with meaning, a portent, a warning, a signifier of ghastly things humans do to each other, to themselves. A concept burning with horror, the Holocaust incubating, its impulse very alive today.

Death and life drives: Klein

Melanie Klein's formulations are rooted in Freud's death drive: "I hold that anxiety arises from the operation of the death instinct within the organism, is felt as fear of annihilation (death) and takes the form of persecution" (Klein 1946, p. 296). A destructive force in the organism translates to global annihilation dread, distilled as particular object fears. Objects may be internal or external, images, persons or parts of persons, affects, character traits, attitudes, somatic functions. Conscious or semi-conscious persecutory fears tap generic unconscious destructive currents rooted in the organism. The psycho-organism, under tremendous destructive pressure from within, filters some of the latter through objects.

One scenario is for intrinsic annihilation dread to be felt as caused by objects. We try to control annihilation anxiety by controlling objects we imagine responsible for it. One such process is to introject the object, taking in and circumscribing disturbance one hoped to expel. If only one can concentrate disturbance, packet it, export it, place it elsewhere. Like the return of the repressed, projected/introjected annihilation works partly, for a time.

A scenario we dumbly repeat is to split off and project disturbance and try to kill it off by killing objects we think cause it. In effect, we try to kill the death drive by killing objects symbolizing it. Horror escalates as attempts to annihilate signifiers of annihilation fail in unconscious aim. This is not to say we are not afraid of murderers or that murder is not real. Likewise, disease and death. This is not a stupid theory. There are many sources of anxiety. Psychoanalysis adds unconscious surplus: global, pervasive unconscious dread of destruction, rooted in the organism, magnified by unconscious fantasy, working by projection–introjection. Conscious dreads tap unconscious dreads. Klein compounds some of the latter (death and birth anxiety, separation anxiety, bodily frustration) into the term "primary anxiety," dread with many faces, at many levels of being.

We have moved from reading symbolic displacements of repressed sexuality, to symbolic traces and enactments of death-work: from sexual-aggressive anxiety to annihilation anxiety. Freud wrote that every psychic act combines death and life drives. Klein emphasizes the function of life drive as defense against death drive. The life drive works to offset the death drive, to mitigate destruction. It is as if the death drive is more basic and powerful and the life drive tones it down for a time. Life as defense against death, a postponement. One reason we feel the press of time is that life is hard pressed to keep up with death. For Klein, life drive and objects function to regulate, offset, modulate the death drive.

Splitting and projective identification

The ego splits in order to modulate the flow of death, toning death down by distributing it across affect and object fields: "The result of splitting is a dispersal of the destructive impulse which is felt as a source of danger" (1946, p. 297). Klein links "the primary anxiety of being annihilated by a destructive force within," and the ego's splitting or falling to pieces, with schizophrenia. Schizophrenia results from an annihilative process defending against further annihilation.

Splitting can proliferate, multiply, go on forever, the result being a fading or thinning of affect, a sense of being unreal, oscillating with hyper-real, depending on whether the diffusing or intensifying aspect of splitting dominates at a given time. While psychosis is an all too rigid, stable organization, a good deal of fluctuating extremes go on in it, the personality obsessively-hysterically shifting grounds, in a panicky, paranoid driven way within a quasi-delusional mode. Psychosis is both a result of and an attempt to regulate destruction, the latter usually quite visible in the individual's concerns and fears. It is as if a person in the grips of psychosis is asking, "Will this destroy me? Will this destroy me?" – as he or she bounces from one thought or feeling or image or external danger to another. Another way of putting it: "What will I have to think or do, in order to preserve the world and myself?" Since splitting the destructive drive works through any psychic function or product and does not stop, spreading anywhere and everywhere, no safe haven can be found for long, neither out nor in. The idea that there will not be destruction is as delusional as the idea that there is only destruction. We modulate, even transform, destruction as we can, but there is no end to it.

In Klein, splitting acts to separate good from bad, but also goes on in the destructive domain. In the first case, splitting tries to protect good from bad, separate them, split off and project the latter. As noted earlier, good–bad may apply to affects, objects, ego states. To preserve good objects or self-states in face of inner attack is a necessary, thankless task. The psyche's work is never done. There is no end to maintaining a modicum of goodness in the midst of destructive tendencies. Islands of goodness in a sea of destruction. A bit like the sorcerer's apprentice, bailing out the psyche, a ship full of holes. To compound difficulty, the psyche tries to control destruction by splitting the destructive tendency, projecting it, diffusing it, dispersing it throughout internal–external universes. Psyche works overtime, keeping bits of goodness good, flushing out bad in ways that multiply the latter.

This sounds a bit like St. Paul's portrayal of the law. Laws multiply to preserve justice, goodness, purity – partly degenerating into superstition. Which side of the bed to get out of, which leg to put down first, which shoe to put on first become ritualized. Something destructive may result if the regulating rule or law is not followed correctly, faithfully. The magical fallacy of such rules does not mean the destructiveness they respond to is unreal. On the contrary, it shows to what extremes we are driven under destructive pressures. The Bible is a kind of handbook to regulate destruction, with more or less success in various contexts. It may send us off in wrong directions, but is filled with important hints.

Klein encapsulates her vision by postulating an early *paranoid-schizoid position*, in which psyche handles disturbance and pain by attacking it, splitting it off, projecting it. It hates disturbance and makes it go away. If hate disturbs, it hates hate, tries to make hate go away. However, it is inwardly identified with the exiled elements, since they are all parts of oneself. One is in the position of banishing parts of one's mind in order to regulate psychophysical disturbance. Thus the term, projective identification: split-off aspects of the self one unconsciously identifies with, but which are projected elsewhere to minimize disturbance. The offshoot is a chronic state of re-routing annihilation anxiety via splitting and projection, while remaining unconsciously identified with exiled aspects of death threats. Outer and inner universes become peopled with projective displacements of annihilation anxiety linked to a destructive force within.

Klein points out the self-defeating nature of this primitive operation. For example, one introjects objects containing our projections, re-infecting ourselves with what we try to get rid of, compounded by the other's projective work as well. Ideally, the other will work over our projections, transform them for the better, so that what comes back is not as bad as what went out. Klein stresses that projective–introjective identifications are fantasy formations. So that distress is magnified imaginatively – a witch, rather than mother, a devil, rather than father, a pit of hell, not simply a stomach. We try to regulate destructive feelings with destructive fantasies, attempt to relocate destruction, shift it away, an operation doomed to boomerang.

Double nuclei, goodness, idealization, denial of psychic reality

Klein posits a double beginning or a doubleness in beginnings, in keeping with Freud's dual drive theory, life and death drives. The phrase, "in the beginning," appears in her work repeatedly. Over and over she says that aggression and hatred (death drive deflected outward by projection) play an important role from the beginning of life and that from the beginning the first internal good object does as well. The "first internal good object acts as a focal point of the ego. It counteracts the processes of splitting and dispersal, makes for cohesiveness and integration, and is instrumental in building up the ego" (1946, p. 297).

This is a momentous shift of emphasis. An internal good object, outreach of the life drive, functions not as a primary source of anxiety (sexual excitement), but to allay, mute, bind anxiety about destruction. The good object, with its sense of wholeness, functions to counteract outreaches of death-work, splitting and dispersal, themselves attempts to distribute destruction in order to survive or ease it.

States of frustration intensify the workings of the death drive, leading to attacks on breast, object, ego. If things are bad enough, destructive attacks extend to sensation, feelings, thoughts, the mind or body itself, splitting self and other into bits and pieces, worlds of hate-filled shards. Amalgams of sensation, affects, ego and object, imaginings, body elements and functions fuse and fly in different directions, threatening to pull self apart even more, issuing into bits of threatening figures everywhere, inside and outside the body. One's own destructive feelings, spread through one's organs, real and imaginary, populate inner and outer horizons.

As the quote above suggests, a good object is present too, counteracting destructive divisiveness, tending towards cohesion (the unifying life drive) and development. "I hold that the introjected good breast forms a vital part of the ego, exerts from beginning a fundamental influence . . ." (1946, p. 295). The good object from the beginning helps mediate growth of self and object relations.

What we have, in part, is a psychoanalytic phenomenological/visionary working out of ways life and death drive work through unconscious fantasy (projective/introjective identification), distributing through creative–destructive ego and object relations, including maturation of affective connection. The support of a good object/ego/affect nucleus from the outset is crucial, or there would be only destructiveness, i.e. nothing at all. Inherent tension between goodness and destruction seems to be basic. A variation of this is the Catholic notion that evil feeds on good, a positive for destruction to destroy. Today, I suspect we wonder if destruction needs only itself to work on.

The good breast makes one feel complete, is felt to be complete itself (1946, p. 297). A completeness shaken by frustration, pain, anxiety. A sense of completeness makes one more secure, a necessary illusion perhaps, but one that can be dangerous. Sometimes the completion of goodness feels suffocating and one tries to break through it. One tries to break self or others apart to recover fragmentary states. At times, destruction feels more real.

We have, then, a kind of gradation. Good feelings that support the self, good feelings that suffocate it. A sense of completeness that adds cohesion and completeness that feels unreal and invites fragmentation. Klein notes that extremes of good feeling correlate with persecutory fears. Not simply that we feel persecuted by good feeling (something she does not consider fully), but that good feeling – idealization, idealized good feeling – binds or counteracts persecutory anxieties. Idealization and persecution as two sides of a split coin: exaggerated good breast or object protects against the annihilating bad breast or object. Translate this as you will, the function pointed to is important.

There are splits within splits within splits. Good–bad breasts or other objects, aspects of breasts or other objects, idealization–persecution, and so on. After delineating the good object as a pivotal nucleus at the heart of personality, necessary to support growth, she develops what I feel to be a quintessential Kleinian theme: use of goodness to deny, even obliterate, psychic reality. Exaggerated goodness, idealized goodness or an idealizing function of goodness perhaps. Or more profoundly, hallucinated goodness, partly built from good memories, perceptions, fantasies.

Klein amplifies Freud's fantasy of an infant hallucinating a good feed when hungry, substituting pleasure for pain, satisfaction for distress, a wish-fulfillment. Freud's hallucinated satisfaction slides into perfection, a beatific or ideal state. A sense of wholeness, completion, fullness when one is helplessly on the verge of dread, panicky hate, falling apart, screaming oneself to oblivion, dying. Good feeling masking persecutory anxiety, the latter a more limited profile of generic destructive force. How easily Freud threads into Klein.

Instinctual desires, aiming at unlimited gratification, "create a picture of an inexhaustible and always bountiful breast – an ideal breast." Also called, "an idealized object" and "ideal object." Splitting and hallucination work together, a hallucinatory splitting off of the good, making it all good, making goodness all (1946, p. 299). An affective sensation that finds its way into and supports the wish or belief or intimation or conviction or goal: to live forever in a state of happiness.

We reach an amazing insight: "In hallucinatory gratification, therefore, two interrelated processes take place: the omnipotent conjuring up of the ideal object and situation, and the equally omnipotent annihilation of the bad persecutory object and the painful situation" (1946, p. 299). Is it the life drive that is annihilating the death drive or the death drive annihilating itself? Individuals and groups attack one another, partly in hope of annihilating annihilation, only to discover pain, often horror, that hallucinatory positions fail to cover.

As Freud suggests, reality breaks through wish-fulfillment as time goes on, but this does not end the pull towards hallucinatory scenarios. Klein points to double aspects of hallucinatory splitting: revving up the good, erasing the bad. Whether such a state is felt to be good or bad varies. Groups and individuals tenaciously fight to maintain hallucinatory positions, disabling a full range of contact with potential difficulties: reality in the service of hallucination, rather than the reverse. Unconscious madness, rather than the challenge of channeling hallucinatory tendencies in creative social, psychological, political, aesthetic, and religious work.

The far-reaching effect of destruction by hallucinated goodness (i.e. the use of goodness to destroy or mask or obliterate destruction, to hallucinate destructiveness out of existence) is sharply noted: "Omnipotent denial of the existence of the bad object and painful situation is in the unconscious equal to annihilation by the destructive impulse" (1946, p. 299). Denial of psychic reality, its full range of pluses and minuses, is a form of annihilation. The attempt at self-preservation (good object supporting life drive) turns against itself, falling to the temptation to blot out the death drive and annihilative tendencies. To blot out a portion of psychic reality, its ugliness and awfulness, is to preserve oneself by annihilating portions of self, psyche, the way life feels. Life drive blotting out death drive amounts to a strange victory of death indeed: good feeling in the service of obliteration.

Death drive as necessary instrument of survival perhaps, at great price. What survives is hallucinated survival, life in the service of annihilation. Relationship to others suffers deformation as connection between self and other must bear annihilative pressures it may not be able to withstand.

Klein has built an astounding nexus of interlocking operations envisioned to distribute destructive impulses throughout the psycho-social economy. Splitting, projective–introjective identifications as privileged operations of unconscious fantasy, idealization, denial of psychic reality, manic defense, omnipotent hallucinated substitution of good for bad states – all significant parts of the paranoid-schizoid position. More can be said. Love and good-ness can be split off and projected too, depleting personality, keeping it vulnerable to imaginary virtues of others. Hallucinated destruction can edge out sincerity, devotion, love of the good, making one doubt any good-ness in oneself or others or in life. Still, enough has been said to point out Klein's emphasis on a primordial destructive gradient that runs through psy-chic processes and human productions, a destructive tendency that will not go away.

Guilt and reparation: from paranoid-schizoid to depressive positions

If Klein has a solution it has an element of tragedy, and is not a "solution" so much as a developmental trajectory. She pictures the infant moving from the paranoid-schizoid to the depressive position, a more mature state. The infant's use of splitting and projection is supplemented by growth of introjec-tion and ambivalence. The infant comes to realize that the bad object it tries to attack and get rid of and the good object it wants are one and the same person.

The depressive elements include several components. One can no longer uninhibitedly attack the bad and take in the good. From this point on, good is not all good, bad is not all bad. The baby moves from a more totalized, absolutized to a more relativized universe. Aggression is not only inhibited by fear of retaliation by a bigger, stronger figure, but by love conjoined with guilt: one repents injuring the good when striking the bad.

To think of self or other as all-good or all-bad appears delusional, hallucinatory, fantastic. Yet there is an absolutizing tendency at work in organizing experience and Klein fingers parts of it. She posits unconscious fantasy of all-good or all-bad objects, their splitting, their fusions, and the developmental task of encompassing and integrating splits as one grows into a more differentiated, complexly nuanced space–time world. From terrified hate expelling psychic reality, to guilty love taking in and making room for a fuller view of the situation. A great developmental task: making room for tensions, conflicts and interplay of paranoid-schizoid and depressive modes of organizing psychic life, with dominance of the latter.

The depressive position opens a field of appreciation for what the good in another does. One feels guilty for injuring the good when attacking the bad and seeks to make reparation. We reach a place in infant–mother relations, where each tries to make the other feel good. Mother tries to diminish persecutory dreads in the infant and, in time, the growing baby tries to make up for its hate wishes and destructive attacks. One of Klein's great achievements is her depiction of arrays of fantasies clustering around injury and repair beginning from infancy on. Clusters of fantasy nebulae involving destruction, fear, guilt, pleasure, pain, destructive satisfactions, anxieties, agonies, and what soon enough comes to be organized as the near-ubiquitous "I'm sorry." So much torment comes from the interplay of loving and destructive urges, wishes, fantasies.

Klein depicts an affective fantasy underpinning that plays a role in organizing schizophrenic and depressive tendencies, with many possible permutations. It almost seems in human history, in all times and places, there are two main ways of going mad, and Klein supplies some structures and contents in processes involved. The fact that paranoid-schizoid and depressive organizations are expected parts of life gives reason to view psychotic and psychotic-like processes as parts of a spectrum of experiences and behaviors. This cuts both ways. Severe clinical psychoses may involve extreme crystallizations of more widespread capacities, supporting hope for help or change. At the same time, psychotic anxieties, conflicts and operations, as intrinsic and pervasive parts of humanity, do not go away. We are challenged to become partners in development with our capacities, including ways we approach madness. We joke about there being no such thing as normalcy, that we're all mad, even normal to be mad. Klein fleshed out part of the story.

Envy and gratitude

In the later part of Klein's career, envy and gratitude became prime coordinates or expressive poles of destructive and generative tendencies (1957). While twisting her writings to stay within the Freudian (now Freudian–Kleinian mold), they, in effect, constitute a complex visionary phenomenology of polar dynamic organizations, with envy a nucleus of the "bad," gratitude a nucleus of the "good."

She placed a lot on the nursing situation as privileged example of the interplay of destructive–creative forces. It functioned at once as reality and image of a dialectic between good and bad objects coupled with inner tendencies. A central issue was whether a sense of goodness survived destructive anxieties, or whether envious attack against the good gained an upper hand. Resentment, greed, jealousy were associated with an envious core. Klein, especially, was concerned with envy's need to spoil the good breast, the good object, to denigrate the good, nourishing, enriching, creative aspects of life.

A scenario she emphasizes is whether, to what extent, an infant can experience the good in the feeding situation, and to what extent he feels the breast is selfish, holding back and keeping the best for itself. To what extent can the baby enjoy a full emotional feed, and to what extent does it feel it is missing out, getting short-changed, or that its aggressiveness is spoiling things. The baby may want inexhaustible, total fullness and spoil what goodness reality offers. Grievance versus gratitude.

Here we have a partial clue for the origin of the current slang, "It sucks, life sucks." Sucking meaning something negative, disappointing. An eternally disappointing feed, spoiled by great expectations and destructive impulses. The expression, too, denigrates the act of sucking, dependency, helplessness, needing care – slurring a baby activity that epitomizes vulnerability and closeness. It also suggests a time before teeth, a lack of bite, oral castration. Teeth provide some power, aid digestion, but also cause pain. Problems revolving around impotence, aggression and pain are close to Klein's concerns. Earlier than genital potency, is fecundity of giving and receiving milk, image of life's nourishing aspect, associated with care, trust, faith. The arena of nourishment is also one of struggle, conflict, destruction. Can nourishment provide a context for destruction, or vice versa, or are there ever variable oscillations?

Klein depicts tensions between envious spoiling (creativity envy) and gratitude for life. We repeatedly come through attacks against the good, reform, and make use of guilt as a signal to take responsibility for destructive impacts. We learn to protect, nourish and take care of the good object within, a vital faith center. We learn to preserve a nourishing center from our attacks against it.

Klein has done something un-Nietzschean with Nietzsche. For Nietzsche, gratitude qualifies as a servile attitude, perhaps belonging with pity and resentment as part of the psychology of the weak. For Klein, gratitude is a center of strength and growth, a less paranoid ground for relationships. For Nietzsche, goodness is a trap, for Klein a primal object that supports life. Two affect–object worlds: a core of gratitude for the good versus envious destructiveness that spoils An inheritance from this double nucleus is a lifelong need and challenge to make use of and encompass internal divisions.

Discussion, dissension and conclusion

Klein has left a powerful legacy that puts destructiveness and love center stage. She views both as constitutional, although they vary in strength and quality for any number of inner or outer reasons. She describes vicious circles showing how attacking good objects or states intensifies mistrust and leads to further attacks. Destructive tendencies do not go away but, to some extent, can be worked with. She seems to feel that a good feed at the center of life goes a long way. Gratitude for a good internal object can lay a foundation for weathering destructive surges and anxieties, especially attacks against the good.

Winnicott (1990) does not feel that the destructiveness that Klein highlights need be explained by a death drive. He is closer to early Freud in seeing it as part of aliveness. Destructive and aggressive tendencies are part of life's vitality. What happens with them is the big question. Winnicott takes care to say he is not merely speaking about aggression in response to frustration, quite real in its own right. Destructive urges are an intrinsic aspect of basic aliveness and have developmental trajectories, partly depending on how they are responded to. Winnicott believes environmental trauma is crucial in personality formation, and has much to do with quality of life and relation to feelings. But if trauma helps structure aggression, it does not account for the latter's existence in the first place. An innate aggressive capacity contributes to life in many ways.

Winnicott (1989; Eigen 1993, ch. 11), also, is not entirely happy with guilty reparation as a way to heal splits. He acknowledges the importance of the role of guilt in developing humane feelings. To accept responsibility and make up for destructive tendencies is part of caring. To care about injuring others is an affective core of ethical growth, a core that is violated on a daily basis.

Nevertheless, Winnicott also emphasizes how early destructive surges are responded to. Fantasies of total destruction are disconfirmed by the other's survival, filling out a sense of the realness of otherness. How the other survives attacks is crucial. Merely to retaliate, cave in or become depressed deforms or collapses the sense of other; whereas, maintaining oneself undefensively catalyzes awareness of otherness beyond fantasy control. Joy, more than guilt, characterizes this coming through.

In a similar vein, Elkin (1972) points out a reciprocity of injury: mother and child injure each other. The fact that hurt feelings are mutual mitigates the child's guilt. Something like, "After all, she hurt me too!" This does not mean there is no guilt. The guilt strand is operative too – or should be. But there are relatively guiltless threads of self and other that are part of the weave. Elkin points out the importance of forgiveness in healing splits, not just guilt (which can split one more, depending on how it functions). If a parent is not too self-justifying, insensitive, bullying and know-it-all, the child is more likely to forgive injury and remain in decent enough contact. Forgiveness rather than gratitude as a healing nucleus. But in a good circle, forgiveness and gratitude probably reinforce each other and open paths of feeling and development.

One of Bion's (1970; Eigen 1996, 1998, 2004) differences from Klein comes from another side. He feels her paranoid-schizoid position too organized a place to start. Her infantile defenses against psychotic anxieties are not psychotic enough. Splitting–projective identification is a relatively highly structured way of dealing with originary breakdown. Bion posits an exploding O (origin, emotional reality) at the beginnings of personality, breakdown states that the evolving personality tries to encapsulate and diffuse, if not encompass. Much psycho-social life distributes psychotic breakdown, versions of madness, throughout the political, cultural, familial body, awaiting capacity for emotional digestion to evolve.

Lacan (1977, 1978) situates Klein's projective–introjective worlds in the imaginary register. Some Kleinians might situate the paranoid-schizoid position in the imaginary, and the depressive position in the symbolic. To do this justice goes beyond the limits of this chapter, but I would like to touch some nodes that bear on certain emphases in Kleinian clinical work. I would like to bring out imaginary aspects of both positions, with particular attention to imaginary threads in the depressive position.

In the Lacanian imaginary, the ego imagines itself (the subject imagines the ego) as more whole than it is, a kind of megalomanic conduit of desire, molding to fit the other's desire, desiring to capture desire, seductive, paranoid, aggressive, enslaved by influence, pretending to be master of attentional fields. Klein's depictions of splitting and projection as ways to keep a contracted ego core on top of things fit in with and amplify Lacan's defensive, self-centered, imaginary I.

It is important to note the imaginary in the depressive position as well. On the one hand, the depressive position attempts to integrate ambivalence. Seeing the good and bad of the other, recognizing loving and destructive aspects of self. Certainly, growth towards reality. Nevertheless, emphasis is on valorizing and protecting an introjected good object core, particularly in face of one's destructive urges. At times, apotheosis of the good internal object gets cloying (I suspect it made Bion claustrophobic, hence his emphasis on the co-equal value of tearing apart as well as putting together; Eigen 1986, 1993, 1996, 1998).

For Lacan, Kleinian emphasis on analyzing defenses against dependency gets too literal. Too much emphasis is placed on analyst as good object needing to be internalized and how patients spoil and destroy this need. The internal sense of wholeness and security attached to the good internal object involves an illusion reciprocal to the wholeness of the I – imaginary wholeness requiring maintenance by subterfuge.

Lacan has a mistrust for wholeness, whether of object or self. He has an inveterate fear of being suffocated by versions or fantasies of wholeness driven by unconscious desires. An extreme, perhaps paranoid view of wholeness, but also freeing. I suspect this partly explains the moralistic, heavy-handed tone of much Kleinian literature. The patient is somehow denigrated for not making the depressive position, for remaining an ungrateful being who bites the feeding hand, a somewhat lesser being. For Lacan (an irrepressible biter), the moral superiority of a more whole being, like wholeness itself, is a signifier requiring contextual analysis.

Lacan keeps us alert as to how terms like good or whole are used by people always enmeshed in politics of desire. Psychoanalysts are not exempt. To be enslaved by goodness or wholeness is a danger Lacan rebels against. A Kleinian might want to analyze Lacan's scathing, paranoid aspect, but Lacan would try to represent symbolically the former's aim in doing so. Nevertheless, even Lacan affirms, at times, the goodness of goodness, the importance of good faith. And as his work evolved, death-work became ever more important.

Our debt to Melanie Klein is far from over. Reading her work is as eye-opening today as when I first began reading it over forty years ago. It is work that grew up in times of war. Mad destruction was a focus. She situated destructiveness in tendencies already at work in infancy, psychotic agonies at the heart of nursing at the breast, this most heart-opening situation, in which a good core of feeling must work to prevail in face of annihilating elements in the total situation. She sensitizes us to momentary quivering between annihilating fantasies in tension with life-affirming ones, as well as long-term ways annihilation dread is organized. Whatever one's critique, Klein makes it impossible to bypass vulnerability to destructive fantasies, anxieties, conflicts, actions, rooted in our natures, our psycho-organisms. Her work drives home the realization that no matter how much of life's injustices we correct – and it is important we try to do so – unless we catch on to destructive forces in our very beings, our success is likely to be shaky.

References

Abraham, K. (1973) *Selected Papers*. London: Hogarth Press.

Bion, W.R. (1970) *Attention and Interpretation*. London: Tavistock.

Eigen, M. (1986) *The Psychotic Core*. London: Karnac Books, 2004.

—— (1993) *The Electrified Tightrope*, ed. A. Phillips. London: Karnac Books, 2004.

—— (1996) *Psychic Deadness*. London: Karnac Books, 2004.

—— (1998) *The Psychoanalytic Mystic*. London: Free Association Books.

—— (2004) *The Sensitive Self*. Middletown, Conn.: Wesleyan University Press.

Elkin, H. (1972) On selfhood and the development of ego structures in infancy. *The Psychoanalytic Review* 59: 389–416.

Ferenczi, S. (1955) *The Selected Papers of Sandor Ferenczi, M.D.: Problems and Methods of Psychoanalysis*, vol. 3. New York: Basic Books.

Freud, S. (1920) Beyond the pleasure principle. *Standard Edition* 18: 1–64.

—— (1937) Analysis terminable and interminable. *Standard Edition* 23: 216–253.

—— (1940) An outline of psycho-analysis. *Standard Edition* 23: 141–207.

Klein, M. (1946) Notes on some schizoid mechanisms. In *Developments in Psychoanalysis*, ed. M. Klein, P. Heimann, S. Isaacs and J. Riviere. London: Hogarth Press, 1952, pp. 292–320.

—— (1957) *Envy and Gratitude*. New York: Basic Books.

Lacan, J. (1977) *Ecrits*, trans. A. Sheridan. New York: Norton.

—— (1978) *The Four Fundamental Concepts in Psychoanalysis*, trans. A. Sheridan, ed. Jacques-Alain Miller. New York: Norton.

Winnicott, D.W. (1989) *Psychoanalytic Explorations*, ed. C. Winnicott, R. Shepherd and M. Davis. Cambridge, Mass.: Harvard University Press.

—— (1990) *Human Nature*. New York: Random House.

Chapter 4

Projective identification

Robert Maxwell Young

The *locus classicus* of Klein's concept of projective identification is a passage in her 'Notes on Some Schizoid Mechanisms', which appeared in 1946. Klein concludes seven pages on the fine texture of early paranoid and schizoid mechanisms as follows:

> So far, in dealing with persecutory fear, I have singled out the oral element. However, while the oral libido still has the lead, libidinal and aggressive impulses and phantasies from other sources come to the fore and lead to a confluence of oral, urethral and anal desires, both libidinal and aggressive. Also the attacks on the mother's breast develop into attacks of a similar nature on her body, which comes to be felt as it were as an extension of the breast, even before the mother is conceived of as a complete person. The phantasied onslaughts on the mother follow two main lines: one is the predominantly oral impulse to suck dry, bite up, scoop out and rob the mother's body of its good contents . . . . The other line of attack derives from the anal and urethral impulses and implies expelling dangerous substances (excrements) out of the self and into the mother. Together with these harmful excrements, expelled in hatred, split-off parts of the ego are also projected onto the mother or, as I would rather call it, *into* the mother. [Klein adds a footnote at this crucial point, to the effect that she is describing primitive, pre-verbal processes and that projecting '*into* another person' seems to her 'the only way of conveying the unconscious process I am trying to describe'.] These excrements and bad parts of the self are meant not only to injure but also to control and to take possession of the object. In so far as the mother comes to contain the bad parts of the self, she is not felt to be a separate individual but is felt to be *the* bad self.
>
> Much of the hatred against parts of the self is now directed towards the mother. This leads to a particular form of identification which establishes the prototype of an aggressive object-relation.
>
> (Klein 1946, pp. 7–8)

Six years later Klein adds the following sentence: 'I suggest for these processes the term "projective identification" ' (*ibid.*; see also pp. 68–9 where she spells out the complementarity of projective and introjective processes).

The concept is introduced to explain a quite early, primitive form of unconscious phantasy and is depicted only in negative terms, albeit offered as the prototype of all aggressive object relations. (Note: this is a very large claim.) Subsequent developments in her and others' thinking will lead it to be seen as a mechanism used for positive and loving feelings, as well (p. 69). It will also come to be seen as an ubiquitous unconscious mechanism in human communication and internal thought processes, i.e. between people and between parts of a given person's mind. Wilfred Bion depicted it as the basis for all communications between therapist and patient. Moreover, after reviewing the development of the concept, E. Torres de Beà writes,

> These authors consider that projective identification is the basic mechanism of empathy and primitive communication and also of the defence mechanism which consists of dissociating and projecting anxiety in order to be rid of it. I agree with this and think also that what we call projective identification is the active element in every communication from empathy to the most pathological and defensive.
>
> (Torres de Beà 1989, p. 266)

He concludes that it is 'the mechanism basic to all human interaction' (p. 272).

Indeed, projective identification is the single most influential concept originated by Klein. It plays a central role in the two basic stances taken up by the mind at all times and at all levels of development from infancy to maturity and on to senescence: the paranoid-schizoid and depressive positions. The former is characterised by extreme splits, part-object relations, punitive and brittle guilt feelings and violent projective identifications. The depressive position also includes splits but not extreme ones, whole object relations ('concern for the object'), reparative guilt (the urge to make reparation for the damage done to the object) and taking back projective identifications, i.e. taking responsibility for our feelings. Irma Brenman Pick writes, 'Constant projecting by the patient into the analyst is the essence of analysis; every interpretation aims at a move from the paranoid/schizoid to the depressive position' (Brenman Pick 1985, p. 158). The tacit injunction to our patients – 'Take back the projections' – is a useful way of characterising the goal of helping her or him to dwell as much as possible in the depressive position.

I believe that projective identification is the most fruitful psychoanalytic concept since the discovery of the unconscious. Of course, as soon as something like that is said, competing claims are made, for example, the significance of the Oedipus complex. Suffice it to say, then, that it is *very* important. Elizabeth Spillius describes it more modestly as Klein's most popular concept

(Spillius 1988, vol. 1, p. 81), and Donald Meltzer called it the most fruitful Kleinian concept over the past thirty to forty years (Meltzer 1991). R.D. Hinshelwood suggests that as well as being a, if not the, most fruitful Kleinian concept, it is also the most confused and confusing one (Hinshelwood 1991, pp. 179–208). Thomas Ogden presents the ideas of Harold Searles, Robert Langs, A. Malin and James Grotstein and describes projective identification as the essence of the therapeutic relationship. Therapy is said to *consist of* dealing with it. It is the basic unit of study of the therapeutic interaction (Ogden 1979, p. 366). He also tells us that Bion 'views projective identification as the most important form of interaction between the patient and therapist in individual therapy, as well as in groups of all types' (p. 365). In 'Attacks on Linking', Bion says, 'Thus the link between patient and analyst, or infant and breast, is the mechanism of projective identification' (Bion 1967, p. 106). In the course of a careful review of developments of the concept from its initial formulation in 1946, to the present, Hinshelwood says that for Bion it became 'the basic building block for generating thoughts out of experiences and perceptions' (Hinshelwood 1991, pp. 189–90). At this same level of generality Segal has described projective identification as 'the earliest form of empathy' and 'the basis of the earliest form of symbol-formation' (Segal 1973, p. 36). Looking to later developments and more broadly, Hinshelwood describes Bion's notion of 'container–contained' as 'an attempt to raise the concept of projective identification to a general theory of human functioning – of the relations between people, and between groups; of the relationships between internal objects; and of the relationships in the symbolic world between thoughts, ideas, theories, experiences, etc.' (p. 191).

This same mechanism is seen to be operative at the heart of autism by Meltzer and his co-workers. He also describes it as '*the* mechanism of narcissistic identification . . . and the basis of hypochondria, confusional states, claustrophobia, paranoia, psychotic depression and perhaps some psychosomatic disorders' (Meltzer *et al.* 1975, p. 228). It is also the sovereign defence against separation anxiety (Grinberg 1990, p. 64). Relinquishment of excessive projective identification is described as the precondition of achieving a fully dimensional inner world (Meltzer *et al.* 1975, pp. 226–7). As Meltzer says in his essay on 'The Relation of Anal Masturbation to Projective Identification',

> The feeling of fraudulence as an adult person, the sexual impotence or pseudo-potency (excited by secret perverse phantasies), the inner loneliness and the basic confusion between good and bad, all create a life of tension and lack of satisfaction, bolstered, or rather compensated, only by the smugness and snobbery which are an inevitable accompaniment of the massive projective identification.
>
> (Meltzer 1966, p. 104)

In his book on claustrophobic phenomena Meltzer describes it as central to the most social Darwinist forms of ambitious, competitive, survivalist conformism, in his concept of 'the claustrum', in which patients use excessive projective identification as a desperate defence against schizophrenic breakdown (Meltzer 1992). Another Kleinian, Leslie Sohn, recalls that the original thoughts on projective identification in the British Psycho-Analytical Society conceived of it 'as a defence against intolerable envy and as an outcome of hatred of dependence' (Sandler 1989, p. 190).

Elizabeth Spillius begins her overview of the concept by telling us that 'the term has gradually become the most popular of Klein's concepts, the only one that has been widely accepted and discussed by non-Kleinians – especially in the United States' (Spillius 1988, vol. 1, p. 81). The problem is that she goes on to say that 'it is often discussed in terms that are incompatible with Klein's conception' (*ibid.*). Hinshelwood draws a similarly disconcerting conclusion when he writes, 'There appears to be no consensus on the value of the term "projective identification" outside the Kleinian conceptual framework' (Hinshelwood 1991, p. 204). It is in danger of degenerating into what he calls 'a catch-phrase for all interpersonal phenomena' (p. 196), a fate similar to that which befell the concept of object relations at the hands of Greenberg and Mitchell, who mistakenly reduced all objects to people so as to bring Klein into closer affinity with American psychoanalytic ideas and those of Harry Stack Sullivan (Greenberg and Mitchell 1983; cf. Kohon 1985).

Having sketched the origin and scope of the concept, I shall devote the remainder of this chapter to what is intended as a *tour de force* of the kinds of projective identification, including examples, which have appeared in the Kleinian literature and some debates about them.

A number of people have told me that they had trouble getting their minds around the concept of projective identification and have said that the following example was helpful to them. Imagine a fly fisherman (I have in mind some lovely scenes from the film *A River Runs Through It*), casting his line gracefully through the air in a lazy arc across the waters of a lake. The line hits the water some distance away, penetrating it and teasing fish to the surface in the hope of catching one. It lures the fish to the surface, hooks it and reels it in. The fisherman is doing the projecting. The fish swimming around some distance away is the repertoire of responses in the personality of the person being projected into. The response which the casting of the line evokes would not otherwise have risen to the surface. It is lured to the surface; the response is evoked. That is the moment of identification in projective identification.

Relinquishing now the fishing analogy and elaborating the example further, we have unconscious feelings that we want to disown or, alternatively, want to entrust to someone. We unconsciously project them into that person's unconscious and call up what we want to evoke from their range of potential responses. We thereby create a symbiosis and impoverish our own egos (hence the ego-strengthening therapeutic value of 'taking back the projections'). You cannot evoke any old response; it has to be a potential one in that person's personality. Freud adumbrated the concept and illustrated my point when he was talking about the projections of jealous and persecuted paranoiacs, of whom it is said that they project onto others that which they do not wish to recognise in themselves. He continues,

Certainly they do this; but they do not project it into the blue, so to speak, where there is nothing of the sort already. They let themselves be guided by their knowledge of the unconscious, and displace to the unconscious minds of others the attention which they have withdrawn from their own. Our jealous husband perceived his wife's unfaithfulness instead of his own; by becoming conscious of hers and magnifying it enormously he succeeded in keeping his own unconscious.

(Freud 1922, p. 226)

Brenman Pick illustrates this point further in saying that

the patient does not just project into an analyst, but instead patients are quite skilled at projecting into particular aspects of the analyst. Thus, I have tried to show, for example, that the patient projects into the analyst's wish to be a mother, the wish to be all-knowing or to deny unpleasant knowledge, into the analyst's instinctual sadism, or into his defences against it. And above all, he projects into the analyst's guilt, or into the analyst's internal objects.

Thus, patients touch off in the analyst deep issues and anxieties related to the need to be loved and the fear of catastrophic consequences in the face of defects, i.e., primitive persecutory or superego anxiety.

(Brenman Pick 1985, p. 161)

In drawing these illustrations from Brenman Pick's important article on 'Working Through in the Counter-transference' I am coming upon a point which surprised me when I first realised it: that Klein did not grasp that countertransference is a species of projective identification. As I see it, the approach adopted by Brenman Pick takes it as read and as normal that powerful unconscious feelings are moving from patient to therapist and back again, through the processes of projection, evocation, reflection, detoxification, interpretation and assimilation. These feelings are all normal, as it were, in the processes of analysis. More than that, as she puts it, they are the essence of the therapeutic process.

Kleinians have not always taken this view of countertransference. Klein had begged her protégé Paula Heimann not to deliver her first paper on countertransference and told Tom Hayley in the late 1950s that she thought countertransference interferes with analysis and should be the subject of lightning self-analysis (Grosskurth 1986, p. 378). According to Spillius, 'Klein thought that such extension would open the door to claims by analysts that their own deficiencies were caused by their patients' (Spillius 1992, p. 61). Having said this, it is important not to be too literal about the use of the term 'countertransference'. Klein's subtle interpretations of her patients' inner worlds – especially their pre-verbal feelings and ideas – only make sense in the light of her ability to be resonant with their most primitive feelings, and Bion's injunction to 'abandon memory and desire' is made in the name of countertransference, whatever term we attach to the process. Indeed, it can be said that his writings are about little else.

It took a considerable time for ideas about the concept of countertransference to reach the point that its congruence with projective identification become apparent. Freud had seen countertransference just as Klein did – unworked-through neurotic material in the therapist. In the period after the Second World War a number of people began to see it in broader terms. I am thinking of D.W. Winnicott on 'Hate in the Countertransference' (1947) and Margaret Little (1950, etc.). Among Kleinians, Paula Heimann wrote two important papers in which she argued that we can learn from the countertransference (1949–50), but saw as the goal of doing so the reduction of instances of it (1959–60). Roger Money Kyrle (1956), however, saw it as normal, and that view has come to prevail among Kleinians. This position is best argued by Brenman Pick in the article quoted above.

The form of projective identification most often referred to in the literature is when one person projects into another, whether a therapist or someone else – mother, friend, enemy, object of affection, etc. – and evokes unconscious feelings. These may or may not be processed and may or may not lead to altered behaviour. In the case of projecting into a therapist, the therapist's task – often a difficult and sometimes a nearly impossible one – is to experience the countertransferential feeling without intemperately reprojecting it, make sense of it, detoxify it by neutralising the violent feelings involved, interpret it internally, and formulate it into an interpretation which is of some use to the patient. This is an analytical version of what a parent or other loved one does in dealing with the distressed feelings of those near and dear to them, for example, comforting a baby, soothing a toddler, counselling an adolescent, sorting out feelings with a lover.

American analysts have taken up the concept with enthusiasm and have written extensively about it. Although the best of this work is interesting and rich in clinical examples, these writers have often tended to concentrate largely on the interpersonal form of the mechanism at the expense of the purely intrapsychic one. In my opinion this impoverishes the concept and does not allow sufficient scope and space for the inner world and internal objects (Grotstein 1981; Ogden 1979, 1982; Scharff 1992). The key issue here is whether or not a real, external 'other', who has been affected by the projection, is essential to the concept. British Kleinians say no; some American interpreters say yes.

Spillius' summary is helpful in clarifying this matter:

> Considerable controversy has developed over the definition and use of the concept. Whether there is a difference between projection and projective identification is perhaps the most frequently raised question, but others have been important too. Should the term be used only to refer to the patient's unconscious phantasy, regardless of the effect on the recipient, or should it be used only in cases in which the recipient of the projection is emotionally affected by what is being projected into him? Should the term only be used for the projection of aspects of the self, or should it also be used for the projection of internal objects? What about the many possible motives for projective identification; should all be included? Should the term be used only in cases where the patient has lost conscious awareness of the quality and part of the self he has projected, or does it also apply to cases in which such awareness is retained? What about the projection of good qualities and good parts of the self; should the concept be used for these as well, as Klein so clearly thought, or should it be reserved for the projection of bad qualities, which has been the dominant tendency? Is a specific bodily phantasy always involved in the projection, as Klein thought, or is it clarifying enough to speak of the phantasy in mental terms?
>
> Of these many questions, by far the most discussion has been devoted to the question of whether and how projective identification should be distinguished from projection. . . . In these discussions the most usual basis for the distinction between projection and projective identification is held to be whether or not the recipient of the projection is or is not affected emotionally by the projector's phantasy . . . . But to restrict the term projective identification to such instances greatly diminishes the usefulness of the concept and is in any case totally contrary to what Klein herself meant by it. The English view is that the term is best kept as a general concept broad enough to include both cases in which the recipient is emotionally affected and those in which he is not . . . . The many motives for projective identification – to control the object, to acquire its attributes, to evacuate a bad quality, to protect a good quality, to avoid separation – all are most usefully kept under the general umbrella.
>
> (Spillius 1988, vol. 1, pp. 81–3)

Hanna Segal's definition seems to side with those who call for an external object which is affected: 'In projective identification parts of the self and internal objects are split off and projected into the external object, which then becomes possessed by, controlled and identified with the projected parts' (Segal 1973, p. 27). Bion also includes projection 'into an external object'

(Bion 1992, p. 159). Unless we assume that they are written from the point of view of the projector's phantasy, these definitions do not embrace both sides of Spillius' broad approach, which allows for projective identification into an internal object as well as into an external one. It is important to emphasise that projective identification can occur wholly inside the unconscious of the projecting person and need not be involved at all with behaviour that elicits a response from another person. The 'other' can dwell exclusively in the inner world of the person who creates the projective identification and supplies the response from his or her phantasy of the dramatis personae in the mind. In this case it is a relationship between one part of the inner world and another. Where behaviour is involved, the process of eliciting the unconsciously desired resonance from the 'other' can be very subtle indeed. Betty Joseph has made the detailed understanding of these interactions an area of special study. In particular, she draws attention to the patient's uncanny ability to 'nudge' the therapist to act out in accordance with the patient's projection – to evoke the disowned feelings from the therapist's repertoire and induce the therapist to experience and perhaps reproject them (Joseph 1989, esp. chs 7, 9–12).

There are further elaborations:

> Projective identification has manifold aims: it may be directed towards the ideal object to avoid separation, or it may be directed towards the bad object to gain control of the source of the danger. Various parts of the self may be projected, with various aims: bad parts of the self may be projected in order to get rid of them as well as to attack and destroy the object, good parts may be projected to avoid separation or keep them safe from bad things inside or to improve the external object through a kind of primitive projective reparation. Projective identification starts when the paranoid-schizoid position is first established in relation to the breast, but it persists and very often becomes intensified when the mother is perceived as a whole object and the whole of her body is entered by projective identification.
>
> (Segal 1973, pp. 27–8)

Mutual projective processes are powerfully described in an essay by Tom Main. He provides excellent analyses of projective mechanisms in individuals, couples and large and small groups:

> Although projective processes are primitive attempts to relieve internal pains by externalising them, assigning or requiring another to contain aspects of the self, the price can be high: for the self is left not only less aware of its whole but, in the case of projective identification, is deplenished [*sic*] by the projective loss of important aspects of itself. Massive projective identification of – for instance – feared aggressive parts of the

self leaves the remaining self felt only to be weak and unaggressive. Thereafter, the weakened individual will remain in terror about being overwhelmed by frightening aggressive strength, but this will now be felt only as belonging to the other. Depending on the range of this projective fantasy the results will vary from terrified flight, to appeasement, wariness and specific anxieties about the other, even psychotic delusions about his intentions.

The above instance concerns only the projector's side of the projective relationship: but projective processes often have a further significance. What about the person on the receiving end of the projection? In simple projection (a mental mechanism) the receiver may notice that he is not being treated as himself but as an aggressive other. In projective identification (an unconscious fantasy) this other may find himself forced by the projector actually to feel his own projected aggressive qualities and impulses which are otherwise alien to him. He will feel strange and uncomfortable and may resent what is happening, but in the face of the projector's weakness and cowardice it may be doubly difficult to resist the feelings of superiority and aggressive power steadily forced into him. Such disturbances affect all pair relationships more or less. A wife, for instance, may force her husband to own feared and unwanted dominating aspects of herself and will then fear and respect him. He in turn may come to feel aggressive and dominating toward her, not only because of his own resources but because of hers, which are forced into him. But more: for reasons of his own he may despise and disown certain timid aspects of his personality and by projective identification force these into his wife and despise her accordingly. She may thus be left not only with timid unaggressive parts of herself but having in addition to contain his. Certain pairs come to live in such locked systems, dominated by mutual projective fantasies with each not truly married to a person, but rather to unwanted, split off and projected parts of themselves. Both the husband, dominant and cruel, and the wife, stupidly timid and respectful, may be miserably unhappy with themselves and with each other, yet such marriages although turbulent are stable, because each partner needs the other for pathologically narcissistic purposes. Forcible projective processes, and especially projective identification, are thus more than an individual matter: they are object-related, and the other will always be affected more or less.

(Main 1975, pp. 100–1)

None of the above descriptions sufficiently emphasises *projective identification into parts of one's own mind*, a topic well expressed (in the context of envy) by Joseph Berke, whose book *The Tyranny of Malice* (1989) can be seen as a compendium on splitting and projective identification:

Projection and projective identification are activities that influence different parts of the self. These, of course, include phantasized or internal representations of actual relationships. Thus a person can indeed feel under attack because he is attacking mental images of his own father or teacher or therapist.

However, a more ominous reaction occurs when, beset by envy, the envier tries to preserve himself from himself by splitting up and projectively identifying his spite and malice with and into parts of his own mind. Consequently the envier contains a multitude of envious others all threatening to attack him from within. These exist as split off and extremely hostile representations of his own envious self or of envious parents and parental substitutes.

(Berke 1989, p. 67)

This process leads to an over-severe and envious superego and saps the individual's progressive and creative capacities.

In order to avoid such a psychic catastrophe, whereby a host of inner enviers assault each other, the afflicted person may utilise projective processes to deflect these enmities outward. The net effect is like picking out a pack of piranhas and throwing them into the air. Because of the action of projective identification, when these vicious little enviers land on something, and they always do, the envious person (fleeing from his own envious selves) inevitably converts elements of external reality (benign people, places, or things) into malevolent entities (witches, evil influences, bad omens). But instead of solving the problem, this manoeuvre compounds it, for the individual feels threatened by malignity emanating from within himself and from without. Thus the envier becomes the envied, and the hunter becomes the hunted.

(ibid.)

Donald Meltzer's book, *The Claustrum* (mentioned above), is entirely devoted to projective identification into internal objects. He is at pains to reveal the evolution of his thinking. He had for some years been uncomfortable with a bias in Klein's paper 'On Identification' (1955) and came to 'discover the real reason for my dissatisfaction: the tendency of Mrs. Klein's paper to continue treating projective identification as a psychotic mechanism and one which operated with external objects, primarily or exclusively' (Meltzer 1992, p. 13). He emphasises that an important part of mental space is inside internal objects (p. 118) and that entry into projective identification is a 'ubiquitous phenomenon in early childhood' (p. 118). More generally, he concludes that 'the existence of one or another infantile part either living in projective identification or easily provoked to enter the claustrum of internal objects is fairly ubiquitous' (p. 134; cf. p. 153).

There is an aspect of projective identification to which I want to revert before moving on to a broader canvas. I have already mentioned it in my analogy to fly fishing. I have already stressed the intrapsychic form, where both parts are played inside the inner world. I now want to draw attention to a feature of the process when it occurs between people. In much of the literature on this topic, reference is made to 'projecting *into* the 'other', whether externally or internally. I believe that there is an important distinction which is, as yet, not fully worked out. It concerns putting something into another person as distinct from eliciting something from the repertoire of their responses, exaggerating it and evoking a reprojection of that aspect of their personality. The process is one of the projection finding a home and of unconscious collusion on the part of the person receiving the projection. In my opinion this is by far the most common manifestation of the interpersonal form of the process, as distinct from being invaded by something entirely alien, a strange feeling in oneself. What is strange in the case of evoked and exaggerated feelings is the intensity. The recipient reprojects a degree or strength of feeling that is surprising, but, though an exaggeration or enhancement, it is still his or hers.

The person who has made most of this point is Harold Searles, who is not a Kleinian and does not stress the term. His writings have centred on the honesty required to acknowledge the patient's prescience. In describing his findings in his first paper on the subject, he says of himself that he

> has very regularly been able to find some real basis in himself for those qualities which his patients – *all* his patients, whether the individual patient be more prominently paranoid, or obsessive-compulsive, or hysterical, and so on – project upon him. It appears that all patients, not merely those with chiefly paranoid adjustments, have the ability to "read the unconscious" of the therapist. This process of reading the unconscious of another person is based, after all, upon nothing more occult than an alertness to minor variations in the other person's posture, facial expression, vocal tone, and so on, of which the other person himself is unaware. All neurotic and psychotic patients, because of their need to adapt themselves to the feelings of the other person, have had to learn as children – usually in association with painfully unpredictable parents – to be alert to such nuances of behavior on the part of the other person.
> (Searles 1978–9, pp. 177–8, 1979; cf. Young 1992)

In my view, much of the striking originality of Searles' work stems from this important insight, one which has been grasped by some Kleinians, for example, Irma Brenman Pick (1985, esp. p. 41), Betty Joseph (1989) and Michael Feldman (1992, pp. 77, 87), but its implications are far from being taken in by most writers on the subject. There is too little awareness of how nearly fully interactive the processes are, and I believe this is a remnant of objectivist attitudes on the part of therapists, who do not grant the fundamental role of the countertransference in therapy, as in the rest of life.

Kleinian ideas are difficult of access, partly because they are largely about unconscious, pre-verbal and pre-conceptual psychodynamics. Moreover, it cannot be said that Klein wrote with conceptual clarity to match her profound understanding of the inner world and its vicissitudes. For a long time practically the only way to learn about her ideas was to work with them and to get supervision from people who had worked with her or with the supervisees of people who had worked with her. Kleinians travelled, most significantly, to Los Angeles, Italy and South America, where they gave seminars and supervisions. The effect in South America and Italy was electric, while in Los Angeles it almost led to the disenfranchisement of the Los Angeles Psychoanalytic Institute from the American Psychoanalytic Association, so strongly did the orthodox Freudians take exception to this alien way of thinking (see Kirsner 2000, ch. 4). Splits in the institute and the formation of a breakaway one resulted from this sectarianism.

This situation of paucity of expository writings changed dramatically in the late 1980s with the publication of two volumes of key Kleinian papers edited by Elizabeth Spillius, *Melanie Klein Today* (1988), one volume of which was subtitled *Mainly Theory* and the other *Mainly Practice*. A year later there followed a book which, in my biased opinion (I had the idea to do it, commissioned Bob Hinshelwood to write it, edited it and published it), is the single most helpful secondary source in the Kleinian literature: *A Dictionary of Kleinian Thought*, admirably and exhaustively compiled by R.D. Hinshelwood. The models for this volume were Raymond Williams' *Keywords: A Vocabulary of Culture and Society* (1976) and *The Language of Psycho-Analysis* by Jean Laplanche and J.-B. Pontalis (English trans., 1983). Hinshelwood set out to provide, and largely succeeded in providing, conceptual definitions and historical accounts of the major and minor concepts in the Kleinian literature. The book was revised two years later in the light of criticisms and is currently being rewritten by a committee – in some ways a good thing and in some ways regrettable. Hinshelwood's chapter on projective identification remains the best single account of the concept and its ramifications, as the book is of so much of Kleinian theory.

More recently there have appeared several other helpful secondary sources, some of which contribute subtle understandings of Kleinian and post-Kleinian concepts. In her *Melanie Klein: Her Work in Context*, Meira Likierman appropriately confines her discussion of projective identification to Klein's ideas but gives a sophisticated rendering of them based on a close reading of Klein's works (2003, pp. 156–61). My book, *Mental Space* (1994, on which I have drawn in this essay), devotes several chapters to projective identification in its interpersonal, intrapsychic and social aspects. I argue that projective identification lies at the heart of many group, social and political processes, for example clubs, gangs, sports, team supporters, class, racism, nationalism, political parties, class conflicts, fan clubs, idealization of music and movie stars, charisma, religions – any process where feelings are strongly felt and projected into others.

My book is a largely theoretical and conceptual exploration, while *Inside Lives: Psychoanalysis and the Growth of the Personality* by Margot Waddell (2000, revised 2004) is widely regarded as the most evocative rendering of Kleinian and post-Kleinian concepts and includes a number of clinical vignettes which vividly illustrate projective identification (e.g. pp. 167–70, 199–200). The appendix provides a particularly helpful discussion of projective and introjective processes (pp. 253–8).

The Dictionary of the Work of W.R. Bion, by a Venezuelan psychoanalyst, Rafael E. Lopez-Corvo, suffers from the brevity of its entries and a translator who did not make sure of using the accepted English equivalents of his Spanish terms. His one-page entry (Hinshelwood's is thirty pages long) on projective identification in Bion stresses its use by the psychotic part of the personality, where it is employed to evacuate the unconscious of whole aspects of ego functioning (2003, pp. 220–1).

There are much more extensive discussions of projective identification in *Introduction to the Work of Donald Meltzer* by Silvia Fano Cassese (2004), an Italian psychotherapist who attended Meltzer's lectures, supervisions and seminars for many years during which he frequently taught in Florence. Her entire first chapter is devoted to 'Projective Identification with Internal Objects'. She discusses Meltzer's ideas on massive projective identification, intrusive identification, adhesive identification and *folie à deux*, and introjective identification.

I will close with a vignette from my own clinical practice in which projective identification and countertransference are as one. I saw a man for a considerable time who appeared on the surface to be successful. He had attended an excellent school and one of the best universities in the country, from which he graduated with highest honours. He trained in his father's profession and worked for a leading firm. Yet he thought of himself as unable to handle his responsibilities and kept resigning from jobs and moving down the pecking order of employment and finally worked in a job ancillary to his profession. He also failed to sustain a relationship with a woman, always ending relationships soon after they began. His grounds for rejecting them were usually somatic – too thin, too hairy, one even too representative of a way of being characteristic of a certain region. He even got to the point that he could begin and end several potential relationships in an evening of telephone dating.

He came from a family that was, on the surface, also successful, but behind this was a struggle on his father's part to stave off bankruptcy that extended over many years and was ultimately avoided, but they had to sell the grand home and ostentatious car. His mother had always felt that my patient's own spontaneous efforts were never good enough and had employed tutors for him at every stage of his education. He ended up with a very angry 'not good enough' internal object. His younger brother had responded to the family dynamics by setting himself very low career expectations.

My patient had been in therapy for a decade before coming to me, but his therapist finally threw in the towel, saying that he had too much hate in him which the therapist had been unable to shift. Needless to say, I was at an early stage declared not good enough, either. Whenever I made an interpretation of which I was particularly proud, he would say in a rather weary, patronising voice that it was not quite right. I soldiered on, only to learn that he had embarked, without discussing it with me, on another course of therapy in parallel and in competition with his work with me. He also went through the introductory year of several therapy trainings, only to declare each, in turn, a disappointment.

Needless to say, the effect of all this was to make me doubt my abilities and to make me exceedingly frustrated and eventually angry and demoralised about his refractoriness. On the other hand, he kept coming, brought good material and dreams and even imitated my taste in transport. But he frequently put me on notice and threatened to leave imminently, saying what a disappointment I was to him.

Now comes the culmination of the intense countertransferential part where he succeeds in putting into me and evoking within me his disowned feelings that I eventually acted out. It so happened that my young daughter was at that time being cared for by a woman who lived a few houses up the road. My partner and I liked to walk together to pick her up at the end of the working day just after I saw the patient I have described. However, this became impossible, because on each occasion – and completely inconsistent with the general tone of our relationship – I would become so bad tempered and rejecting during our short walk that an argument would invariably occur in the couple of minutes it took to reach the child minder's house. More accurately, I would always pick a fight completely unreasonably. My only recourse was to stay at home and clear my head so I could greet them warmly when they returned.

I wish I could end this story by saying that steady interpretation of a detoxified understanding of his distress over not having unconditional love finally diminished his rejection of self, his abilities, his girlfriends and his therapists, but it did not. You could say that the well was poisoned or that there was in his inner world a father that failed and a mother that continually found fault. My interpretations somehow got converted into inadequate parenting. In the course of our work I once increased his fee. (I had been making allowance for his need to pay off some debts.) His response was to say that in the light of what he got for his money he was already being overcharged. One day he fired me and moved to another country in search of an adequate therapist and a worthy training.

I trust that this account starkly illustrates the power of projective identification and offers a convincing example of countertransference as a species of this fundamental Kleinian concept, one that lies at the heart of human nature.

I have attempted to offer definitions and examples of the various aspects of the concept of projective identification. I hope I have managed to convey the scope and richness of the concept and justified the claim that it is basic to all communication. I am confident that the concept of projective identification will continue to undergo important clinical and theoretical development at the intrapsychic, interpersonal, group, institutional and political levels and look forward to discussions and elaborations of the concept in the psycho-analytic literature.

References

(Place of publication is London unless otherwise specified.)
Anderson Robin (ed.) (1992) *Clinical Lectures on Klein and Bion*. Routledge.
Berke, Joseph (1989) *The Tyranny of Malice: Exploring the Dark Side of Character and Culture*. Simon and Schuster.
Bion, W.R. (1967) 'Attacks on Linking', in *Second Thoughts: Selected Papers on Psycho-Analysis*. Heinemann Medical, pp. 3–109; reprinted Maresfield, 1984.
—— (1992) *Cogitations*. Karnac.
Brenman Pick, I. (1985) 'Working Through in the Counter-transference', *International Journal of Psycho-analysis* 66: 157–66; reprinted in Spillius (1988), vol. 2, pp. 34–47.
Cassese, Silvia Fano (2004) *Introduction to the Work of Donald Meltzer*. Karnac.
Eigner, J.B. (1986) 'Squid and Projective Identification', *Free Associations* 7: 75–8.
Feldman, Michael (1992) 'Splitting and Projective identification', in Anderson (1992), pp. 74–88.
Freud, Sigmund (1922) 'Some Neurotic Mechanisms in Jealousy, Paranoia and Homosexuality'. *SE* 18, pp. 221–32.
—— (1953–73) *The Standard Edition of the Complete Psychological Works of Sigmund Freud*, 24 vols. Hogarth (*SE*).
Greenberg, Jay R. and Mitchell, Stephen A. (1983) *Object Relations in Psychoanalytic Theory*. Harvard University Press.
Grinberg, L. (1990) *The Goals of Psychoanalysis: Identification, Identity and Supervision*. Karnac.
Grosskurth, Phyllis (1986) *Melanie Klein: Her World and Her Work*. Hodder and Stoughton.
Grotstein, James (1981) *Splitting and Projective Identification*. Aronson.
Heimann, Paula (1949–50) 'On Counter-transference', in Heimann (1990), pp. 73–9.
—— (1959–60) 'Counter-transference', in Heimann (1990), pp. 151–60.
—— (1990) *About Children and Children No Longer: The Work of Paula Heimann*. Routledge.
Hinshelwood, R.D. (1991) *A Dictionary of Kleinian Thought*, 2nd edn. Free Association Books.
Joseph, Betty (1989) *Psychic Equilibrium and Psychic Change: Selected Papers*. Routledge.

Kirsner, Douglas (2000) *Unfree Associations: Inside Psychoanalytic Institutes*. Process Press.

Klein, Melanie (1946) 'Notes on Some Schizoid Mechanisms', reprinted in *WMK* III, pp. 1–24.

—— (1955) 'On Identification', reprinted in *WMK* III, pp. 141–75.

—— (1975) *The Writings of Melanie Klein*, 4 vols. Hogarth. Vol. I: *Love, Guilt and Reparation and Other Works, 1921–1945*. Vol. II: *The Psycho-Analysis of Children*. Vol. III: *Envy and Gratitude and Other Works, 1946–1963*. Vol. IV: *Narrative of a Child Analysis*. All reprinted Virago, 1988 (*WMK*).

Kohon, Gregorio (1985) 'Objects are Not People', *Free Associations* 2: 19–30.

Kreeger, Lionel (ed.) (1975) *The Large Group: Dynamics and Therapy*. Constable; reprinted Maresfield.

Laplanche, Jean and Pontalis, J.-B. (1983) *The Language of Psycho-Analysis*. Hogarth; reprinted Maresfield.

Likierman, Meira (2003) *Melanie Klein: Her Work in Context*. Continuum.

Little, Margaret (1950) 'Countertransference and the Patient's Response to It', in Little (1986), pp. 33–50.

—— (1957) ' "R" – The Analyst's Total Response to His Patient's Needs', in Little (1986), pp. 51–80.

—— (1985) 'Winnicott Working in Areas where Psychotic Anxieties Predominate', *Free Associations* 3: 9–42.

—— (1986) *Transference Neurosis and Transference Psychosis: Toward Basic Unity*. Free Association Books/Maresfield Library.

—— (1987) 'On the Value of Regression to Dependence', *Free Associations* 10: 7–22.

—— (1989) Review of *Selected Letters of D.W. Winnicott*, *Free Associations* 18: 133–8.

—— (1990) *Psychotic Anxieties and Containment: A Personal Record of an Analysis with Winnicott*. Aronson.

Lopez-Corvo, Rafael E. (2003) *The Dictionary of the Work of W.R. Bion*. Karnac.

Main, Tom (1975) 'Some Psychodynamics of Large Groups', in L. Kreeger (ed.) (1975), pp. 57–86; reprinted in *The Ailment and Other Psychoanalytic Essays*. Free Association Books, 1989, pp. 100–22.

Meltzer, Donald (1966) 'The Relation of Anal Masturbation to Projective Identification', *International Journal of Psycho-Analysis* 47: 335–42; reprinted in Spillius (1988), vol. 1, pp 102–16.

—— (1992) *The Claustrum: An Investigation of Claustrophobic Phenomena*. Strath Tay: Clunie.

Meltzer, Donald, Bremner, John, Hoxter, Shirley, Weddell, Doreen and Wittenberg, Isca (1975) *Explorations in Autism: A Psycho-Analytical Study*. Strath Tay: Clunie.

Money-Kyrle, Roger (1956) 'Normal Counter-transference and Some of its Deviations, *International Journal of Psycho-Analysis* 37: 360–6.; reprinted in *The Collected Papers of Roger Money-Kyrle*. Strath Tay: Clunie, 1978, pp. 330–42, and Spillius, (1988), vol. 2, pp. 22–33.

Ogden, Thomas K. (1979) 'On Projective Identification', *International Journal of Psycho-Analysis* 60: 357–73.

—— (1982) *Projective Identification and Psychotherapeutic Technique*. Aronson.

Sandler, Joseph (ed.) (1989) *Projection, Identification, Projective Identification*. Karnac.

Scharff, Jill S. (1992) *Projective Identification and the Use of the Therapist's Self.* Aronson.

Searles, Harold (1978–9) 'Concerning Transference and Countertransference'. *Journal of Psychoanalysis and Psychotherapy* 7: 165–88 (written in 1949).

—— (1979) *Countertransference and Related Subjects.* Madison, CT: International Universities Press.

Segal, Hanna (1973) *Introduction to the Work of Melanie Klein.* Hogarth; reprinted Karnac, 1988.

Spillius, Elizabeth B. (ed.) (1988) *Melanie Klein Today,* 2 vols. Routledge.

—— (1992) 'Clinical Experiences of Projective Identification', in Anderson (1992), pp. 59–73.

Torres de Beà, E. (1989) 'Projective Identification and Differentiation', *International Journal of Psycho-Analysis* 70: 265–74.

Waddell, Margot (2004) *Inside Lives: Psychoanalysis and the Growth of the Personality,* 2nd edn. Karnac.

Williams, Raymond (1976) *Keywords: A Vocabulary of Culture and Society.* Fontana.

Winnicott, Donald W. (1947) 'Hate in the Countertransference', in Winnicott (1975), pp. 194–203.

—— (1975) *Through Paediatrics to Psycho-Analysis.* Hogarth.

Young, Robert M. (1992) 'The Vicissitudes of Transference and Countertransference: The Work of Harold Searles', *Journal of the Arbours Association* 9: 24–58; also in *Free Associations* 5(34): 171–95, 1995.

—— (1994) *Mental Space.* Process Press.

Chapter 5

Precious illusions: re-constructing realities

Marilyn Charles

Through her attempts to understand the developmental impediments encountered by her young patients, Melanie Klein opened an extraordinary window into the workings of the primitive mind. Her depictions of conceptualizations such as projective identification and the paranoid-schizoid and depressive positions opened up profound territory for psychoanalytic exploration. Klein's conceptualizations are pivotal understandings to have in mind as we engage in deep analytic work, most particularly in our work with more fragile patients. With individuals such as these, it is often critical to be able to ground ourselves in a coherent theoretical understanding at just those times when rational understanding is least accessible within the process itself.

In this chapter, I would like to highlight a few of the conceptualizations I have found to be most useful in my clinical work. I will first offer a clinical vignette, so that we can anchor the theory and technical considerations in personal experience. I will then outline the theories that informed my clinical work in this case, emphasizing critical pieces from Klein along with useful emendations from key figures such as Bion and Winnicott who expanded on her work, and noting how these conceptualizations have been coloured and refined by current writings of contemporary British Kleinians. I will then offer notes from one week's sessions, so that we can see how the theory informs the process. I will end with a brief conclusion to highlight the technical value of Klein's contributions, which are very useful conceptualizations to have in mind as we engage in this difficult work.

'Mary'

This is a woman with whom I have been working for over two years. We initially met twice weekly, then she cut back to once a week, in part because of a lack of funds. This was clearly not sufficient for any real work to be done. We had come to an impasse. Mary was thinking about giving up, whereas I thought the impasse might be addressed more constructively if she were to come in more frequently. I suggested that she consider coming in three times a week for the total weekly fee she had been paying. She said she would think about it and then agreed to try this path.

At this point in our work together, Mary and I had come up hard against a wall of silence. It had always been difficult for Mary to speak, but now it felt as though she was lost in her own silence. At times, I had rescued us from the silence; however, as our relationship grew and I became more clearly an object on whom she could rely, it began to seem increasingly important to be respectful of Mary's need to locate her own self within the space. When we increased the sessions to three times weekly, the silence persisted, but began to have a different feel. At times, I wondered whether I had made a mistake, torturing myself with this additional silence. Then, a shift came. The space had clearly changed for her. My sense was that being offered the space – without needing to do anything with it – felt like an opening in which she might be able to *be* in a larger sense.

Mary is a 39-year-old African-American lesbian woman, whose childhood home had been chaotic and violent. Mary had learned to survive by being the 'good girl' and walling herself off in a world of books. Her mother had not wanted her and had clearly stated at various points her regrets that the pregnancy had come to term. Mary feels as though she should not have been born and acts out her rage and ambivalence by enacting her own nonexistence in various ways, including ritualized cutting, which seems to be her most gratifying outlet under stress. Her father, now deceased, was by far the warmer of the two parents. The mother is described as depressed, angry, and often inaccessible through a fog of alcohol. Mary has three older brothers who fought verbally and physically with her father throughout her childhood. Most of the family violence was catalyzed by the acting-out behaviour of Mary's youngest brother. This was the brother who had shown her the most care and affection but also seems to have sexually abused her, though this is not always clear to her.

I have likened my experience of working with Mary to 'playing in an empty room' (Charles 2004a). In many ways, imagining the room as empty serves as a defence against encountering an other who might recognize Mary and those aspects of self and experience she prefers not to know. She is caught between annihilating her past and thereby her future, or acknowledging truths that make the present seem impossible to bear.

Mary's one positive escape in childhood had been into the world of books. The academic environment had been the one realm in which she could affirm her own value. In her advanced studies, Mary encountered the theory of 'repressed memories', which offered her the escape of believing that she had just 'made up' the abuse. This had been a more satisfactory resolution than believing it had actually occurred. We had visited this domain once previously in our work together, and then it receded from our overt content. It reappeared, however, in the sessions being reported here.

In the hours leading up to the sessions being reported, the theme of fantasy versus reality had been playing around the edges. The confusion between these two becomes a soft fog that Mary can hide behind, blurring the sharp edges that threaten to penetrate into conscious awareness. The other major theme was of victim/perpetrator: I easily become the persecutor/prosecutor, forcing Mary to know what she prefers not to know, intruding my own sharp edges. The intensity of this engagement at times is such that it brings to mind Melanie Klein's conceptualization of the paranoid-schizoid position, which characterizes this type of deadly interplay in a way in which one might achieve some life-saving distance while also being sufficiently affectively engaged to participate in the work. Working our way *through* these moments has been facilitated by conceptualizations that expanded on Klein's work, such as Winnicott's (1971) ideas about how play becomes possible only when one has assured one's self of the viability of both self and other; and Bion's (1977) notions of 'myth' as a vital form of play. These important psychoanalytic threads are built upon the crucial foundation, of Klein's characterizations of self under assault.

Mary and I 'play' around the deadly issues confronting her in small skirmishes in which we attempt to make contact without undue harm. Humour has become one way of masking truth sufficiently that we can survive the encounter. We also use myth and metaphor as means for communicating dense realities that must to some extent remain hidden (Charles 2004a). At times, this occurs through images of distorting mirrors and Pandora's boxes, whereas at other times we move into the realm of poetry, as Mary brings in snippets of songs to which she has been resonating. It is often easier to speak in the displacement, through the voice of another. The displacement, however, becomes another hall of mirrors, easing the encounter but also reinforcing the wall. Encounter is so difficult for Mary that she can barely make eye contact. For some time, when she would try to look at me, her eyes would shift to the side: they could not meet mine. Learning to engage with one another without undue harm (by omission *or* commission) was an ongoing dilemma.

Conceptualizing the case

Before we move on to the actual sessions, let's pause to locate ourselves within the conceptual space in which I was orienting myself as I attempted to find my way. As I mentioned, it was extremely useful in my work with Mary to be able to look at her predicament through the lens of Kleinian theory and technique, which, in turn, is deeply embedded in classical Freudian technique, with a profound respect for the importance of the frame in bounding the treatment (Segal 1981). Klein, however, gives particular emphasis to what Betty Joseph (1985) has termed 'the total transference', in which the experience of the moment *illuminates* the internal objects, including the wealth of experiential, relational, and situational elements. If we are to truly understand the other's object world, we need to be willing to participate in it, to experience the 'transference as a living relationship in which there is constant movement and change' (Joseph 1985, p. 453). Klein's willingness to be present in the moment, and to engage with impossible realities, gives her work a potency and vitality that is quite remarkable.

Perhaps Klein's greatest contributions to technique lie in her theories, which, in turn, were informed by her attempts to understand the factors that move us in our earliest years and in the most primitive recesses of our beings. Klein opened up a new universe of psychoanalytic thought and technique, bringing us right into the heart of our most basic needs, desires, and fears. She helps us to find our way through the primal terrors we experience when taxed to our utmost resources. Through it all, she maintains an appreciation of the ambivalence that is inevitably found at the heart of human relationships. In acknowledging the good and the bad, the hostility and the care that can intermingle and obscure one another, we help to heal the splits that arise under extreme pressure.

Klein (1930) builds upon Freud's drive theory, linking early anxieties to an excess of sadism that is expelled (because it is ego-dystonic and therefore unknowable), but then becomes dangerous (and therefore retaliatory). Always, in Klein's work, there is the affirmation that what is explicitly not known is still held within the individual at some level of awareness. Whatever cannot be consciously known is carried in the less conscious regions through what Klein (1957) has called 'memories in feeling': the 'language of the body' (Charles 2002). These feelings 'mark the spot' (Charles 2004b) of the distress, holding the place of what must ultimately (yet cannot now) be known, so that we can master the anxiety sufficiently to survive.

This was the type of crucible that represented an essential dilemma for Mary, who seems to have reached an uneasy balance in her attempts to master this type of potentially overwhelming anxiety. Her relational needs had brought her to points of seeming annihilation, via both the mother's angry, critical, controlling nature and the brother's ostensibly 'loving' sexual assaults. It remained for me to help her to affirm and acknowledge these unknown meanings, and to believe that we might know them together without imminent annihilation.

In this endeavour, it was crucial that I be able to mark the feelings (and their relative absence) that characterized Mary's presentations and also the process between us. What could not be known was integrally tied to what could not be felt without invoking annihilation anxieties. In delineating both the dilemma and the path towards resolving it, Klein (1930) links the experience of annihilation anxiety to the creation of symbols, pointing to the desperate struggle to hold on to meaning in adverse circumstances.

The ability to create meaning is a crucial step towards ultimately building relationships between two separate beings. Initially, however, the beings are not entirely separate, nor are the symbols. According to Klein (1930), early symbols take the form of 'symbolic equations', a type of proto-symbol in which no distinction is made between the object and the representation. Symbolization processes offer a means of relief from these untenable equations, providing respite from the intensity of the affective charge. Through the creation of the symbol proper, an object can be internally represented and more explicitly thought about, and thereby used more freely in the service of meaning-making and communication (Segal 1957).

Symbols give us conceptual anchors. They provide relief from anxiety by linking objects while also obscuring problematic aspects of reality, so that we can keep the dilemma in mind with sufficient distance to be able to think about it more freely. In this way, the internal object is protected by virtue of the very forces that keep it at peril. If we are aware of the representative nature of the internal object, we have some way of thinking about it and thereby taming its more terrible aspects. This transformation entails also coming to terms with the ultimate separateness of self and other (Grotstein 1982–3).

The process of differentiation of good and bad, self and other, requires us to be able to note similarities and differences, while keeping the boundaries sufficiently permeable and sufficiently separate to be able to make real contact, without the type of symmetrization of self and other that can occur when primary process thinking holds sway (see Matte-Blanco 1975, 1988). Generalization helps us to link similar objects, which helps us to organize our world, but can impede development if insufficient discrimination is made *between* objects. Severe anxiety (fear) impedes symbolization, so that we can fail to make critical distinctions between dangerous and not dangerous aspects of others, thereby impeding the capacity to ground one's observations in reality.

Whereas Klein's early work was closely tied to Freud (focusing on anxiety as a signal of distress, rather than noting the signal functions of affect more generally), later followers expanded upon these ideas. Bion (1977), for example, noted the essential relationship between meaning and feeling, placing emotion at the heart of meaning (see Meltzer 1981). In this way, Bion highlights an essential hallmark of Klein's work, which is also a hallmark of any good psychoanalytic work. He terms this quality 'passion', to denote the quality of feeling that marks the essential truth of an experience. Valuing the feelings that we experience in our relationships with patients helps us to mark these essential truths, so that we can attend to them more carefully and perhaps come to understand them better over time (Charles 2002).

Klein's ability to track emotional realities seems to have been quite profound. She links the experience of anxiety to the experience of dependence, noting the delicate balance between the need to rely upon the other, and the terrible vacuum that ensues in the absence of sufficient responsivity to the child's experienced needs. When there is a lack of fit between the child's needs and the mother's capacities, the excess of dependency needs can feel like a chasm ever waiting. The ensuing rage then loops back into the relationship, further toxifying need, self, and other. For Mary, the resolution to the terrible danger to which her relational needs exposed her was to attempt to have no interpersonal needs. She created a vacuum in which sleep, substance use, and ritualized cutting attenuated her longing and despair and thereby ostensibly kept her safe from the far more perilous world of human relations.

This desire to have no needs also becomes a desire to have no words, no way in which to symbolize – and thereby make more palpable – thoughts that seem too distressing to think about. Klein notes this tension between the need for words and the fear of knowing. Discussing her work with a very disturbed child, she writes:

> In general I do not interpret the material until it has found expression in various representations. In this case, however, where the capacity to represent it was almost entirely lacking, I found myself obliged to make my interpretations on the basis of my general knowledge, the representations in Dick's behaviour being relatively vague. Finding access in this way to his unconscious, I succeeded in activating anxiety and other affects. The representations then became fuller and I soon acquired a more solid foundation for the analysis.
>
> (Klein 1930, pp. 228–229)

Klein's attunement helped her to verbalize and to thereby detoxify feelings that had seemed impossible to know together. In my work with Mary, I, too, have learned to speak to what is missing as well as that which is present, as a way of affirming that one might know impossible things without imminent annihilation (see Charles 2004b). Mary often points to a problem by noting an absence, as was the case in the material to follow. In this material, not only were the connecting links missing, but also the very words by which the feared representations might be known.

Anxiety can be titrated through an interpretation that allows for a re-distribution and re-construction of elements in a way that is more tolerable to the self. In this regard, writing of her work with a very disturbed young boy, Klein writes: 'From the theoretical point of view I think it is important to note that, even in so extreme a case of defective ego-development, it was possible to develop both ego and libido by analyzing the unconscious conflicts, without bringing any educational influence to bear upon the ego' (1930, p. 229). At the more primary levels of unconscious fears and phantasies, *implicit* education is more readily integrated than explicit, 'rational' instruction. We are putting forward an alternative way of thinking, an alternative way of being.

For Klein, the individual under attack becomes caught between the pain, the urge to fend off the pain through counterattack, and the fear of retaliation (which is also the fear of one's own hostility):

The ego's excessive and premature defence against sadism checks the establishing of a relation to reality and the development of phantasy-life. The further sadistic appropriation and exploration of the mother's body and of the outside world (the mother's body in an extended sense) are brought to a standstill, and this causes the more or less complete suspension of the symbolic relation to the things and objects representing the contents of the mother's body and hence of the relation to the subject's environment and to reality.

(Klein 1930, p. 232)

The apparent lack of anxiety is bought at the price of interpersonal engagement and of contact with one's own affect and being.

Whereas Freud (1917) tends to speak in terms of whole objects, implicit in Klein's theory is an appreciation of the role of part objects and the various meanings of these, along with the meanings of whatever links or lack thereof might also be present. Klein's metaphors are very concrete, developed in her work with small children. In the work of more contemporary Kleinians, there has been a tendency to shift from a focus on structure to one on function. 'It is capacities for seeing, touching, tasting, hearing, smelling, remembering, feeling, judging, and thinking, active as well as passive, that are attributed to and perceived in relation to part objects' (Spillius 1988, p. 5). Klein's own language, however, vivifies the dilemma of these primal aspects of self that entangle us in their particular emotional realities. In the following passage, for example, Klein speaks to the abject and primary terror experienced when faced with impossible realities:

One of the earliest methods of defence against the dread of persecutors, whether conceived of as existing in the external world or internalized, is that of scotomization, the *denial of psychic reality*; this may result in a considerable restriction of the mechanisms of introjection and projection and in the denial of external reality.

(Klein 1930, p. 262; italics in original unless otherwise noted)

In my work with Mary, we often came upon these crevasses in her reality, in which facts that might be knowable at one moment were eminently unknowable at the next turn. Whereas Freud (1917) posits the loss of a (whole) loved object as the fundamental cause of despair, Klein (1935) suggests that early losses are more difficult because the relationships are with part and not whole objects, thus enhancing splitting processes and impeding the type of integration of good and bad that is required for real mourning and successful resolution of loss to occur. Klein notes that the reciprocal attempts to introject the good and expel the bad are each inherently doomed. The need for reparation to (and hence reunion with) the good object exists side by side with the need to placate (and hence avoid being destroyed by) the bad object.

In order for this resolution and integration to occur, the internalization of affect regulation is critical. Klein (1935) points to the crucial function of affect regulation in ensuring healthy development and adaptation to reality constraints: 'Every internal or external stimulus (*e.g.* every real frustration) is fraught with the utmost danger: not only bad objects but also the good ones are thus menaced by the id, for every access of hate or anxiety may temporarily abolish the differentiation and thus result in a "loss of the loved object"' (p. 266).

In her attempts to understand this internalization process, Klein (1935) details her fantasies/extrapolations/interpretations of the internal world of the infant that result in particular dilemmas. Whether or not one accepts the details overlying Klein's analyses more concretely or more metaphorically, the processes she is depicting are crucial in understanding the dilemmas with which many of our patients are faced. These depictions parallel quite closely the fundamental processes of cognitive and affective self-regulatory development that have been detailed by researchers such as Stern (1985), Fonagy and Target (1997), and Tronick (1989), augmented by those theorists who have described the constraining effects of trauma upon those same processes (Krystal 1988; Van Der Kolk and Van Der Hart 1991).

These early tensions between good and bad part objects are linked not only to affect regulation, but also to the development of superego functions. Klein (1935) notes that anxiety becomes complicated by the need to fulfil demands of the 'good' object, who turns persecutor when the demands cannot be met. The resistance this evokes from within, in Klein's view, is experienced as hatred, which in turn causes

> uncertainty as to the 'goodness' of a good object, which causes it so readily to become transformed into a bad one – all these factors combine to produce in the ego a sense of being prey to contradictory and impossible claims from within, a condition which is felt as a bad conscience. That is to say: the earliest utterances of conscience are associated with persecution by bad objects.
>
> (Klein 1935, p. 268)

This results in a terrible dilemma when the primary object relations are weak or impeded, in that 'the stronger the anxiety is of losing the loved objects, the more the ego strives to save them, and the harder the task of restoration becomes, the stricter will grow the demands which are associated with the super-ego' (Klein 1935, p. 269). For Mary, this has resulted in an impossible bind in which goodness (mother) is equated with self-annihilation (as not-mother and therefore as bad). Psychic survival, however, is predicated on preserving self from mother (preserving her difference). The resolution of this dilemma has been to avoid the bad mother and to long for a (re)union with mother that will never and can never come. In this way, as attempts to find a 'mother' who will love and accept her have been sabotaged by her attraction to 'motherly' women (critical, self-absorbed, narcissistic women whose love is annihilating), Mary has reinforced her notions of self as inherently unlovable and utterly valueless. This position protects her from further disappointments but also keeps her isolated and alone, thereby perpetuating the negative self-reflections.

In our work together, this idea of self-reflection has come up repeatedly, as Mary's eyes slide to the side in attempts to not see herself being seen. We have discussed how repugnant she found herself in her childhood mirror, and how mirrors have become sources of fear, aversion, and self-loathing. This inhibition seems to add a terrible edge to Winnicott's (1971) description of the baby who *must* find herself in the mirror of the mother's eyes. Not only could Mary not find herself in any positive sense, she has lived in fear of being annihilated by the other's gaze.

Klein (1935) suggests that this fear of annihilation is more fundamental than the fear of loss. This is the paranoid-schizoid reality, in which the individual finds herself in the odd position of residing in a world that is 'in a state of dissolution – in bits' (p. 269). This dissolution – this 'unlinking' (Bion 1977) and unknowing – both feeds and titrates the underlying anxiety. We are inevitably persecuted by whatever it is we are not-knowing. The enforced blindness of projection and expulsion does not eliminate the feared objects, but only dislocates them. The lie remains, continually yearning to right itself. One aspect of this attenuation of reality is the coexistence of the bad object with the fantasied perfect object, without possibility of integration or diminution. The wish for perfection further vilifies the imperfect self who cannot attain the longed-for perfect object. This desire for perfection may also be seen as a desire to protect (and to heal) the flawed object from our own destructive attacks.

When our needs are insufficiently met, they become increasingly problematic. From Klein's (1935) framework, this leads to the ego's hatred of the id. The seemingly irresolvable clash within the self results in extreme despair and feelings of unworthiness. The hatred may be seen as a function of the inability to tolerate one's own pain, a fear of one's own lethality, and also a projected fear that this intense level of hatred may reside in the other. The excess of hate and associated persecution anxieties impede the ability to integrate good and bad aspects of object and self, in this way perpetuating both the split and the fear. Paranoid anxiety, invoked as a means of warding off danger, may be seen as the type of hypervigilance that has been linked to the sequelae of trauma (Krystal 1988). This level of anxiety tends to promote distortions because of the lack of reality-testing resulting from an enhanced focus on negative over positive aspects of self and other.

Klein (1935) links paranoid anxiety to the fear of destroying or damaging the internalized loved objects. One means, then, for protecting both self and other may be by defensively withdrawing from the external world. This type of defensive withdrawal seems, at times, to have been Mary's only resolution to her desires for and terror of connection. Immuring herself in her own internal world, she seems to have folded into herself by way of creating a womb in which she might, perhaps, be born anew. Her means for lulling herself into this position, however, had been quite lethal. It was only when she entered analysis and was confronted with my view of the lethality of these 'comforts' – and my conception that a womb might actually be a place from which one might emerge and be recognized – that she was confronted with an alternative creation myth.

It is in a footnote in her 1935 article that Klein affirms her use of the term 'position' to describe these early developmental anxieties and defences. In this way, she attempts to bridge the experience of primal anxiety across time, expressly unlinking this dilemma from any explicit chronology or pathology (see Charles 2001a). In Klein's view, the destruction of the self represents both the murder and the saving of the loved object. In killing the bad parts of self and other, there is a fantasied reunion with the object. Mania may be seen as a denial of dependence; an unknowing that is a denial of the importance of the objects and also of their dangers. Attempts to master and control the anxiety through the control of the environment represent a denial of the need and of the dread. In kind, Mary describes needing to repudiate all ties with the object world when her anxieties become aroused. Experiencing my caring, in particular, has been almost intolerable, resulting in defensive acts of self-annihilation. From this perspective, Mary's avoidance of eye contact may be seen not only as an avoidance of the feared vilification she might read in the eyes of the other but, perhaps more importantly, as an avoidance of becoming entrapped by her desires for love and acceptance.

When Klein (1946) talks in terms of psychotic anxieties, she seems to be literally referring to anxieties that preclude the type of effective reality-testing that might serve to attenuate them. In her term the 'paranoid-schizoid' position, she integrates Fairbairn's (1952) notion of a schizoid position into her ideas of a persecutory phase. In this composite, the term 'paranoid' refers to the anxiety, and 'schizoid' to the resultant distance/alienation prescribed as the price of safety from the feared object relations, whether in the service of keeping self or other safe. In Klein's view, the failure to successfully resolve primary persecutory fears becomes further reinforcing of this paranoid-schizoid position. In line with Winnicott's (1945) views on the lack of integration of the early ego, Klein (1946) assumes that the early months of life are characterized by a tendency towards disintegration or 'falling into bits' (p. 4). The fear of annihilation 'takes the form of fear of persecution' (p. 4) so that experientially, at a certain level of intensity, persecution and annihilation become interchangeable.

Klein believes that the splitting of the object is inextricably tied to a splitting of the ego. Although 'it is in phantasy that the infant splits the object and the self . . . the effect of the phantasy is a very real one, because it leads to feelings and relations (and later on, thought-processes) being in fact cut off from one another' (1946, p. 6). This splitting also leads to a dislocation of parts of self and other. Klein describes projective identification as an identification that takes the form of an aggressive object-relation, such that whatever is vilified is not seen within the bounds of self but only outside, in the other. When the primary impulse is to harm or control, the other is felt, reciprocally, to be the persecutor. If, in contrast, it is the good parts that are projected excessively, the other becomes the ego-ideal, resulting in an over-dependence on the other and a reciprocal weakening and impoverishment of the self. Mary's difficulties in integrating good and bad aspects of self and other leave her caught in relationships in which she is inevitably persecuted by either the withholding good object or the actively bad object.

Introjective processes, when excessive, result in the same type of impasse, in which the dependency and subservience are in relation to an internal rather than external object. 'With an unassimilated idealized object there goes a feeling that the ego has no life and no value of its own' (Klein 1946, p. 9). With excessive introjection, the disintegration results from the concomitant attempts to unite with the ideal internalized object while also fending off the internal persecutors. For Klein, parental love and understanding are the forces that help this integration process to occur, a theme explored most pointedly by Winnicott (1971). Bion (1977) then expands our views of this containment process by noting the crucial 'reverie' function of the maternal object who digests the child's evacuations and feeds them back in tolerable chunks so that meaning can be made. This is also the role of the analyst, who digests the evacuated elements and attempts to put them into words that can be integrated by the other.

When maternal containment or reverie is insufficient, the lack of integration of good and bad aspects into a coherent whole lends itself to impoverished relations with self and others: 'as-if' relationships that do not evolve, develop, enrich, or grow. Klein (1946) links this type of relating to loneliness, isolation, and fears of parting. This is the type of constricted imprisoning cocoon in which Mary finds herself when her anxieties begin to supersede her desires for relationship. From this perspective, the self is experienced as inevitably bad and wanting, and the other appears to be in danger from this deprecated self. For Klein, the resolution of this conflict comes in the form of a drive to make reparation, which she sees as a function of the move towards the depressive position. If reparation cannot be made (in Mary's case, her inability to find the good mother or evade the bad brother), then the anxieties and the fear and splitting are reinforced.

Much as Klein (1946) describes in her depiction of schizoid defences, Mary appears to have split off those parts of self that seemed to be dangerous or hostile to the other. The destructive impulses are then turned towards the self and are experienced as an *external* danger because of the projection. This splitting helps to allay the anxiety that seems to stem from a fear of killing/

losing the other whose well-being is felt to be essential to the self. Klein notes that interpretations regarding the causes of the splitting that integrate an understanding of the anxiety and its impact in the transference – and also in the past – must include details of the situations that encourage regression to these schizoid states. These details help to anchor the individual to the functional elements of the problematic interchanges, rather than becoming lost in the surface aspects of the apparent context. Although confronting reality in this way can lead to depression in the short term, it also leads to greater integration and to fundamental positive changes in object relations. This crucial developmental milestone, in which good and bad are integrated into one object, is what Klein terms the 'depressive position'. This position is not an ultimate end to be achieved, but rather a point in an ongoing developmental process achieved through recursive phases of fragmentation and integration across the life span (Bion 1977; Klein 1952a).

With the mourned loss of the idealized object, the demonized object, too, loses its power. Without this integration, persecution prevails. At the extreme, there can be an apparent lack of anxiety (as in schizoid states), which Klein (1946) links to fragmentation. 'The feeling of being disintegrated, of being unable to experience emotions, of losing one's objects, is in fact the equivalent of anxiety' (p. 21). The inner deadness results, in this case, not from an absence but rather from a surfeit of affect. For Klein, it is through our interpretations that we re-link whatever has become unlinked due to the intolerable anxiety. In the moment, however, it may be very difficult for us to maintain the links sufficiently to be able to offer them up for consideration:

> Interpretations which tend towards synthesizing the split in the self, including the dispersal of emotions, make it possible for the anxiety gradually to be experienced as such, though for long stretches we may in fact only be able to bring the ideational contents together but not to elicit the emotions of anxiety.
>
> I have also found that interpretations of schizoid states make particular demands on our capacity to put the interpretations in an intellectually clear form in which the links between the conscious, pre-conscious and unconscious are established.
>
> (Klein 1946, pp. 21–22)

In these difficult moments, we find ourselves in opposition to the other's fear of knowing that is being experienced by them as persecutory anxiety. This is the type of dilemma in which I often found myself in my work with Mary. Klein's metaphors help us to position ourselves in these odd engagements in which a battle is being played out for psychic survival and the sides can change quite rapidly. She describes persecutory anxiety as a primitive form of protection of object and self, positing splitting as a function of the death instinct and integration as a function of the life instinct. 'Persecutory anxiety relates predominantly to the annihilation of the ego; depressive anxiety is predominantly related to the harm done to internal and external loved objects by the subject's destructive impulses' (Klein 1948, p. 34).

Depressive anxiety implies the injury of the good object, which is then lost. In this way, 'depressive anxiety is closely bound up with guilt and with the tendency to make reparation' (p. 34), whereas persecutory anxiety is about psychic survival. Klein suggests that persecutory anxieties provide a means for avoiding guilt and despair, whereas the reparative tendency is a more adaptive function of the sense of guilt. You will see in the material from the case how the progression in these sessions is presaged by Mary's growing awareness that she is not merely a helpless victim, but rather a complicit one. She, too, plays an active part in the drama in which she feels imprisoned.

This growing awareness helps to bring Mary out of the dichotomized experience of self and other, in which, according to Klein (1952b), omnipotence is the corollary of persecutory anxiety. This distance gives us a bit more room for reflection rather than being so overwhelmed by the affect of the moment. Being able to be present with both the thoughts and the feelings helps us to better understand the transference, in which one must be able to appreciate not only the present moment but also 'the fluctuations between objects, loved and hated, external and internal . . . [and] the interconnections between positive and negative transferences' (1952b, p. 53). For Klein, to truly understand the transference, we must be able to 'explore the early interplay between love and hate, and the vicious circle of aggression, anxieties, feelings of guilt and increased aggression, as well as the various aspects of objects towards whom these conflicting emotions and anxieties are directed' (p. 53).

Through these explorations, recognition of the splitting helps to contain our ambivalence, so that we might more constructively illuminate the patterns, not only of relationships or characteristics, but also of modes of being and of defence, reactivity, and adaptation that are being repeated. We can notice, for example, how internal and external loci of aggression feed the persecutory anxiety, while the projection and introjection of loving feelings serve to strengthen one another and to decrease persecutory anxiety. Recognition of these patterns helps us to better understand how to contain the affect sufficiently to build ego resiliency, which in turn enhances the ability to know and to link, thereby providing further aid in perception and reality-testing.

We all titrate our knowing through the reciprocal processes of fragmentation and integration that help to contain anxiety, optimally allowing further development without too much anxiety. As we move towards greater integration, however, greed can threaten the internal and external objects. 'The ego therefore increasingly inhibits instinctual desires . . . [which may lead] to serious inhibitions in establishing both affectionate and erotic relations' (Klein 1952a, p. 73). This certainly seemed to be the case with Mary, who became destabilized when the possibility arose of allowing anyone entry as a valued or valuable object. In the transference, encounters with a caring object seemed more difficult to tolerate than disdain. The identification with the injured object (and the attendant guilt and anxiety) leads to denial of feelings or connecting links, even to the extent of disavowing any care for the object. This may be seen as a manic defence that precludes care or relatedness, which pulls away from acceptance of the inevitable duality of being and back towards the paranoid-schizoid position.

It is our ability to confront and engage with the world that facilitates development. 'The continued experience of facing psychic reality, implied in the working through of the depressive position, increases the . . . understanding of the external world' (Klein 1952a, p. 74), thereby reducing distortion, enhancing reality-testing, and reducing anxiety. Being able to differentiate between internal and external sources of danger and disequilibrium helps to reinforce more adaptive ways of coping, which reduces both aggression and guilt, and aids in effective sublimation of these. For Klein, the urge to make reparation becomes the primary means for keeping depression at bay, which helps in making this important transition. Real successes and new achievements are felt to be reparative, thereby strengthening object relations as well as the ego.

Ego development is sorely challenged by early environments such as Mary had endured. Severe deprivation results in a diminished capacity to receive goodness and to make crucial distinctions between inside and out. When insufficient distinction is made between internal and external sources of danger, real self needs may be abdicated in the hope of repairing the other. Excessive anxiety also leads to rigidity and a lack of porousness and permeability between conscious and unconscious, impeding further phantasy, symbolization, and integration. At the extreme, self-denial and injury become the ultimate gift, in hope of reparation. If the underlying hostility remains split off, self-harm can become a very dangerous manic defence. We can see this tension in Mary, in her impulse to give life by giving to the other, while denying the self. This always seemed to be the price of connection. Receiving had been the greater hazard, in that so much of what had been received had been toxic: from mother, anger; and from brother, sex.

When early objects have been toxic, it is particularly important for the patient to be able to come into contact with, and to thereby integrate, bad as well as good aspects of the analyst. Failing this, any growth or resolution will inevitably be unstable. It is important to build in this resilience, which helps us to tolerate the ongoing struggles between paranoid-schizoid and depressive modes of being and between aggression and libido that are 'renewed at every mental or physical crisis' (Klein 1952a, p. 93). This struggle can be quite taxing and may, at times, be beyond the capacity of the individual to bear. The potency of the destructive impulses can reach a point such that life-enhancing activities are foreclosed, leading to what contemporary Kleinian theorists have termed 'narcissistic' (Rosenfeld 1971), 'defensive' (O'Shaughnessy 1981) or 'pathological' organizations (Steiner 1987, 1990). These terms attempt to characterize an interim state in which the individual is caught between the fragility of the ego and the intensity of the anxieties with which it is faced, resulting in oscillations between exposure and restriction (O'Shaughnessy 1981).

This type of an interim position may offer some respite from the fragmentation and confusion of the paranoid-schizoid position, and from the anxiety and anguish of the depressive position (Steiner 1987). It may be characterized as a kind of no man's land, wherein no growth may occur. Yet, as O'Shaughnessy (1981) points out, within the containment provided by the analysis, this interim position may enable the ego sufficient respite that growth is eventually possible. This may be one way of understanding the hours of silence in my work with Mary that eventually gave way to the clinical material being presented.

Rosenfeld (1971) notes that in the narcissistic organization, the destructive aspects of narcissism are highlighted and linked with envy, which aligns with the powerful parts of the destructive other as a means for psychic survival. This characterization would seem to help us better understand another aspect of Mary's dilemma: her alliance with her pain that seemed to keep her from straying too far from its sources. At this level, pain and pleasure seem to be closely aligned; we find ourselves in the region of the alliance with whatever has become 'home' (see Novick and Novick 1996).

The sessions

For Mary, the issue of home – how it might be characterized and whether it might ever be a place in which any real nurturance or sustenance might be found – was a pivotal one. Crucial in this regard was not only how home was to be defined, but who might do the defining. During the hours leading up to the sessions being reported, an issue that had become salient was the possibility of actually coming to the fore in her own life, rather than allowing others to destroy her. This would require her to integrate good and bad aspects of self and other. Keeping others in the persecutor role keeps her safe from taking risks of incurring new assaults, but also keeps her immobilized.

During this time, Mary reported a dream in which she was encircled by barbed wire in an empty room. She was trying to chew her way out but not meeting with much success. As she was describing the dream, I had a sense of her allegiance to the pain, her alliance with it – there seemed to be a perverse element in all of this. The real enemy seemed to be her love of the pain.

'Who is saving whom from what?' I wondered to myself.

Processing this dream led us to her relationships with her mother and with a previous lover, both of which were extremely sado-masochistic. An interpretation had then led Mary to more actively consider her own part in this loop. Seeing herself as an actor in the drama, rather than merely a passive victim, had shaken her.

'I'm still kind of raw from last week,' she said, when she returned after the weekend break, 'thinking that I might need to forgive my mother and J. and realizing that I've probably been doing to them exactly what I've been accusing them of. It's good – the realization – but it's hard.'

Mary had brought in the lyrics of two songs by Alanis Morissette and read them to me. One was about 'little rejections' that become internalized affirmations of lack of self-worth, ending with the challenge of *not* abandoning one's self. In the lyrics, I could clearly hear Mary playing with the possibility of acknowledging the victim stance in which she positions herself. Hearing these words left a charge in me – we were clearly entering into new territory in this possible reconfiguration of self.

The other song was about 'precious illusions', beginning with a playful recognition that in playing out the urge to be rescued, one reaffirms the victim role and thereby re-enacts the victimization. In these lyrics, there is an acknowledgement of the comfort inherent in whatever has become 'home'. No matter how self-destructive, there is always the longing to return to the known. At this point in the session, the charge in the affective field is heightened as we sit with the hope, juxtaposed with the sadness and the loss. Each is palpably present in the room, accelerating the intensity. There is so much waste, so much lost time, making it difficult for Mary to come to grips with all that has occurred. When we hit that waste, it is like a vast chasm of pain that opens.

We come, then, to the week's sessions being reported. Although I had hoped to present this particular case at an upcoming clinical seminar, I had found it very difficult to write out the process. In part, this is an inhibition against attempting to remember, which I find difficult. There was also an inhibition against inviting judgement, in my own little eddy into the paranoid-schizoid position. More deeply, however, this represents a fundamental dilemma in which, as I think about remembering, I realize that this focus takes me out of the session. I become caught between my wish to hold on to the process so that I might report it, and the need to abandon this desire and immerse myself in the session.

I often find the sessions so taxing that the idea of writing about them afterwards can be quite repugnant. The following transcriptions are what I have managed to retrieve from this tension. They represent one week of work.

Monday morning

'I'm realizing that I miss things', says Mary. 'There was a party Saturday night with my co-workers. They're mainly straight. We were playing charades and the word was "blow" and the guy decided to get to "blow" by using the word "blow-job". He said something about "sexual perversion" and then "jobs" and I'm thinking "jobs . . . sexual perversion . . . what the hell is this" and I'm just not getting it. And everyone is laughing and laughing. And I just couldn't get it. Was my face red.'

She sat for a few moments, then said: 'Then, I was listening to this Tori Amos song, these lines: "boy you best pray that I bleed real soon – how's that thought for you" and finally I get it and I think "God, how stupid."'

(I'm thinking that she is now thinking it's about pregnancy, which is outside of her realm, and that previously she had thought it had to do with cutting, which is within her realm. I'm not certain whether her old thought or her new thought is 'correct', only that my reading has been more consistent with her old thought; wondering what that means . . .)

'I feel so stupid', she says.

'Why stupid?' I ask.

'Just not wanting to even think about pregnancy or any of that. Just not getting it.'

'It's interesting that you would decide that you're stupid', I say. 'We all miss things. I'm thinking that with the first example, with everyone laughing, it makes sense that you would feel stupid, but with the second example, you were alone, up against your internal critic. I'm wondering about when you were young – your experience of feeling laughed at or ridiculed or criticized.'

She smiles wry acknowledgement. 'Oh, that. There was certainly a lot of that.'

(But then a wave hits. Lots of distress in her face.)

'What?' I ask.

'I feel like I just went down the rabbit hole.'

(Silence. She curls up into a ball on the chair, sideways.)

'I feel really weird.'

'How so?' I ask.

'This white noise hit. . . . That's how I feel when I wind up cutting.'

(I'm thinking 'blow-job' – 'blood' – 'brother' – thinking we're back on this track we had gone down before but been diverted from. I'm wondering how much to say; not say; wondering if she is even aware of these headlines that are screaming in *my* head. When the spasm ebbs a bit, I say, tentatively: 'I'm thinking of where the session began.'

(She nods, but isn't able to say much. I just sit, hoping the pain will ebb. I ask her how she's doing. She describes the pain in bullet points:

- 'intensity,
- noise,
- voices'.

(She curls up. I watch as the pain hits again, and she curls further into herself.)

'I don't know if I can do this', she says.

'I don't know if you can afford not to', I say, after a pause.

(Some time passes, then the pain and distress intensify.)

'I can't stand it', she says.

'Then let it go', I respond. 'Maybe that's enough for today.'

Mary calls mid-afternoon:

'I need a little contact with reality', she says. 'I'm not doing so well.'

'Would you like to come in this evening?' I ask.

'Yeah.'

That evening

'I'm trying to avoid climbing into a bottle or cutting myself', Mary begins. 'Sleep seemed to be the best option.'

'I just can't figure out what's going on. I've been going over and over it and I just can't get it. I feel like I keep missing something.'

'How do you put it together?' I ask.

(I'm wondering once again about the blow-job and the blood: those refrains keep going through my head. They're so palpable in the room I am never certain to what extent they are present for her or, to the contrary, are exactly that which is not being seen. I'm not wanting to assault her with something she already sees, yet not wanting to be complicit in the not-seeing.)

'I came in, talking about not being able to put things together, then I started thinking about childhood and all the things I couldn't make sense of, and they just kept marching across, the whole progression and then this pain and this wailing and "stop it!" and "don't do that!" and I just can't make sense of it.'

(She's holding the sides of her head with her hands rigid at this point.)

'It seems to have something to do with "blow-job" and "blood" and not being able to stop it or get anyone to help', I suggest.

'I just can't tell what's true and what's not. I spent so much time convincing myself it wasn't true and most of my adult life putting it to rest. I just can't even tell what's true.'

'It seems like a story I told myself', she continues after a pause.

'*That* may be the story you tell yourself to lull yourself', I reply.

'Seems like a dream.'

'A dream you dream to avoid the nightmare?' I ask.

'I don't know.'

(Mary turns to the other side and curls up tightly in the chair.)

(I'm wondering how she might be able to speak to whatever *is* there. I'm feeling pretty lost. Not knowing what is known and what is not known or how we might know together.)

'Tell me about the nightmare', I say.

(She smiles – she sees the ruse and is grateful for the respite offered by the displacement. She works with me: 'It's very dark. I'm very small . . . and I'm scared . . . and in pain.'

'Where do you hurt?' I ask, hoping for some bit of detail through which we might orient; more fragments to piece together – hoping to be let in – to know more of what she knows. But she surprises me completely by saying: 'My heart, my soul – it's like broken. I'm broken.'

(The brokenness is palpable. It has taken over the room. I want there to be some way she can be not broken. I want to have not broken her. Inwardly, I challenge the brokenness. I am not willing to believe in it. Not ultimately.)

'I wish I was dead', she says, cutting the silence with raw emotion.

(I'm thinking that that was in line with her mother's stated wish that Mary had never been born and also with this experience she describes with her brother, of having been killed. I'm thinking she acts this out in the blood-letting – ritualizing the killing of herself, keeping it within herself, under her control.)

'That was certainly the message you got', I reply, after a pause. 'Hard to know how to survive that then.'

The line of a song is running through my head, a song I know she listens to, and it's persistent. I wonder about saying it aloud to her and finally tell her: 'This line is running through my head: "Hold on – hold on to yourself – this is gonna hurt like hell".'

(She smiles, grimacing a bit, but nodding. Her resonance is palpable. We have come into synchrony. A bit of respite. The lighter side of the silence.)

'Sara McLachlan', she says, rolling her eyes, but acknowledging the meeting.

(Then I say something referring to having been betrayed by the people who ostensibly loved her. This is the part that seems to be difficult to know or to believe in.)

(We are at the end of the hour. I ask her if she thinks she can go home and get some sleep without 'crawling into a bottle'.)

She smiles. 'I'll give it a shot', she says. 'Thank you.'

'See you tomorrow', I say, affirming the bridge.

Tuesday morning

Mary brings in a poem she had written some years before. I realize she has given it to me before, a long time ago, but accept it as though I am seeing it for the first time, which gives an uncanny feel and yet seems resonant to *her* experience of proffering something new – a gift.

Through the fog of things past
and forgotten . . .
In the darkness of night where
the moon is obscured . . .
I see a little girl child

hidden in fear . . .
In this place called childhood
there is no laughter
only silence and death.
I see in this place, a big man-boy
moving towards the little girl child
A malicious glee parts his lips
in a smile of satisfaction . . .
The satisfaction of the conqueror
of the victor . . .
He moves to her and strikes
with the speed of a rattlesnake . . .
He comes back to her again
and again and
again . . .
He says to her don't tell, don't tell
don't tell
DON'T EVER TELL!
Or no one will ever love you
And the six year old little girl child
listens and believes . . .
She believes the lies of the big man-boy
because she trusts him.
She does what he wants
because he is family.
I see the little girl child crack and split
split and crack, beneath the weight
of the big man-boy.
Finally, he leaves . . .
The little girl child sits in a darkened
room . . .
The little girl child cries out
in anguish and pain.
Pain that scars so deep
it leaves little visible sign
Save the eyes which had
fallen into yesterday's hell of tomorrow.
The moon disappears,
Night is complete in this place
of no light, no air . . . no love.
I move to the little girl child
and I take her in my arms and
hold her, I rock her in my cradled arms.
For now, for the Goddess, forever . . .

I take the little girl child with me
through the years after Him.
I show her how I pieced together the
broken dreams.
We journey to another family,
one of love and safety,
of comfort and growth.
We see the pain of coming out and
the joy within.
I take the little girl child
to a place of today . . .
and together we look back
to where we have been,
and where we are headed.
We look at today and
come together, healing at long last.

'That's an optimistic note', I say. 'What was going on then?'

'That's when I was in grad school – J. (her former lover). When I was in grad school, the repressed memory issue came up and I went underground. Seems like a safer place to be.'

'You're not six any more', I say, trying to separate now from then; trying to give her a bit of respite from the intensity of the affect of being six and overwhelmed; perhaps to give us both some respite.

'I'm not so sure', says she.

(I had an image as she was talking of being submerged and gasping for air, but being afraid of going back: being caught in between.)

'I have the sense that you feel as though if you went back there it would be the same', I say. 'Kind of like you were drowning and need to get up above the surface to gasp for air, but terrified of going back there. You're stuck between needing to know and needing to not know.'

(I don't have the whole flow of this session. I know that I was preoccupied once again with the blow-jobs and the bleeding and thought once again back to her comment in which she referred to 'suddenly knowing' the 'real' meaning of the line from the song.)

'How had you interpreted the bleeding before your "epiphany" ', I ask, after a period of silence.

(She does not connect with this: it was too rough. I had wanted to insert some distance between myself as the 'holder of truth' and this 'truth' she had discovered, but mainly managed to insert distance between us.)

I try again: 'The line from the song – how had you interpreted it before you saw it in the new way?'

'As cutting', she says, smiling with some embarrassment.

'What makes you think you were wrong?' I ask.

She just looks at me for a bit, taken aback, then says: 'My willingness to assume that the other person is right, damn it.'

(She shakes her head violently, and then floods with tears.)

After a long time has passed, I say: 'What's going on?'

'I'm thinking that I'm going to need to let you in more', she says.

'And I'm wondering why you're doing this. Why you're willing to take this journey.'

'I think you know why, but you're afraid to believe you could get what you hoped for', I reply.

'I'm afraid of being dependent and then having the rug pulled out again', says she.

(I'm thinking that there is a lot of pushing and pulling, lightening and deepening, in this relationship; that this game between the two of us is a way of making safe her surrounds. That in many ways that *is* the work: making *her* the frame of reference. I say something about that but am not certain at this point what it was that I said.)

Thursday evening

I open the door and Mary looks taken aback, like a deer in headlights.

'You looked surprised as I opened the door', I say.

'I wasn't expecting you so quickly', says she.

(As we sit down, I am thinking of the irony of this – the image comes to mind of her knocking on a door and being surprised (and not so pleased) that someone would answer. The image is persistent enough that I say: 'I have the image of you knocking on someone's door really quietly and then being disappointed when they answer.'

'I've done that.' She nods, smiling, seeming pleased, albeit a bit sheepish, at being recognized in this way.

There is silence and then: 'I'm not wanting to be here', she says. 'I'm having a hard time. I've been going back to my journals from the last time I got to this place and it's like ridiculous. It was ten years ago, but it's like the same thing over and over. I turn the page and it's like: "yep, been there, done that".'

(There's a lot of turbulence in all of this. I'm aware of a certain nausea that has been present since the beginning of the week and wondering to what extent it has to do with my sense of trying to disgorge something being forced into her/our mouth.)

'Same old shit', I say, in keeping with the feeling.

(I'm thinking: blow-jobs and blood, and feeling nauseated. I'm wondering how much of this is in reaction to her material. In kind to my own turbulence, she says: 'I'm thinking it's not real.'

I'm wondering how we might talk about something that is not real. I decide, once again, to accept her conditions, and say: 'So tell me about your dream nightmare.'

She smiles. She curls up into her chair and begins telling me, once again: 'It's fragments . . . Darkness . . . Force of the hand at the back of the head.'

(She stops. I'm thinking that we have been here before. Wondering what other experiential bits of memory we might be able to pull, wondering how to get to them, how to help her to speak of them; how to bring the past into the present sufficiently that we might give words to each, and so distinguish between the two, thereby marking her survival.)

'And the front of the head?' I ask.

'Eyes closed. "Open your mouth." "Just a little." "Kiss it" ', she says, in her other-person mode, mouthing the words with repugnance.

'Crying', she says, in reporting mode once again. Then: ' "I don't want to" ', she says, in her first-person-past voice.

'Oh God,' she says finally, in anguish, holding on to the sides of her head: 'my head!'

Silence, then: 'I can't go there.'

'It's there', I say. 'It's already happened. Not knowing it just keeps you from being able to move on.'

Silence, then: 'I don't even know if it's true.'

'You know what you feel', I say. 'He betrayed you. And then you betrayed yourself by pretending. That's how you survived. But now it's killing you.'

Silence, once again, then I say: 'It's hard because you can't afford to force yourself, because that's part of the problem.'

She makes a gesture of helplessness, then says: 'What do I do?'

(I'm acknowledging her dilemma, but not wanting to take a position that would once again move her out of the centre of *her* life, *her* experience; not wanting to pre-empt her in any way; wanting to preserve the core of her that seems to need strengthening.)

I say: 'You're on a tightrope and the important thing is to find your balance at any given moment – to take care of yourself – to keep yourself as the frame of reference and not get lost.'

(There is silence once again, but the tension has eased. She opens up a bit, looks less distressed. We're at the end of the hour.)

Conclusion

The week's sessions reported here represented a turning point in our work together. Mary had changed. She was no longer so persecuted by her past and by powerful others in her surround, but rather was beginning to locate herself as an active agent in her universe. Increasingly, our hours were filled with Mary's descriptions of experiences of insight achieved and challenges met. She began to dare to spend more time with others and was better able to keep her eyes open in these encounters. She could locate deficit and disjunction, not only within self, but also within the other. Through these interactions, Mary develops an enhanced awareness of the tensions and the enticements she experiences with others, and can begin to make sense of these.

A crucial factor in this work was our ability to build a space in which we might coexist without annihilating self or other. In this process, my attunement to Mary was the fundamental crucible within which the work and meaning itself were tested. Mary repeatedly wondered aloud at my persistence with, and apparent valuation of, her. This type of recognition of both the experienced and the potential self can be an essential precondition for any real work to take place (see Charles 2001b). Irma Brenman Pick (1997), for example, notes how fundamentally the transference/countertransference experiences of patient and analyst are tied to constructive working through in the analysis. 'I wonder whether the issue of truly deep versus superficial interpretation resides not so much in terms of which level has been addressed but to what extent the analyst has worked the process through internally in the act of giving the interpretation' (p. 352).

Our ability to track the other's affect and patterns of meaning grounds our recognition in ways that make it useful to the other in their attempts to ground their own experiences of self and other more adaptively. As Mary builds resilience through encounters with real (rather than demonized or idealized) others, she is better able to experience her distress and, along with it, her enjoyment. She can struggle with tensions rather than becoming annihilated by them. Winnicott (1974) talks about the fear of a breakdown that has, in actuality, already occurred. My sense was that the pivotal turning point in my work with Mary came at the point where she recalled feeling as though she was being annihilated by her brother, but recalled it in the present tense, as an imminent and ongoing annihilation that could not be directly faced, but only avoided. Locating the *breakdown* in the past and the *survival* in the present helped Mary to be able to see her survival as well as her surrender. This ability to see what had been unseeable – to know what had been deemed unknowable – represented a profound shift in terms of Mary's ability to locate and ground her strengths along with her vulnerabilities in the present moment and to utilize these strengths in the service of her own development.

One of the sequelae of extreme trauma is the abdication of one's own being. One becomes quite literally not present in the moment. The capacity to dissociate under extreme stress can allow us to survive the unsurvivable. And yet, in our inability to be present in our own experience, to some extent we have *not* survived. Paradoxically, we have lived through our own annihilation. Perhaps in part because of this type of dissociation under stress, trauma impedes the encoding of memory and also the ability to think one's way through the traumatic event to a more tolerable conclusion.

One of our roles, as analysts working with individuals who have experienced severe trauma, is to become the one who knows. Through our interactions, we build, at both verbal and nonverbal levels, an understanding of the experience of the other. We find ourselves in the odd position of being in sufficient proximity to profoundly resonate to – and in this way to 'know' – the experience of the other, while also having sufficient distance to be able to think about this experience and to begin to find our way towards a more adaptive conclusion. This is the role of the interpretation, as Klein (1946) depicts it. From her framework, the most useful interpretation is one that binds past to present by highlighting the salient elements of the interaction. This brings us to the essence of the dilemma, rather than becoming lost in the particulars. We can mark the pattern in a way that makes it more recognizable in spite of whatever costumes it might wear.

If an interpretation is to be useful, it must not only highlight the functional aspects of the dilemma; we must also be able to anchor our awareness in the affective cadence of the lived moment, while titrating the affect sufficiently to maintain our capacity for reflection. This is the crucial balance between feeling and thinking, pointed to by Matte-Blanco (1988) and others, that was always a reference point guiding my work with Mary. Ever lurking in the background was the tension I experienced between the potential of failing to confront difficult issues, and overwhelming her affectively. In this way, we struggled to maintain our bearings between the Scylla of allowing her to remain lost in the darkness created by her fear of knowing, and the Charybdis of retraumatization and despair.

In our work together, Mary and I needed some way of maintaining an interim space in which unknowable meanings could be deposited and transformed into meanings that might be knowable. One magnificent mark of the creativity of the unconscious is our uncanny ability to know while not-knowing; to reveal important truths while also obscuring them sufficiently to tolerate the exposure. This titration process is a crucial aspect of our work as analysts. In Bion's (1963) terms, we ease our patients' encounters with the infinite by transforming and translating the primary experience into tolerable and meaningful chunks that can then be further elaborated and integrated. This process is facilitated by our ability to use symbols, which enable us to 'mark the spot' (Charles 2004b) of important meanings, while also titrating the exposure. Symbols allow us to play with potential meanings that might be too dire to consider without the safety of distance. Over time, this titration process becomes internalized and our patients learn to ease their own encounters with the infinite, which, in turn, affords them the opportunity to play with their own experience, to consider potential meanings rather than being locked into foreclosed realities that offer neither relief nor escape (Winnicott 1971; Charles 2004a).

The reversal of the symbolization process is the *unlinking* of associations described so vividly by Bion (1962). The denial of meaning can be an important safeguard against the traumatic onslaught of overwhelming affect, but can also leave the individual immobilized, unable to grow. This was the dilemma Mary put before me quite explicitly when she re-introduced the poem that had become un-known between us, even though it had been shared knowledge at some time previous. In this way, Mary was telling me that there were gaps in her memory; gaps that were not necessarily repaired by the mere introduction of knowledge. We would have to find some way of repairing this damage; some way of making links that could persist over time. The key, she was telling me, lay somewhere within these thoughts that could not be thought about, regarding memory; blow-jobs; and blood.

My ability to carry these words – along with their potential meanings in light of Mary's history – in my mind, enabled me to begin to confront Mary with the knowledge she needed to have, but was afraid to encounter. In this process, she relived, quite vividly, the felt sense of having been killed by her brother through his sexual assaults. Experiencing herself being killed in this way seemed to evoke, at another level, the affective sense of having been a failed abortion. Her mother had wanted to bleed, but had not. Mary had been the cause and the result of this abortion that had remained unfulfilled. Her life had been won at the expense of her mother's. In some fashion, she appeared to have been living out her expiation for this crime, by letting her own blood in the fantasied atonement to, and re-union with, the mother.

My work with Mary was extremely difficult and taxing. At times there was no hope in the room, only silence and darkness. In these dark and dire moments, having a sense of the conceptualizations first articulated by Klein, and then further delineated and augmented by her followers, offered me a conceptual map through which to find my way. These conceptualizations helped me to locate myself in psychic space, as I struggled through the long and at times torturous hours we spent together. This conceptual map was an essential ally in my ability to tolerate being in these dark and terrible spaces with her, and was also an important guide in working together towards a place where these dangers became less imminent and healing became possible.

Note

The author would like to express her gratitude to 'Mary' for her gracious willingness to share this material. Appreciation is also due to all of the members of the London Clinical Seminar Group, whose generosity of spirit and thoughtful comments greatly enriched my appreciation of elements of this case.

References

Bion, W.R. (1962) *Learning from Experience*. London: Heinemann.
—— (1963) *Elements of Psycho-Analysis*. London: Heinemann.
—— (1977) *Seven Servants*. New York: Jason Aronson.
Charles, M. (2001a) A 'confusion of tongues': conflicts between developmental and psychoanalytic theories. *Kleinian Studies*, 2: n.p.
—— (2001b) Stealing beauty: an exploration of maternal narcissism. *Psychoanalytic Review*, 88: 549–570.

——— (2002) *Patterns: Building Blocks of Experience*. Hillsdale, NJ: Analytic Press.

——— (2004a) *Constructing Realities: Transformations through Myth and Metaphor*. Amsterdam and New York: Rodopi.

——— (2004b) *Learning from Experience: A Guidebook for Clinicians*. Hillsdale, NJ: Analytic Press.

Fairbairn, W.R.D. (1952) *Psychoanalytic Studies of the Personality*. London and New York: Routledge.

Fonagy, P. and Target, M. (1997) Attachment and reflective function. *Development and Psychopathology*, 9: 679–700.

Freud, S. (1917) Mourning and melancholia. *Standard Edition*, 14. London: Hogarth Press, 1971, pp. 239–258.

Grotstein, J.S. (1982–3) The significance of Kleinian contributions to psychoanalysis III. The Kleinian theory of ego psychology and object relations. *International Journal of Psychoanalysis and Psychotherapy*, 9: 487–510.

Joseph, B. (1985) Transference: the total situation. *International Journal of Psycho-Analysis*, 66: 447–454.

Klein, M. (1930) The importance of symbol-formation in the development of the ego. In *Love, Guilt and Reparation and Other Works, 1921–1945*. London: Hogarth Press, 1975, pp. 219–232.

——— (1935) A contribution to the psychogenesis of manic-depressive states. In *Love, Guilt and Reparation and Other Works, 1921–1945*. London: Hogarth Press, 1975, pp. 262–289.

——— (1946) Notes on some schizoid mechanisms. In *Envy and Gratitude and Other Works, 1946–1963*. London: Hogarth Press, 1975, pp. 1–24.

——— (1948) On the theory of anxiety and guilt. In *Envy and Gratitude and Other Works, 1946–1963*. London: Hogarth Press, 1975, pp. 25–42.

——— (1952a) Some theoretical conclusions regarding the emotional life of the infant. In *Envy and Gratitude and Other Works, 1946–1963*. London: Hogarth Press, 1975, pp. 61–93.

——— (1952b) The origins of transference. In *Envy and Gratitude and Other Works, 1946–1963*. London: Hogarth Press, 1975, pp. 48–56.

——— (1957) Envy and gratitude. In *Envy and Gratitude and Other Works, 1946–1963*. London: Hogarth Press, 1975, pp. 176–234.

Krystal, H. (1988) *Integration and Self-Healing: Affect, Trauma, Alexithymia*. Hillsdale, NJ: Analytic Press.

Matte-Blanco, I. (1975) *The Unconscious as Infinite Sets: An Essay in Bi-Logic*. London: Duckworth.

——— (1988) *Thinking, Feeling, and Being: Clinical Reflections on the Fundamental Antinomy of Human Beings and World*. London and New York: Routledge.

Meltzer, D. (1981) The Kleinian expansion of Freud's metapsychology. *International Journal of Psycho-Analysis*, 62: 177–185.

Novick, J. and Novick, K.K. (1996) *Fearful Symmetry: The Development and Treatment of Sadomasochism*. Northvale, NJ: Jason Aronson.

O'Shaughnessy, E. (1981) A clinical study of a defensive organization. *International Journal of Psycho-Analysis*, 62: 359–369.

Pick, I.B. (1997) Working through in the countertransference. In R. Schafer (ed.), *The Contemporary Kleinians of London*. Madison, Wisc.: International Universities Press, pp. 348–367.

Rosenfeld, H. (1971) A clinical approach to the psychoanalytic theory of the life and death instinct: an investigation into the aggressive aspects of narcissism. *International Journal of Psycho-Analysis*, 52: 169–178.

Segal, H. (1957) Notes on symbol formation. *International Journal of Psycho-Analysis*, 38: 391–397.

—— (1981) Melanie Klein's technique. In *The Work of Hanna Segal: A Kleinian Approach to Clinical Practice*. New York and London: Jason Aronson, pp. 3–24.

Spillius, E.B. (1988) General introduction. In E.B. Spillius (ed.), *Melanie Klein Today: Developments in Theory and Practice. Vol. 1: Mainly Theory*. London and New York: Routledge, pp. 1–7.

Steiner, J. (1987) The interplay between pathological organizations and the paranoid-schizoid and depressive positions. *International Journal of Psycho-Analysis*, 68: 69–80.

—— (1990) Pathological organizations as obstacles to mourning: the role of unbearable guilt. *International Journal of Psycho-Analysis*, 71: 87–94.

Stern, D.N. (1985) *The Interpersonal World of the Infant: A View from Psychoanalysis and Developmental Psychology*. New York: Basic Books.

Tronick, E. (1989) Emotions and emotional communication in infants. *American Psychologist*, 44: 112–119.

Van Der Kolk, B.A. and Van Der Hart, O. (1991) The intrusive past: the flexibility of memory and the engraving of trauma. *American Imago*, 48: 425–454.

Winnicott, D.W. (1945) Primitive emotional development. In *Through Paediatrics to Psycho-Analysis*. New York: Basic Books, 1975, pp. 145–156.

—— (1971) *Playing and Reality*. London and New York: Routledge.

—— (1974) Fear of breakdown. *International Review of Psycho-Analysis*, 1: 103–107.

Chapter 6

Klein's theory of the positions revisited

James S. Grotstein

"Only connect."

Howard's End, by E.M. Forster

PART ONE

Introduction

Klein's uncovering first of the depressive position (1935) and then of the earlier and more primitive paranoid-schizoid position (1946) occurred during the hegemony of the one-person psychoanalytic model, i.e. the concept of the experiencing analysand being analyzed by a neutral and objective analyst. In about a decade, three of her followers, Paula Heimann, Roger Money-Kyrle, and Wilfred Bion, began exploring the two-person (interpersonal or intersubjective) model. Bion (1959, 1962a, 1962b) in particular conceived the most far-reaching notion of the irreducible intersubjective model in his "container/contained" ($\female\male$) hypothesis. Meanwhile, analysts from different schools simultaneously began to explore the positive clinical uses of counter-transference responses, a trend which culminated in the formalization of a new heterogeneous field of intersubjectivity and/or of relationism and of the two-person analytic model. One of the main characteristics of this paradigm change was the idea of "social constructivism" or "co-creationism" (by analysand *and* analyst as well as by infant *and* mother (Hoffman 1992). Yet another developmental trend began to emerge around this time from an erstwhile supervisee of Klein's, John Bowlby (1969), who, speaking from the cultural anthropological perspective, presented the concept of "bonding" (by mother) and "attachment" (by infant). After a long, quiet incubation, this last concept seems to have taken hold in a major way in infant develop-ment research and now in psychoanalysis itself as a major factor in the analysand–analyst relationship (Fonagy 2001).

My plan in this contribution is twofold. First, I wish to create bridges between Klein's theory of the positions and these new parallel trends in regard to the basic nature of relationships. Second, I seek to re-examine the "position" of Klein's positions in light of current thinking and new possibilities. Ultimately, I seek to unite all the above under the embrace of the concept of a "covenant," a sacred treaty that implicitly exists between infant and mother (and analysand and analyst) in which each member avows absolute fidelity to the bond between them and promises to vouchsafe it for the common good of the analytic endeavor.

The paranoid-schizoid and depressive positions: the Kleinian version of epigenesis and development

Klein originally followed the orthodox/classical protocol of the sequences of autoerotic epigenesis (i.e. oral→anal→phallic). Her thinking about development is best captured in Susan Isaacs' (1952) paper "The nature and function of phantasy" in which the latter presents the concept of the *"principle of genetic continuity,"* by which is meant that developmental sequencing evolves from oral→anal→phallic, that is, from the beginning of life. The orthodox and classical schools of analysis, on the other hand, long held that the (phallic) oedipus phase is the prime position of infant development because, according to their thinking, it represents the first true object relationship, objectless primary narcissism being its forerunner. The oedipus complex, according to them, retrospectively constellates (organizes and gives meaning to) the pregenital stages of development. Yet it must be remembered that Abraham (1924) had constructed a protocol of autoerotic development parallel with part-object development. What Freud and orthodox and classical analysts derived from his seminal work was the validity of the existence of orality and anality but they seemed to have emphasized their retrospective importance as regressive elaborations of the oedipus situation (the first real object relationship, i.e. following autoerotism and narcissism) (Freud 1917b, pp. 340–341).

This way of thinking was linked to the orthodox/classical notion that primary narcissism preempted the *primacy* of the object-relations significance of the autoerotic or pregenital stages. When the analysand associates to oral, anal, or phallic material, orthodox and classical analysts regard these references as regressive elaborations of or defenses against the emergence of oedipal anxieties rather than constituting significant object or part-object relations in their own right. In other words, they felt that the infant lacked a mental life until the oedipus complex came on line. Isaacs (1952), a follower of Klein, presented the concept of "developmental continuity" in her now famous paper, "The nature and function of phantasy," in which she explicated Klein's view that the infant actively relates to objects from the beginning of life.

Later, Klein came more and more to realize from her experience in analyzing very young children that there was significant overlapping of each of the so-called autoerotic phases in the clinical material. Further, she began to observe clusters of anxiety that seemed more comprehensible as quasi-permanent *positions* rather than being time-bound or sequential stages or phases. She first postulated the *depressive position* as a cluster of anxiety beginning about 4 months of age which represented clinical depressive illness in the infant (Klein 1935). She also included such entities as the *obsessional* and the *manic positions* along with the depressive position. Ultimately, she dropped these latter two positions and transformed the "manic" into a defense organization that triumphs over, controls, and contemns dependent relationships upon the whole objects which emerge in the depressive position.

She subsequently amended this notion with the introduction of the para-noid-schizoid position, the seat of persecutory anxiety ("It is the object's fault that I suffer"), which she hypothesized began around 3 weeks of age (Klein 1946). When this position is worked through, then the infant passes into the depressive position, in which the infant accepts its own sense of responsibility for its suffering and for the suffering it believes that it had inflicted on its objects ("It is my fault that I – and they – suffer"). The Kleinian concept of the depressive position is in need of redefinition. Klein originally thought of it as a stand-alone position, which, like Freud's infantile neurosis, represented the pathological crisis of infancy, i.e. infantile depres-sive *illness*. When she later formulated her concept of the paranoid-schizoid position, the persecutory anxiety originally associated with the (pathological) depressive position then became shifted to it.

Infantile *depressive* illness, a defense against mourning object loss, in contrast to infantile *paranoia*, should, in my opinion, be assigned to the depressive position. As time passed, Klein switched from stating that the infant must "work through" the depressive position to the infant must "achieve" the depressive position, thereby transforming the latter from a pathological position to a sublimated one. Later in this chapter I shall deal at length with how I believe the depressive position should be reconceptualized (see Likierman 1995; Britton 2001; Grotstein 1993, 1995a, 1995b, 1996, 2000). Subsequently, Ogden (1989) posited an *autistic-contiguous* position that antedated the paranoid-schizoid position. Steiner (1993) then posited the concept of a position intermediary between the paranoid-schizoid and depressive positions, the *psychic retreat* position. Grotstein (1993, 1995a, 1995b, 1996, 2000) conceived of the *transcendent position* to succeed the depressive position to accommodate Bion's (1965, 1970) concept of trans-formations in O. Bion defines O as the absolute truth about an ultimate reality that is always unknown and unknowable. It includes Plato's Ideal Forms and Kant's noumena in the unrepressed unconscious on one hand and also designates the ever present, constantly evolving (ongoing) stimuli from external and internal raw experience on the other. It is initially unmentalized and must be mentalized by the individual's "alpha-function," a transformative function.

The relationship between the positions, container/ contained, and attachment theory, and the concept of the *covenant* which unites them

Schemata of infant development

When Freud (1905) formulated the concept of infantile sexuality, i.e. autoerotism and the oedipus complex, the innocent infant of Wordsworth and Blake died, and a new, more formidable and disingenuous infant emerged, one that Freud and especially Abraham (1924) conceived of as undergoing a hitherto undreamed of metamorphosis under our own and their own unseeing eyes. The first schema of development, the psychosexual one (oral, anal, phallic (passive and active), and oedipal), was prominent for many years. It was modified and extended by Erikson (1959) into psychosexual-cultural modes and modalities of relating to objects. Others, like Ferenczi (1913) and Fairbairn (1944), offered their own unique schemata, but they never captured the fancy of mainstream psychoanalysis. Mahler (1968) proffered a different kind of schema of infant development, one based upon the degree of fusion-to-separation of the infant's relationship to its object. It remained for Klein and Bowlby, her erstwhile supervisee, to create their own unique schemata which were fated to collide at the Tavistock Clinic in London, the fires from which controversy are only now beginning to be banked. Bion's container/contained, on the other hand, seems to span both of theirs non-controversially.

Thesis

I propose that Klein's theory of the paranoid-schizoid (P-S) and depressive (D) positions, Bion's theory of container/contained, and Bowlby's theory of attachment fundamentally relate to one another complementarily on differing levels and vertices of experience and observation, the last being conscious and viewable externally (anthropologically or ethologically), the first (Klein's positions) being unconscious and to be inferred only from within the internal world of the infant, and the second (Bion's container/contained) also being unconscious but to be inferred by both partners. Together, they constitute a master plan for the continuing ontology of the infant and its relationship to caretakers. I believe that attachment, the positions, and container/contained are part of a profounder bond that, along with primary identification, emerges from the mists of intra-uterine existence and designates a primary belongingness of one to the other. This bond I call the *covenant*. One may, using Trevarthen's (1988) concept of "communicative musicality," poetically capture the essence of this inchoate covenant, one aspect of which disappears upon the onset of primal repression, and which I designate the "lost c(h)ord" (Grotstein 2000).

Bion (1977) assigns the quality of intersubjectivity to exist beyond the caesura into early fetaldom, as does Trevarthen (1988, personal communication 2004), who believes that his concept of communicative musicality transcends attachment theory. Parenthetically, one may consider the phantasy of infantile omnipotence to be a post-natal "yolk-sac" or placenta to help the infant deal with his/her post-natal helplessness and incompleteness.

Stein Bråten (1993), an infant developmentalist, presents an interesting new view about the origins of the infant's capacity for object relationships. He states:

> The infant is born with a virtual other in mind who invites and permits fulfilment by actual others in felt immediacy. Thus, the normal developing and learning mind recreates and transforms itself as a self-organizing dyad (i) in self-engagement with the virtual other, as well as (ii) in engagement with actual others who fill and affect the companion space of the virtual other and, hence, are directly felt in presentational immediacy.
>
> (p. 26)

One may think of Bråten's concept as a Kantian "empty form." Trevarthen (1988) and Stern (2004) speak of new empirical evidence for the existence of what they term the "intersubjective matrix." Stern cites the new discovery of the "mirror neuron" (2004, p. 79) mentioning the works of Gallese (2001) and Gallese and Goldman (1998) and others. I consider the intersubjective matrix hypothesis and the function of the mirror neuron to be aspects of Bion's theory of container/contained.

Whereas Klein postulated that the paranoid-schizoid (P-S) and depressive (D) positions were both normal as well as pathological, it is the quality, let alone the presence, of attachment that fundamentally determines or defines the manner in which these categories are experienced. Similarly, the expression of the positions would also be a function of container/contained – and the reverse, i.e. how the infant or analysand experiences being in either or both of the positions would partially account for how successfully the containment is functioning. Parenthetically, Bion (1970) regards "patience" as the normal version of P-S and "security" as the normal version of D.

One might accurately say that all mental health as well as all psychopathology become functions of the quality of the bonding and attachment *and* of container/contained between mother and infant – and, consequently, how P-S and D play out. Considerations of attachment and container/contained, consequently, bestow new dimensions on the positions. An infant who is securely attached and/or contained will experience P-S as its entitlement to protest to a good mother about a bad mother – and fear minimal repercussions or retaliations.

Attachment (and/or communicative musicality), the positions, and container/contained are all subsumed, in my opinion, by an overarching and supraordinating concept of an *unconscious covenant* between fetus–infant and mother (what Trevarthen and Stern term the "intersubjective matrix") that goes back to the very beginning and includes Bion's concept of Faith (Bion 1970, p. 31) – during the "dark night of the soul" when maternal absence releases doubt and the demons begin to appear. I conceive of the covenant as an ontological and spiritual dimension that subsumes the sanctity of the interrelationship between infant and mother (and analysand and analyst). To these I should also add "*Innocence*" because one of the functions of the attachment bond, in providing affect attunement, is to vouchsafe the illusion of a world of innocence in which it is safe for the infant to develop. The phenomenological aspect of the covenant may be expressed in terms of "the terms of endearment" (McMurtry 1975), which also heralds the onset of the depressive position. This idea can be epitomized in the slogan, "cherish or perish!"

The psychoanalytic way in which we might speak about attachment, consequently, is Klein's positions and Bion's (1962) theory of container/contained, Faith, and his own version of Klein's positions: patience (P-S) and security (D), which he interrelates as P-S↔D. The function of the positions, attachment, and container/contained is the mediation, not merely of the infant's emotions per se, but of the impact of evolving "O" and its resultant careening beta-elements (Bion 1965, 1970) on the infant's emotional frontier and the need to facilitate their transduction into mentally acceptable elements that can ultimately be felt as feelings – albeit, through the intermediary, initially, of its mother's predigestion via her reverie and alpha-function.

The contingent and non-contingent infant

A feeling tone one gets in reading the attachment and infant development literature is a concept of a non-contingent, as well as a contingent, infant; that is, an infant in its own right who, despite its dependency on its objects, constitutes a being which is to be distinguished from the dependent infant. I posit the existence of a contingent and a non-contingent infant-self. The infant's development is, according to Kleinian theory, solely contingent on its dependency upon its objects and is solely defined by its relationship to them. The non-contingent infant is the infant in its own right, the one celebrated by Fairbairn, Winnicott, and Kohut. The non-contingent infant, as well its contingent twin, is to be held in trusteeship by its objects whose sacred task it is to vouchsafe its innocence and shepherd it along with its endowment of *entelechy*,[1] which is, from one point of view, independent of the objects, and constitutes inner, spontaneous, creative echoes from the farthest coasts of eternity in the non-contingent infant's imaginative creativity.

The conflict between attachment theory and psychoanalysis

One of the problems that besets an integration between attachment theory and psychoanalysis revolves on the realization that the provenance of the former lies in ethological observation with a bent toward cognition, similarly to infant development research, and its purview lies in the external reality of the relationship between the infant and its mother – in contrast to the psychoanalytic purview, particularly the Kleinian, which lies almost exclusively in the internal world of the infant and is cast in unconscious phantasies in contrast to cognitive working models. When attachment does relate to the internal world, it is as working models of external relationships without any consideration of phantasied distortion.

Furthermore, attachment comes on line at 6 months of age, according to Bowlby and his followers, sometime after both Klein's positions have begun operation. Bowlby could not observe attachment before then because, I believe, his observational instrument was ethology. Klein observed from psychoanalytic intuition. The most patent connection between attachment theory and psychoanalysis seems to have escaped general notice. The infant–mother attachment must certainly remind us of Freud's (1910, pp. 142–144) transference and countertransference and Klein's theory of mutual projective identification – i.e. unconscious phantasy!

Put succinctly, attachment is the consciously and pre-consciously experienced and observable portion of a vaster and profounder phenomenon of mutual connectedness that inextricably binds two or more individuals together, which can otherwise be understood as a manifestation of an unconscious (implicit) covenant between them with definitive and binding rules of engagement. Attachment, P-S and D (and T), transference/countertransference, and container/contained are phenomenological and ontological manifestations of this covenant.

The "covenant" as a supraordinating concept for infantile development

The "covenant" is the unconscious psychologically experienced of a powerful unity that inheres with primary identification. It is my belief that the concept of the covenant effectively supraordinates the functions of attachment, Klein's positions, and container/contained. P-S and D become vastly different experiences when one considers whether or not a mutually experienced covenant between infant and mother is in place. Weaning and trauma constitute dire challenges to the maintenance of attachment, which may range from secure to the various categories of insecure, and which therefore may dictate how the infant fares as it proceeds through P-S and thus to and through D. The normal infant who is dominated by the P-S state of mind and who can take for granted that all the while it is protesting its frustrations, it is being supported by reliable, caring parents has a radically different prognosis than the infant in P-S who experiences any of the insecure attachment patterns. In other words, the normal infant must feel secure with a good relationship to its caretaking object to be able to complain to this "good mother" about a "bad mother." The same situation applies to the analysand in psychoanalysis.

Generally, a supportive and trustworthy covenant between analysand and analyst subtends the treatment while the former undergoes the experiences of being in P-S as well as D. In the extremes of infantile and childhood trauma and catastrophe, however, one may witness the emergence of "orphans of the Real" (Grotstein 1995a, 1995b) whose persecutory anxiety constitutes a confusion between the parents as persecutors and parents as true enemies.[2] In these situations the infant's and the analysand's experiences of being in P-S and D are quite altered. Consequently, we must consider that both P-S and/or D in any particular infant lie on a gradient that is constrained to the consideration of the quality of attachment and covenant between the infant and the parent. Obviously, it is more complicated in the analytic situation, yet similar considerations apply. Klein recognized this situation. In the "Editor's Note" in *Envy and Gratitude* the editor, Edna O'Shaughnessy, states, "[S]he was able to begin effectively to differentiate the normal from the abnormal form of the paranoid-schizoid position" (Klein 1957, p. 326).

The concepts of intersubjectivity and of the two-person model of psychoanalysis speak to this issue. For our purposes here the idea of the covenant is congruent with bonding and attachment, the experience of which is conveyed by Jessica Benjamin's (1995) idea of "mutual recognition" and what *I* should say as the recognition that the two (or more) partners inextricably *belong* to one another, a phenomenon that emerges from what Lichtenberg (1992) terms the "affiliation instinct," a notion that is supported by Stein Bråten (1993), cited above, with his concept that the "infant is born with the other in mind." The concept of a "covenant with oneself," a covenant that lies in the shadow of the one with the object, becomes a legacy of the latter. The concept of the covenant transcends that of positive transference – or even of therapeutic alliance. I consider it to be a Kantian primary category.

A brief review of Klein's theory of the positions

Klein (1935) began to uncover the existence of a cluster of infantile anxieties characterized by the occurrence of infantile depressive illness. She postulated two stages: (a) an earlier part-object stage characterized by paranoid anxiety; and (b) a later whole-object stage in which the loss of the object and defenses against it were paramount. She extended her conception of this position in 1940. She thought of position rather than stage because of its tendency to recur. In 1946 she enfranchised the earlier form as the paranoid – and later paranoid-schizoid position. P-S was characterized by a cluster of persecutory anxieties about bad, imposing internal and external objects created by splitting and projective identification. D was characterized by depressive anxieties about lost and/or damaged objects, and introjection of objects was more prominent.

A general classification of the positions would be based on the following characteristics:

(a) the experience of transient, semi-permanent, or permanent clusters of specific anxieties and/or affects, persecutory and depressive respectively;
(b) specific defenses (splitting, projective identification, denial, and idealization in P-S, and the manic and obsessional defenses in D, to which I would add the depressive, paranoid, phobic, and hysterical;
(c) differing states of mind;
(d) differing world views;
(e) differing techniques of relating to objects – paranoid in P-S and loving in D.

The paranoid-schizoid position (P-S)

The individual in P-S would be more prone to be cyclopean (non-reflective) and use symbolic equations (concrete), whereas the individual in D would have access to symbols, a dual-track, and other-mindedness (intersubjectivity and empathy). The newborn infant *must* begin life in P-S in order to be self-protectively omnipotent so as to immunize itself against the "O" (Bion 1965, 1970) of the raw circumstance of the reality into which it has been delivered. Once this infant achieves the depressive position, it not only affirms its future lifetime incompleteness, but also its willingness to bear it and deal with it.

I postulate that P-S mediates the inchoate personal reality of the contingent *and* non-contingent (normal narcissistic) subject, whereas D mediates the subject's social-interpersonal reality and reality-testing, while the transcendent position mediates their relationship to the Absolute Truth about the Ultimate Reality of "O" (Bion 1965, 1970), which represents a state that is beyond the private, personal, *and* social realities of the non-contingent *and* contingent selves.

P-S is a way of talking about the development of normal narcissism, and D is a way of talking about the infant's social need to engage objects as persons who are separate. P-S deals with the non-contingent self, whereas D deals with the (object-) contingent self. P-S is characterized by immature dependency and the defenses against it, whereas D represents the dawn of awareness of mature dependency. Because Klein employed a single-track, one in which D followed P-S, their relationship to each other became inescapably polarized so that P-S inadvertently became demonized (pathological) and D idealized. Bion and Britton have sought to resolve that problem by applying a dual-track

(Grotstein 1978), i.e. in distinguishing between normal and pathological P-S and D. Freud (1911, p. 223) actually anticipated Klein's conception of P-S with his notion of the "purified pleasure ego" which the infant seeks to attain by disavowing its painful stimuli.

Klein believed that D was an advance upon P-S and that the latter could be regressively recruited to defend against the experience of D. Bion's postulation of "O" placed P-S and D as binary-oppositional structures that cooperatively mediate "O." Later in this chapter I shall argue that two more positions exist: the positions of innocence and transcendence. One may consider that P-S mediates dispersal and differences, whereas D mediates wholeness and coherence. P-S↔D, when sublimated, become the poles of differentiation and integration, as in calculus. P-S represents, "Let's pretend," whereas D represents, "Let's put away childish things."

Now, since attachment and affect-attunement and Bion's container/contained, we see P-S as the challenge to the infant's unconscious concept of sophrosyne (balance), which issues from what Plato called "the Memory of Justice."

The depressive position (D)

Klein (1940) states: "[T]he baby experiences depressive feelings which reach a climax just before, during, and after weaning. This is the state of mind in the baby which I have termed the 'depressive position', and I suggested that it is a melancholia in *statu nascendi*" (p. 312). She went on to say: "[P]ersecution (by 'bad' objects) and the characteristic defenses against it, on one hand, and pining for the loved ('good') on the other, constitute the depressive position" (p. 348). According to Kleinian theory the infant must successfully traverse, i.e. work through, P-S in order to attain D. If the infant becomes a victim of a pathological P-S, it may either become stuck there and/or fall into a default position, which Rosenfeld (1987) terms "pathological narcissism," Joseph (1989), "psychic equilibrium," and Steiner (1993), a "psychic retreat." These are varying terms for a mid-position, an eternal "Purgatorio," if you will, between the ultimate "Paradiso" of an unattainable D and the "Inferno" of a misbegotten P-S.

Sometimes the boundaries between P-S and D become blurred. Klein (1946) states:

> Some fluctuations between the paranoid-schizoid and the depressive positions always occur and are part of normal development. No clear division between the two stages can therefore be drawn; moreover, modification is a gradual process and the phenomena of the two positions remain for some time to some extent intermingled and interacting.
>
> (p. 16)

The debate whether D must be achieved or surmounted can be answered in the positive for each option. Yes, D must be achieved so that the infant can reconcile its fragmentations from P-S and become integrated and separate from the object, but the infant must also surmount or transcend D. D allows for the mourning of the object and reparations toward it now that the object is known to depart, return, and disappoint as well as fulfill. Mourning is time-bound, according to Freud (1917a). After a while mourning must end, and the critical time allotted for reparations subsides so that the infant can get on with his/her life. The next position stop is the transcendent position, where the non-contingent self can flower at last – after having "paid its dues," so to speak, as a dutiful contingent self in the depressive position.

It is also noteworthy that it is only after the patient has achieved the depressive position that, in my opinion, the analytic techniques of other schools become applicable. Self psychology, relationism, intersubjectivity, etc. all have a place after the infant has been able to have become separate from his/her object and thereby become able for the first time to regard the object as a person in his/her own right, one justifiably blameworthy, for instance, of defective parenting. One of the tasks of analysis is to assist the patient in being able to discriminate between a *persecutor* and an *enemy*. The latter constitutes an object that the subject has created or altered through projective identification. Thus, the persecutor is always a function of the projecting subject. The enemy never is. More often than not the subject becomes confused between the two because of projective identification. In the depressive position, when separateness between self and object is achieved, the subject may withdraw his/her projections and reveal the enemy.

There is yet another, hitherto unrecognized, feature of D that needs to be stated. The Kleinian and post-Kleinian view of D emphasizes the infant's ultimate regret, sorrow, and contrition about phantasied (and/or actual) damage done to the maternal (and paternal) object while the infant is becoming more evolved as a more developed, separate, and individuated person in his/her own right. In the act of becoming more separate and more individuated the infant projects less and perceives (observes) more objectively. It can now more readily detect the difference between a persecutory object (which always denotes the projecting self) and an enemy, which is always other than the projecting subject. In other words, as the infant achieves the depressive position, it is better able *objectively* to perceive parental errors as unforced parental errors – and only hope that their parents too have entered the depressive position.

P-S↔D or P-S before and after D

When Klein (1935, 1940, 1946) posited the positions, she believed that P-S came on line in the mental life of the infant at approximately 3 weeks of age and D at 4 months of age; thus an epigenetic succession was postulated.

Meltzer (1992) states that he had encountered infants who seem to have been born directly into the D without having to encounter the P-S. Yet Klein states:

> Whereas I have not altered my views on the depressive position setting in about the second quarter of the first year and coming to a climax at about six months, I have found that some infants seem to experience guilt transiently in the first few months of life. . . . This does not imply that the depressive position has already arisen.
>
> (Klein 1957, p. 194)

Or maybe it does, *I* suggest.

Bion further complicated the issue by positing a "binocular vision" paradigm that lifts Klein's one-dimensional, and sequential concept of the positions and places them into an entirely new three-dimensional "dual-track" (Grotstein 1978) in which they are coeval from the beginning and dialectically oppositional but not necessarily conflictual since they each constitute mediating observation posts scanning the individual's emotional intersections with evolving "O." This cooperative, three-dimensional model closely resembles that of the cerebral hemispheres, which too are oppositional and cooperative.

In other words, perhaps we can postulate, following Bion, that the infant is potentially born into "O"[3] but is beneficently prevented from experiencing "O" ("nameless dread") because of being born into the mythic blanket of a protective and blessed innocence by the bonding-containing ministrations of its mother, whose reverie and dream-work-alpha[4] constitute ongoing inoculations against the "nameless dread" of "O." But the protective blanket of innocence is transient and all too vulnerable.[5] The infant and mother have serious ontological work to do; otherwise infantile catastrophe becomes inevitable.

Britton (2001) extends Bion's dialectical schema into a series of sequences that may best be described as helical, i.e., normally, P-S precedes D and succeeds D in another transformation, and then is succeeded again by D in yet another iterative cycle. He also, like Bion, distinguishes between normal and pathological P-S and D. I agree with his and Bion's formulations. One of the problems in moving between Bion's and Britton's versions is whether or not to consider the status of P-S and D as belonging to the unrepressed unconscious or the repressed dynamic unconscious. If the former, then we would be constrained to consider Bion's point of view for the following reason. The unrepressed unconscious is characterized by timelessness and infinity; thus P-S and D would, like the Kleinian infant of the unconscious, be the "once and forever P-S and D." In so far as they might qualify for the dynamically repressed unconscious, they would be time-bound, and Britton's helical model would apply. Personally, I should opt for both, but recognize that Britton's has immense clinical usefulness and is readily applicable.

Whereas Bion and Britton are imaginatively and creatively dealing with the orchestration of two positions, however, I should like to add a third, the *transcendent* position (Grotstein 2000). Briefly, inherent in the operations of P-S is the formation of sensory images of the object[6] (phantasies), and in D, symbolic images (thoughts). I believe there is need to postulate a transcendent position,[7] one that transcends the use of images and symbols and of experiencing one's "being-in-itself, or, as Bion (1970) puts it, to confront the "emotional turbulence" of the interaction with the other without memory, desire, understanding, or preconceptions (imagery or symbols) – to be able to confront the other-in-itself as "Dasein" (Heidegger 1927), the undisguised self. I consequently visualize the three positions as playing existential "musical chairs" in which Bion's mechanism of shifting perspectives comes into play. In this game of musical chairs one position becomes transitorily dominant as the other two recede – as in alternating figure and ground perspectives. When P-S and D operate in parallel, Homer could compose the *Iliad* and the *Odyssey*, some unknown minstrel *Beowulf*, and Dante *The Divine Comedy*. Creativity allows for a natural intercourse between the symbol and the symbolic equation.

Let me summarize. The infant is born potentially into "O" but mediates "O" (with mother's help) with P-S and D strategies. The very act of being born constitutes *ipso facto* an object loss, thus, the occasion for depression-mourning, the undertaking of which the infant is not yet at first developmentally prepared for; thus it finds itself predominantly in P-S with D as an extant latent function that is destined to achieve hegemony over P-S later. Put another way, the infant is born into the depressive position as a default of "O" because of the experience of object loss, but its developmental immaturity necessitates its falling into yet another default, P-S, so as to be able to countenance the complexities of its birth situation.

My proposed revision of the theory of the positions

I suggest that Klein was right the first time when she described the depressive illness in regard to the clinical depressive (melancholic) illness of infancy, which was her version of the infantile neurosis and which dealt with whole objects in the main. When she subsequently unveiled the paranoid-schizoid position, she uncovered infantile paranoid states in regard to part-objects. Because she believed that mourning invariably contained melancholia, she conflated the two, and thereby conflated mourning with reparations, which I think was an error.

Freud painstakingly elaborated their differences, the key ones being: (a) depression (melancholia) constitutes a split in the ego and also constitutes a state in which hatred of the self is equivalent to hatred of the object which has been internalized and identified with in the ego; (b) the presence of self-esteem in the mourner and its absence in the depressive – because of (a). I believe that Klein erred. To me "normal depressive position" now constitutes an oxymoron.

Thus, I propose the following: P-S (the part-object state of dissociation and paranoia), which is the second phase of the position of autochthonous creativity, *seems* to be succeeded by D (the whole-object, still dissociated state of clinical depressive illness, i.e. "Purgatory"), which in turn is succeeded by the position of mourning and reconciliation – and then the transcendent position follows. In this scheme, restorations[8] of the value of the object are conducted in the depressive phase, and mourning and reconciliation in the later phase. Thus, normal versus pathological P-S would be a function of the quality of attachment and bonding. D is axiomatically pathological but normalizes to "M and R."

I just mentioned that P-S *seems* to be succeeded by D. I should now like to alter that statement. It is now my belief, following Bion's concept of the P-S↔D, i.e. that they exist and function simultaneously but either one may achieve hegemony, that the infant exists from the very beginning in the combined state of both positions, which constitute the status of a binary-opposition structure. The infant (or patient) may *seem* to be in P-S, but now we might say, "predominantly P-S, with D as background" until it is ready to assume and to achieve D, at which time P-S slips to the background.

PART TWO

As a consequence of the above I therefore present the following as position statements about the relationship between the two disciplines, psychoanalysis and attachment theory. In the course of presenting them I shall undertake a re-examination of the positions.

The position of the positions

(A) P-S and D occur and operate simultaneously from the very beginning of life, but *appear* to function in tandem (helically), at least early on, because of the necessity for the infant to endow its creative, autochthonous mastery of its personal world view, i.e. the infant must believe that it has created the world and the objects who and which inhabit it in order to establish the foundations of its personal, subjective being and sense of personal agency in this world by imposing its own sense of creative mastery on the objects of its world so that it seems to "create" them as it discovers them (Winnicott 1971). It is as if Mother Nature endows the infant with that manic defense known as omnipotence so as to be able to deal with its unimaginable and unmanageable smallness. In Bion's (1992) terms, the infant must first discover its "narcissism": before it discovers its "socialism."

A necessary shift in the hegemony of the positions occurs after the personal, subjective self-as-agent foundations have been laid, at which time the more objective, other-world-view nature of D comes online along with the development of language with which to engage the others of this outer world. Thus, I believe that the proper name for P-S is the *"creative, solipsistic or autochthonous position of dissociation and protest."* It is also the *"narcissistic position."* Succeeding them is the depressive position of "socialism." Overarching them is the transcendent position.

(B) I believe that Klein may have been short-sighted both in naming her first position the "paranoid-schizoid" and her second position the "depressive." The term "paranoid-schizoid," when we stop to reconsider it, applies only to the second phase of an even larger positional phenomenon and designates only the *results* or *consequences* of a yet earlier or prior act, that of autochthonous *creation* via the unconscious phantasy of projective identification, which is the Rosetta Stone to its arcane hieroglyphic. In support of Klein, however, is the supposition that she named her positions in terms of respective clusters of putative infantile pathologies, i.e. persecutory and depressive, akin to Freud's (1918) postulation of the "infantile neurosis." We must remember that the positions, not unlike many other psychoanalytic discoveries, first emerged from observations about psychopathology. My point is that we must now trek backward to the normal headwaters of the concept before clinical turbulence arose.

However, if we are to regard the larger picture, we will easily see, I believe, that the persecutory anxiety of P-S is the result of the infant's creative, autochthonous, self-determination and organization (via projective identification) of its "O" experiences (not just hate and destructiveness), and that the depressive anxiety of D represents the emergence of the infant's dawning awareness of a world it did *not* create but which created it. Thus, in retrospect, the infant must now reconsider its treatment of its objects which it had previously taken for granted as its own "slave" (and "master') part-objects. It is at this juncture that the infant becomes more sanguinely aware of the existence of a covenant between itself and the object. It must now develop concern for them, thus Winnicott's (1963) notion of the "position of concern." Put another way, the infant must now experience (a) *appreciation* of its own specific needs, (b) *appreciation* of the offerings from the object that specifically match its needs, (c) internalize the appreciative experience, and thus (d) find that the internalized experience *appreciates* with it in the form of burgeoning self-esteem.

(C) In other words, I posit the existence of a *"creative"* or *"autochthonous dissociative narcissistic position"* in which "paranoid-schizoid" is the second phase and the first split-off and then projected consequence. This position is characterized by dissociative splitting between the putatively good and bad aspects of the object (Klein 1946) and by a protest to the object about its mental pain (Bowlby 1969), and in its phenomenology one would find the techniques of approach and withdrawal, enumerated above, which have been postulated by Bowlby. P-S is the first relay station that intercepts and transduces beta-elements from "O" on its emotional frontier. Its putative task is to transduce the infinity, absolute symmetry, and chaos that characterize "O" into tolerable binary-opposition phantasies, like "good breast" and "bad breast," etc. What cannot be tolerated is relayed by the infant to its holding and containing object via projective identification.

(D) I believe that Klein's notion about D, which followed from Freud's (1917) "Mourning and Melancholia," seems in retrospect to be in need of conceptual rehabilitation. In her first "position paper" about D, Klein (1935) described the occurrence of a cluster of depressive anxieties comprising an *infantile depressive illness* in the infant, and associated that occurrence with a position that she then justifiably termed the "depressive position," and she went on to explore it further in a later paper (Klein 1940). In both contributions she suggested that there were two phases: one, an earlier paranoid phase in relation to part-objects, and a later depressive stage that dealt with the internalization of whole objects. In both these contributions Klein disagreed with Freud in so far as he thought that there was a definite cleavage between clinical depressive illness (melancholia) and mourning, whereas Klein believed that depression occurred even in mourning, i.e. she conflated melancholia with mourning even while maintaining that some distinction between them did exist. The critical distinction between mourning and melancholia, according to Freud, is the presence of self-esteem in the former and its absence in the latter. Klein ignored this distinction.

The conceptual problem is this: "depression" is a clinical illness that operates as a defense against the process of mourning. As a matter of fact, Klein, who coined the terms "manic defense" and "obsessional defense," never mentioned a "depressive defense," but *I* have (Grotstein 2000).

Thus, by all but erasing the differences between mourning and depression, Klein complicated the situation of the infantile neurosis. Is it really progress to advance from P-S to D when D represents clinical depressive illness, which is, after all, the inversion of paranoia and equally narcissistic? I believe that P-S is the narcissistic position, and that what is not processed there in terms of part-object transformations, continues forward into whole-object psychology as mania, depression, obsession, phobia, hysteria, and paranoia (Fairbairn's (1943) "transitional techniques") as defenses against the mourning and reconciliatory functions of what Klein and Kleinians later came to mean by the depressive position.

A few years later, Klein (1946) altered her view about the depressive position. She separated out the earlier paranoid aspect and elevated it to the status of a position, the "paranoid" – and then the "paranoid-schizoid" position, in deference to Fairbairn. P-S then took the place of what was once D, and the fate of the latter was to be shifted forward almost intact, but its significance then became "laundered," purified, and "gentrified." Whereas aspects of the clinical depressive illness of infancy became thought of more and more as paranoid and ascribed to the paranoid-schizoid position, others remained in the depressive position proper but in a minor form. The concept of infantile depressive illness was on the wane – in favor of infantile paranoia. In other words, the depressive position, once the seat of infantile depressive illness, became transformed into a position of achievement and a reward for working through P-S, which became polarized as the demon to the ideal in the depressive position.

Klein varied in how she spoke of the now reconstituted depressive position, sometimes stating that it must be "overcome" (e.g. Klein 1940, p. 347) or must be "worked through" (Klein 1946, p. 15), and at other times that it must be "attained" (e.g. Klein 1946; Likierman 1995). The last term, "attained," seems to have captured the thinking of Kleinians ever since. The psycho-pathology that had hitherto been assigned to D, i.e. clinical depressive illness, became amalgamated into the defenses against D, namely the manic and obsessional defenses, to which I have added the "depressive defense" (Grotstein 2000), as I have already stated.

Thus, the reconstituted depressive position evolved into a more complicated role. It now included: (a) residues of the earlier concept of infantile depressive illness with sense of despair and hopelessness in regard to whole objects, (b) mourning and pining for the lost or damaged (whole) object, and (c) a desire to restore one's inner world of good objects by reparations. To use Bion's (1992) terms again, whereas P-S designates the development of narcissism or a sense of a personal reality, D designates the development of "socialism" or a relational reality. Klein (1935, 1940) seems to be in agreement with this since she assigns the beginnings of the oedipus complex to D. Finally, T deals with Ultimate Cosmic Reality.

I should like to add yet another dimension to D. Whereas P-S represents the infant's righteous *protests* against the pain of living a life it didn't ask for, D represents the infant's beginning *reconciliation* with that life and its agreement with the covenant with the object to do its best by itself and with the object to live its life as best it can. It marks the beginning of what I would call the "addiction to being alive." I therefore believe that the proper name for D is *the position of "mourning and reconciliation"* and that depression constitutes a defensive technique to disguise it, along with the manic, obsessional, and even the paranoid, phobic, and hysterical, as suggested by Fairbairn (1943).

(E) Returning to attachment theory and its relationship to container/contained, I should now like to integrate the preceding with Bion's (1965) concepts of "binocular vision," "reversible perspectives," and "shifting verti-ces," the "dual-track"[9] (Grotstein 1978), and "other mindedness" with "self-reflection" and empathy (Fonagy and Target 1996). Psychoanalytic theory, particularly Kleinian, especially since the contributions of Bion, must con-sider the issue of optimal and dreadful binocularity (ambivalence) in the infant–mother relationship. Put archly, the mother's state of mind must have attained, not just the status of D, but even of the "transcendent position" so that her reverie and dream-work-alpha can come online so that, in turn, she can facilitate her infant's emotional navigation through the dangerous straits of "O," which have become confused with P-S in the minds of most analysts, particularly Kleinian and post-Kleinian.[10]

What I mean here is as follows. The containing mother must assist her infant in becoming more successful in P-S so as better to mediate its experience of "O" (nameless dread). Similarly she must assist her infant in cleansing the internal status of its damaged objects, who have become damaged in the first place by becoming faulty containers of "O," not just targets of attack by the infant's death instinct, which itself had been recruited in the first place as a defense against "O." In other words, what the infant must seek to "repair" is the putative damage to its objects, particularly the mother, that resulted from its projecting its beta-elements into her. In proportion as she becomes overwhelmed by them, she becomes internalized as a damaged and damaging internal object. All internal objects, to my mind, are misbegotten or failed containers of "O."[11] The mother must also have "cleared" D and entered the transcendent position (T) in order to achieve reverie so as to facilitate her infant's attempts at mourning, restoration, and reparation. Realistically, the infant as well as the patient are invariably aware of the position status of the mother and the analyst.

The covenant (continued)

In view of the need now to postulate an intersubjective matrix as one of the "psychoanalytic" contributions of attachment theory, I should like to consider the biblical concept of the existence of a *covenant* between each party to account for the hidden order that mediates their interrelationship. A covenant requires an act of sacrifice on the part of each member for a guarantee that each will honor the welfare of the other for the sake of the bonding or partnership. Perhaps that is why splitting, displacement, dissociation, and projective identification play such significant roles in P-S. The infant must experience, process, and express its painful proto-affects as well as its destructive impulses that emerge as a consequence of "O," but it needs a tolerant and accepting "scapegoat object" upon whom to play them out (Grotstein 2000) while another aspect of the object remains available.

Thus, the infant, according to this way of thinking, is born into "the positions," as Bion (1974) succinctly puts it, and the "positions" represent a combination of the properties of P-S, D,[12] and T. Consequently, the infant, like the patient, can indulge more safely in the whole range of its emotional repertoire, on one level, knowing all the while on the other that a protective covenant (bonding and attachment) is in place. The quality of bonding, attachment, containment, and holding, i.e. the *"covenant,"* constitutes the hidden order, the supraordinating missing third that subtends P-S *and* D, but which the mediating activities of P-S and D reciprocally reinforce. The covenant presupposes that the mother and father must be in the depressive position and even the transcendent position while nurturing their infant in P-S and D and that the infant can "play" with its negative self, knowing all the while that it must respect *the terms of endearment* for the object's suffering its developmentally scheduled abuse. Once again, *the positions of the infant and those of the parent constitute an obligatory binary-oppositional structure.*

Imprinting and primary identification

I should like to interpose the ethological concept of "imprinting" (Tinbergen 1951) and appose it to the psychoanalytic notion of "primary identification" (Lichtenstein 1977). Imprinting, like attachment, suggests that the newborn of whatever species instantly identifies and claims its caretaker for itself, silently declares it belongs to this object, and assumes that the object belongs to it as well. Lichtenstein thought that the infant is born into a non-cartesian unity with its mother, that this primary identification lasts a lifetime, and that the infant is destined to live out the life theme that its mother unconsciously foreordains for it to follow. I have encountered the clinical finding in a number of patients in which they believe either that mother and/or father "broke their vows" of belonging to them, never took their vows, or that the patient him or herself broke the vows of belonging to the family and lived thereafter with the bitter and painful secret that they had "divorced" their family in childhood and no one knew it, except their detached and orphaned unconscious.

P-S and D again

(F) Returning to the theme of P-S and D, when one regards the relationship between P-S and D as a sequential one, the two become polarized whereby the former becomes demonized and the latter idealized, a phenomenon that also characterizes Freud's (1923) topographic and structural models. The unconscious, constituting the repressed, becomes demonized as a "seething cauldron." Bion's concepts of dreaming, binocular vision, shifting perspectives, and varying vertices allow for an interesting view of it. The contact-barrier defends the unconscious from consciousness as well as the reverse, and each constitutes mediators of "O," the third element. Similarly, P-S and D, when viewed this way, become cooperatively dialectically oppositional (like thumb and forefinger) modes of transformation of beta-elements (unmentalized elements) that inchoately emerge from evolving "O"'s impact on the individual's emotional receptor frontier. In other words, P-S and D also constitute a binary-oppositional structure.

(G) Following from the above, the putative role of P-S is to mediate transformations from "O" (Bion 1965, 1970) into unconscious phantasies from the subjective, personal, creative (self-as-agent) perspective (via Bion's

(1963) L, H, and K[13] transformative linkages). The putative role of D is to mediate transformations from "O," through P-S, to K (symbolic emotional knowledge) from the objective (self and object as uniquely separate) perspective. On a more pragmatic level P-S deals with the infant's protests of discomfort and pain, for which it holds the object responsible (Bowlby 1969). In D the infant begins to acquire a sense of responsibility for living its own life and respectfully appreciates the help it obtains from its objects in that regard, at which time the infant experiences "tender mercies."[14]

(H) *It follows from the above that, hitherto, P-S has been erroneously demonized and confused furthermore with "O" and its beta-elements.* Put another way, a pathological P-S becomes a post factum statement about its failure to transform the beta-elements from "O," and a statement as well that, in its failure, it has become transformed *by* "O," a phenomenon Bion (1967, p. 116) terms "*nameless dread.*"

(I) Klein's positions have been supplemented by other authors. Bick (1968) and Meltzer (1975) located a cluster of anxiety and a position to designate it, which they believe antedates the onset of P-S, and which they term "adhesive identification," and later, "adhesive identity." These findings emerged from infants and children who suffered from autistic illness, which is a pervasive developmental disorder, thereby adding a factor that renders them and their developmental epigenesis significantly different from normal infants and from infants suffering from exclusively psychological factors. Winnicott (1950, p. 206), as stated earlier, proffered the notion of "position of concern." Marcelli (1983) proffered the notion of an "autistic position," following which Ogden (1989) came forth with an "autistic contiguous position."

While the term "autistic," whose provenance lies in Mahler's (1968) ill-fated and now discarded "autistic phase" of development (presuming the existence of primary narcissism) (Stern 1985), now seems obsolete, Ogden's concept of "contiguous" has merit in calling attention to what *I* believe is an inchoate aspect of P-S, an aspect that designates the earliest object relations between infant and mother, that between their respective skin boundaries and the sense organs related to them.[15] Put another way, to my mind, an object relationship, no matter how inchoate, primitive, or elemental, designates *ipso facto* the existence of either P-S or D. The alternative is to postulate an inchoate existence that precedes P-S, automatically presumes primary narcissism, which presumes in turn an absence of differentiation between infant and mother and therefore the absence of a position.

Brown (1987) posited a "transitional position" to exist between P-S and D in order to reconcile Kleinian developmental concepts with those of Piaget. Steiner (1979) originally posited a "borderline position" between P-S and D and subsequently conceived of "psychic retreat" as occupying an intermediary or default position between them. Fairbairn's (1944) "endopsychic structures" bear a strong resemblance to the structures of a psychic retreat (Grotstein 2002).

Fairbairn's concept is of particular interest since it seems to be the "conjoined-twin" counterpart of Klein's.[16] One recalls that Fairbairn proposed a schizoid position that was followed by a depressive position. Whereas Klein's positions are phantasmal primarily and responsive to external reality only secondarily, Fairbairn's are the reverse. They depict how an infant *realistically* dissociates the image of a good from a bad parent and selectively internalizes only the bad, first in order to protect the need for the illusion of a good parent on whom to depend, and second in order to control the internalized bad parent within. Once the bad aspects of the needed object have become internalized, by a central ego that relates to an ideal object, they become dissociated once again into a rejecting object and an exciting object respectively, with which an antilibidinal ego identifies with the former and a libidinal ego with the latter.

To my mind, Fairbairn's positions constitute the complement to Klein's and fit in with Bion's notion of the importance of the reality of the maternal container function. Fairbairn (1943) also formulated a schizoid and a depressive position, which though at some variance from Klein's conceptions in part, follow her ideas in the main. This binary opposition of both concepts of the positions could include the qualities of attachment.

Grotstein (2000), responding to the ambiguity in the Kleinian conception of the depressive position, i.e. the question as to whether one "*achieves*" it or "*surpasses*" it, and addressing the issue that the depressive position mediates a mourning process that, according to Freud (1917a) has a time-limited duration, proffered the concept of a "*transcendent position*," one that designated that the individual had transcended both P-S and D and had now achieved the serenity and equanimity of a "transformation *in* 'O' " (Bion 1965, 1970), i.e. has transcended the need for iconic images in P-S and the symbolic images of D for the noetic or aniconic (Rhode 2003), non-cartesian objectless state. This is the meditative state that characterizes maternal and analytic reverie.

(J) In discussing the relationship between attachment and the positions, I remind the reader that I am shifting between two vertices, the ethological or sociobiological and the psychoanalytic. I should now like to invoke yet another vertex, the religious. I am invoking this vertex to help answer a conundrum about D. Freud, like the *Talmud*, and like clinical wisdom itself, states that mourning should be time-bound and thus ultimately should end. Klein seems ambiguously to believe that the depressive position should both be worked through and surmounted *and* be attained – and therefore *maintained*. Furthermore, she believes that every individual vacillates between P-S and D over a lifetime. The question emerges: should or does mourning eventually end? Another question then emerges: may not mourning, then, be part of a more profound process that itself never ends? In searching for a resolution to these questions, I returned to the concept of the covenant, but this time from a religious vertex.

In the Catholic ceremony of the eucharist, the parishioner eats a wafer and drinks wine believing as (s)he does so that (s)he is eating the flesh and drinking the blood of Christ and thereby becomes one with him. In other words, the parishioner *must* participate in the phantasied cannibalization of the savior in order ceremonially to recertify his (Christ's) sacralization and their (the parishioner's) sacred attachment to him. On another level there exists the Trinity, which includes the Father, the Son, and the Holy Ghost, the last of which constitutes the holy and numinous *attachment* between God and man. Jung (1958) conceives of a "Quaternary," which includes Mary as one of the deities. In other contributions I suggested that the gods become sacralized by their having been sacrificed and in turn become re-deified with each sacrificial ceremony.

Psychoanalytic investigation runs parallel to these ideas. Freud (1913) discussed the sacrifice of the *father* by the band of brothers in some primeval time, upon which he became the totem god of the clan – and ultimately the ego ideal and then the superego. Klein implicated the sacrifice of the mother, who seemingly becomes benignly idealized during the depressive position following the infant's awareness of his/her putative predatory attacks against her. Fairbairn, Winnicott, and many current schools of psychoanalysis focus on the sacrifice of the child by the parents. My conclusion is that the mother, father, and son in heaven, along with the Holy Ghost, achieve their sacredness by having become sacrificed, which act thereafter seems to consolidate and insure the bond or attachment between the deity (-ies) in heaven or in the mind (superego(s)) and in mankind. Thus, perhaps it is the *sorrow* by the offending partner in regard to his/her putative or actual hurtfulness of his/her object and the latter's *pity* and *tender mercies*[17] that fundamentally organize and choreograph the attachment bond between two or more individuals. Furthermore, I question Klein's (1940) concept of *reparations*. When one stops to ponder the issue, one begins to realize that no one can ever repair emotional injury to an object. One can only feel contrite and seek to honor the beloved victim and *restore* them to grace within oneself.

Put another way, it is my impression that the authority of the superego lies not only in the omnipotence which Klein suggested that the infant projectively attributes to it. Its authority also lies in the results of the experience of one's recognition of the triple ongoing human sacrifices (father, mother, child) and the continuing guilt that constitutes the covenant of the internal family.

"The position of innocence"

As a consequence of the above, I postulate that there exists yet another position, that of *innocence*, that occurs coeval with Klein's P-S and D and my transcendent position and constitutes a parallel developmental line with them. I have in mind here ideas derived from both Wordsworth and Blake, particularly the latter's concept that the infant is born into and with innocence, then must enter the Forest of Experience or Error, and then, if all goes well, it achieves higher innocence. In light of this idea, one can credibly assign the psychologies of Freud and Klein to the belief in the doctrine of "original sin" (psychoanalytic version) and the psychologies of Fairbairn, Winnicott, self psychology, relationism, interpersonalism, and intersubjectivity to the doctrine of innocence. My option is for a dual-track or a binary-oppositional structure that unites the two. In other words, I believe that the infant is born into an ontological dual-track, one track being its fate to wound (sacrifice) the object in order to survive, and requiring a covenant of perpetual sorrow and remorse for the obligatory cruelty of the sacrificial act – and the other that the infant is born innocent of experience and feels anger and disappointment when its caretakers and/or culture prematurely disabuse it of its necessary world view of protective innocence.

Parenthetically, it is my belief that the psychoanalytic psychologies that spring from the doctrine of the infant's innocence become more credible after the working through of the depressive position and not before. After this working through has taken place, the infant is able for the first time to achieve the experience of separateness from its object, as well as to confer separateness to the object. It is only at this time that the infant or child is able to acknowledge the full significance of a defective caretaking object that it can contemplate as being or having been defective in their own right, i.e. as separate from it.

Notes

1 "Entelechy" is Aristotle's term for the activation of one's inherent potential.
2 One of the task of psychoanalysis is to assist the analysand in differentiating between persecutors and enemies. The former always originate in the analysand; the latter never. Clinically, they all too often become confused with one another.
3 "O" is Bion's (1965, 1970) unsaturated and enigmatic term for the Absolute Truth about Ultimate Reality, which is beyond our capacity to know, perceive, or conceive of symbolically. It corresponds in some ways to Lacan's (1966) "Register of the Real." Bion also associates "O" with Kant's noumena and things-in-themselves, Plato's Ideal Forms, "godhead," and "beta-elements" (unmentalized elements).
4 Bion's (1992) other term for "alpha-function," the mental capacity to transform unmentalized beta-elements into alpha-elements that are then suitable for mental "digestion" as thoughts, memories, and dreams.
5 It is of some interest that the corpus callosum and the anterior commissure do not become myelinated (and therefore functional) until about 4 months of age and do not complete their myelination until early adulthood. The function of these structures is to bridge and mediate communication between the two cerebral hemispheres. In another contribution I theorized that perhaps one of the developmental functions of this prolonged delay in their functioning may be correlated with establishing and protecting childhood naivety and innocence. It is of some interest that Bowlby (1969) believes that attachment begins at 6 months. I intuitively believe that it begins much earlier.
6 The infant or patient in P-S is a prisoner of the image or percept.
7 There is need to postulate a transcendent position to account for Bion's (1965, 1970) conception of transformations in "O," of which maternal and analytic

reverie are examples. The formulation and/or proffering of an interpretation would be an example of a transformation from "O" to "K" (knowledge), the latter of which indicates the operation of the depressive position.

8 When one stops to think about it, one begins to realize that one can never *repair* damage done to an object. The damage has already been done and can only heal through "secondary intention." The most one can do is to experience authentic contrition, sorrow, and regret over the alleged wounding of the object and *restore* its value in one's mind.

9 My concept of the "dual-track" resembles Bion's concept of "binocular vision." Basically, it states that the mind, like the brain and even the body, is organized along parallel, complementary lines. Thus, for instance, the unconscious is not so much in *conflict* with consciousness as it is in binary (cooperative) *opposition* with it in mediating a third element, Bion's O.

10 Classical analysts since Freud confuse the id (the "seething cauldron") with "O," and it is my opinion that Kleinians confuse P-S with "O" rather than, as Bion obliquely suggests, consider P-S to be a defensive strategy to contend with "O."

11 Here I can only briefly allude to Fairbairn's (1944) notion that all internalized objects are bad. Good objects are not internalized – except to help defend against the absolute badness of the bad objects, in which case the latter become "conditionally bad." Kleinian analysis depends in no small measure on the patient's being able to mourn the absence or loss of the good object and to accept a substitute from the object – the legacy of the experience with the object in lieu of the object. If a good object becomes internalized, it becomes possessed by the subject and consequently becomes persecuting – and thus "bad." Conclusion: the concept of the internalized good object constitutes *ipso facto* an oxymoron.

12 Consequently, Klein (1935, 1940) may have been more nearly correct in her original assessment of D than she was subsequently in 1946.

13 "Love," "hate," and "knowledge."

14 I am once again indebted to Larry McMurtry.

15 See Mitrani (2001) for a view of this area of development that approximates Ogden's.

16 See Grotstein (2000, 2002) for elaborations on the complementarity between Fairbairn, Klein, and Steiner.

17 Once again I am indebted to Larry McMurtry.

References

Abraham, K. (1924) A short study of the development of the libido. In *Selected Papers on Psycho-Analysis*. London: Hogarth Press, 1948, pp. 418–501.

Benjamin, J. (1995) *Like Subjects, Love Objects: Essays on Recognition and Sexual Difference*. New Haven, CT: Yale University Press.

Bick, E. (1968) The experience of the skin in early object relations. *International Journal of Psycho-Analysis*, 49: 484–486.

Bion, W.R. (1959) Attacks on linking. In: *Second Thoughts*. London: Heinemann, 1967, pp. 93–109.

Bion, W.R. (1961) A psycho-analytic theory of thinking. *International Journal of Psycho-Analysis*, 43: 306–310.

Bion, W.R. (1962a) A theory of thinking. *International Journal of Psycho-Analysis*, 43: 306–310.

Bion, W.R. (1962b) *Learning From Experience*. London: Heinemann.

Bion, W.R. (1963) *Elements of Psycho-analysis*. London: Heinemann.

Bion, W.R. (1965) *Transformations*. London: Heinemann.

Bion, W.R. (1967) *Second Thoughts*. London: Heinemann.

Bion, W.R. (1970) *Attention and Interpretation*. London: Tavistock Publications.

Bion, W.R. (1974) *Bion's Brazilian Lectures: 1 – Sao Paulo 1973*. Rio de Janeiro: Imago Editora Ltd.

Bion, W.R. (1977) *Two Papers: The Grid and the Caesura*. Ed. Jayme Salomao. Rio de Janeiro: Imago Editora Ltd.

Bion, W.R. (1992) *Cogitations*. London: Karnac Books.

Bowlby, J. (1969) *Attachment and Loss. Vol. I: Attachment*. New York: Basic Books.

Bråten, S. (1993) Infant attachment and self-organization in light of this thesis: born with the other in mind. In *Making Links: How Children Learn*. Ed. I. Gomnaes and E. Osborne. Oslo: Yrkeslitteratur, pp. 25–38.

Britton, R. (2001) Beyond the depressive position: Ps (n+1). In *Kleinian Theory: A Contemporary Perspective*. Ed. Catalina Bronstein. London and Philadelphia: Whurr Publishers.

Brown, L.J. (1987) Borderline personality organization and the transition to the depressive position. In *The Borderline Patient: Emerging Concepts in Diagnosis, Psychodynamics, and Treatment. Volume 1*. Ed. J.S. Grotstein, J.F. Solomon and J.A. Lang. Hillsdale, NJ: Analytic Press, pp. 147–180.

Erikson, E.H. (1959) Identity and the life cycle. *Psychological Issues. Volume 1*. New York: International Universities Press.

Fairbairn, W.R.D. (1943) The repression and the return of bad objects (with special reference to the "war neuroses"). *British Journal of Medical Psychology*, 19: 327–341. Also in *Psychoanalytic Studies of the Personality*. London: Tavistock, 1952, pp. 59–81.

Fairbairn, W.R.D. (1944) Endopsychic structure considered in terms of object-relationships. In *Psychoanalytic Studies of the Personality*. London: Tavistock, 1952, pp. 82–136.

Ferenczi, S. (1913) Stages in the development of the sense of reality. In *Sex and Psychoanalysis*. New York: Robert Brunner, pp. 213–239.

Fonagy, P. (2001) *Attachment Theory and Psychoanalysis*. New York: Other Press.

Fonagy, P. and Target, M. (1996) Playing with reality: I. Theory of mind and the normal development of psychic reality. *International Journal of Psychoanalysis*, 77: 217–233.

Freud, S. (1905) Three essays on the theory of sexuality. *Standard Edition*, 7. London: Hogarth Press, 1953, pp. 125–245.

Freud, S. (1910) The psychoanalytic view of psychogenic disturbance of vision. *Standard Edition*, 11. London: Hogarth Press, 1957, pp. 209–218.

Freud, S. (1911) Formulations of the two principles of mental functioning. *Standard Edition*, 12. London: Hogarth Press, 1958, pp. 213–226.

Freud, S. (1913[1912–1913]) Totem and Taboo. *Standard Edition*, 13. London: Hogarth Press, 1957, pp. 1–64.

Freud, S. (1917a) Mourning and melancholia. *Standard Edition*, 14. London: Hogarth Press, 1957, pp. 237–260.

Freud, S. (1917b [1916–17]) Introductory lectures on psycho-analysis: Part III. General theory of the neuroses. *Standard Edition*, 16. London: Hogarth Press, 1963, pp. 243–463.

Freud, S. (1918 [1914]) From the history of an infantile neurosis. *Standard Edition*, 17. London: Hogarth Press, 1957, pp. 3–122.

Freud, S. (1923) The ego and the id. *Standard Edition*, 19. London: Hogarth Press, 1961, pp. 3–66.

Gallese, V. (2001) The "shared manifold" hypothesis: from mirror neurons to empathy. *Journal of Consciousness Studies*, 8 (5–7): 33–50.

Gallese, V. and Goldman, A. (1998) Mirror neurons and the simulation theory of mind reading. *Trends in Cognitive Science*, 2: 493–501.

Grotstein, J. (1978) Inner space: its dimensions and its coordinates. *International Journal of Psychoanalysis*, 59: 55–61.

Grotstein, J. (1993) Towards the concept of the transcendent position: reflections on some of "the unborns" in Bion's *Cogitations*. Special Issue on "Understanding the Work of Wilfred Bion", *Journal of Melanie Klein and Object Relations*, 11(2): 55–73.

Grotstein, J. (1995a) Orphans of the "Real": I. Some modern and post-modern perspectives on the neurobiological and psychosocial dimensions of psychosis and primitive mental disorders. *Bulletin of the Menninger Clinic*, 59: 287–311.

Grotstein, J. (1995b) Orphans of the "Real": II. The future of object relations theory in the treatment of psychoses and other primitive mental disorders. *Bulletin of the Menninger Clinic*, 59: 312–332.

Grotstein, J. (1996) The significance of Bion's concepts of P-S↔D and transformations in "O": a reconsideration of the relationship between the paranoid-schizoid and depressive positions – and beyond. In *Schemas and Models in Psychoanalysis*. Ed. Kirsty Hall and Bernard Burgoyne. London: Rebus Press, in press.

Grotstein, J. (2000) *Who Is the Dreamer Who Dreams the Dream? A Study of Psychic Presences*. New York: Analytic Press.

Grotstein, J. (2002) "We are such stuff as dreams are made on": annotations on dreams and dreaming in Bion's works. In *Dreams in Group Psychotherapy: Theory and Technique*. Ed. C. Neri, M. Pines, and R. Friedman. London and Philadelphia: Jessica Kingsley, pp. 110–145.

Heidegger, M. (1927) *Being and Time*. Trans: John McQuarrie and Edward Robinson. San Fransico: Harper, 1962.

Hoffman, I. (1992) Some practical implications of a social constructivist view of the psychoanalytic situation. *Psychoanalytic Dialogues*, 2: 287–304.

Isaacs, S. (1952) The nature and function of phantasy. In M. Klein, P. Heimann, S. Isaacs, and J. Riviere, *Developments in Psycho-Analysis*. Ed. J. Riviere. London: Hogarth Press, pp. 67–121.

Joseph, B. (1989) *Psychic Equilibrium and Psychic Change*. London: Routledge.

Jung, C.G. (1958) *Psyche and Symbol*. Ed. V. de Laszlo. Trans. R.F.C. Hull. Princeton, NJ: Bollinger/Princeton University Press, 1991.

Klein, M. (1935) A contribution to the psychogenesis of manic-depressive states. In *Contributions to Psycho-Analysis, 1921–1945*. London: Hogarth Press, 1950, pp. 282–310.

Klein, M. (1940) Mourning and its relation to manic-depressive states. In *Contributions to Psycho-Analysis, 1921–1945*. London: Hogarth Press, 1950, pp. 311–338.

Klein, M. (1946) Notes on some schizoid mechanisms. In M. Klein, P. Heimann, S. Isaacs, and J. Riviere, *Developments in Psycho-Analysis*. Ed. J. Riviere. London: Hogarth Press, 1952, pp. 292–320.

Klein, M. (1957) The early development of conscience in the child. In *Contributions to Psycho-Analysis, 1921–1945*. London: Hogarth Press, 1950, pp. 267–277.

Lacan, J. (1966) *Écrits: 1949–1960*. Trans. A. Sheridan. New York: Norton, 1977.

Lichtenberg, J.D. (1992) *Self and Motivational Systems: Towards a Theory of Psychoanalytic Technique*. Hillsdale, NJ: Analytic Press.

Lichtenstein, H. (1977) *The Dilemma of Human Identity*. New York: Jason Aronson, 1983.

Likierman, M. (1995) Loss of the object: tragic motifs in Melanie Klein's concept of the depressive position. *British Journal of Psychotherapy*, 12: 147–159.

McMurtry, L. (1975) *Terms of Endearment*. New York: Simon & Schuster.

Mahler, M.S. (1968) *On Human Symbiosis and the Vicissitudes of Individuation*. New York: International Universities Press.

Marcelli, D. (1983) La position autistique. Hypothèses psychopathologiques et ontogénétiques. *Psychiatrie enfant*, 24(1): 5–55.

Meltzer, D.W. (1975) Adhesive identification. *Contemporary Psychoanalysis*, 11: 289–310.

Meltzer, D.W. (1992) *The Claustrum: An Investigation of Claustrophobic Phenomena*. Strath Tay, Perthshire: Clunie Press.

Mitrani, J. (2001) *Ordinary People and Extra-Ordinary Protections: A Post-Kleinian Approach to the Treatment of Primitive Mental States*. Hove and Philadelphia: Brunner-Routledge.

Ogden, T. (1989) On the concept of an autistic-contiguous position, *Bulletin of the Menninger Clinic*, 53: 394–413.

Rhode, E. (2003) *Notes on the Aniconic*. London: Apex One.

Rosenfeld, H. (1987) *Impasse and Interpretation: Therapeutic and Anti-Therapeutic Factors in the Psychoanalytic Treatment of Psychotic, Borderline, and Neurotic Patients*. London: Tavistock.

Steiner, J. (1979) The border between the paranoid-schizoid and the depressive positions in the borderline patient. *British Journal of Medical Psychology*, 52: 385–391.

Steiner, J. (1993) *Psychic Retreats: Pathological Organizations in Psychotic, Neurotic and Borderline Patients*. London: Routledge.

Stern, D. (1985) *The Interpersonal World of the Infant*. New York: Basic Books.

Stern, D. (2004) *The Present Moment in Psychotherapy and Everyday Life*. New York and London: Norton.

Tinbergen, N. (1951) *The Study of Instincts*. London: Oxford University Press.

Trevarthen, C. (1988) Universal cooperative motives: how infants begin to know language and skills of culture. In *Ethnographic Perspectives on Cognitive Development*. Ed. G. Jahoda and I. Lewis. London: Croom Helm, pp. 37–90.

Winnicott, D.W. (1950) Aggression in relation to emotional development. In *Collected Papers: Through Paediatrics to Psycho-Analysis*. New York: Basic Books, 1958, pp. 204–218.

Winnicott, D.W. (1963) The development of the capacity for concern. In *The Maturational Processes and the Facilitating Environment*. New York: International Universities Press, 1965, pp. 73–82.

Winnicott, D.W. (1971) Creativity and its origins. In *Playing and Reality*. New York: Basic Books, 1971, pp. 65–85.

Chapter 7

Hegel on projective identification

Implications for Klein, Bion, and beyond

Jon Mills

The psychic process known as "projective identification" has become a familiar tenet of psychoanalytic doctrine. The term was coined by Melanie Klein in 1946[1] where it was conceived as an aggressive discharge of certain portions of the ego *into* an external object, the aim of which is to dominate or consume certain aspects of the object's contents in order to make it part of the ego's own internal constitution. Not only has the introduction of this concept revolutionized Kleinian theory, further developments have paved the way toward its progressive application in understanding a number of mental processes, pathologies, and clinical encounters. To be sure, projective identification may be viewed in multiple fashions: (1) as a general process of mental activity, from unconscious structure to conscious thought, (2) as a defensive maneuver motivated by intrapsychic conflict, and (3) as an intersubjective dynamic affecting object relations, especially the process of therapy. But with a few noteworthy exceptions (see Bion 1959), projective identification has been largely overlooked as a basic element of psychic organization.

Although largely unknown to psychoanalytic discourse, Hegel was the first philosopher to articulate the process of projective identification. In fact, Hegel anticipated many key psychoanalytic insights that Freud was to make more intelligible nearly one hundred years later (see Mills 1996, 2002). It is my intention throughout this chapter to highlight the normative functions of projective identification and show how it is an indispensable ontological feature underlying all mental activity. Through a proper appreciation of Hegel's logic of the dialectic, projective identification may be seen as the most elementary process that governs both unconscious and conscious life, a dynamic that brings Hegel into dialogue with Klein, Bion, and contemporary psychoanalytic thought.

Hegel's logic of the dialectic

Hegel's philosophy of mind or spirit (*Geist*) rests on a proper understanding of the ontology of the dialectic. Hegel refers to the unrest of *Aufhebung* – customarily translated as 'sublation,' a dialectical process continuously annulled, preserved, and transmuted. Hegel's use of *Aufhebung*, a term he borrowed from Schiller but also an ordinary German word, is to be distinguished from its purely negative function whereby there is a complete canceling or drowning of the lower relation in the higher, to also encompass a preservative aspect. Unlike Fichte's meaning of the verb *aufheben*, defined as to eliminate, annihilate, abolish, or destroy, Hegel's designation signifies a threefold activity by which mental operations at once cancel or annul opposition, preserve or retain it, and surpass or elevate its previous shape to a higher structure. This process of the dialectic underlies all operations of mind and is seen as the thrust behind world history and culture. It may be said that the dialectic is the *essence* of psychic life, for if it were to be removed, consciousness and unconscious structure would evaporate.

When psychoanalysis refers to dialectics, it often uses Fichte's threefold movement of thought in the form of thetic, analytic or antithetic, and synthetic judgments giving rise to the popularized (if not bastardized) phrase, thesis–antithesis–synthesis[2] – a process normally and inaccurately attributed to Hegel;[3] or it describes unresolvable contradictions or mutual oppositions that are analogous to Kant's antinomies or paralogisms of the self.[4] It is important to note that Hegel's dialectic is not the same as Kant's, who takes contradiction and conflict as signs of the breakdown of reason, nor is it Fichte's, who does not explicate the preservative function of the lower relation remaining embedded in the higher. Furthermore, when psychoanalysts and social scientists apply something like the Fichtean dialectic to their respective disciplines, the details of this process are omitted. The presumptive conclusion is that a synthesis cancels the previous moments and initiates a new moment that is once again opposed and reorganized. But the synthesis does not mean that all previous elements are preserved, or that psychic structure is elevated. In fact, this form of dialectic may lead to an infinite repetition of contradictions and conflict that meets with no resolve.

Hegel's dialectic essentially describes the process by which a mediated dynamic forms a new immediate. This process not only informs the basic structure of his *Logic* which may further be attributed to the general principle of *Aufhebung*, but it also provides the logical basis to account for the role of negativity within a progressive unitary drive. The process by which mediation collapses into a new immediate provides us with the logical model for understanding the dynamics of projective identification. An architectonic process, spirit invigorates itself and breathes its own life as a self-determining generative activity that builds upon its successive phases and layers which form its appearances. Spirit educates itself as it passes through its various dialectical configurations ascending toward higher shapes of self-conscious awareness. What spirit takes to be truth in its earlier moment is realized to be merely one appearance among many appearances. It is not until the stage of Absolute Knowing as conceiving or conceptual understanding that spirit finally integrates its previous movements into a synthetic unity as a dynamic self-articulated complex whole.

Hegel's use of mediation within the movements of thought is properly advanced in the *Science of Logic* (1812) as well as the *Encyclopaedia Logic* (1817) which prefaces Hegel's anthropological and psychological treatment of spirit in the *Encyclopaedia of the Philosophical Sciences* (1817/1830). In the *Logic*,[5] thought initially encounters Being which moves into Nothing and then develops into Becoming, first as the "passing over" into nothing, second as the "vanishing" into being, and third as the "ceasing-to-be" or passing away of being and nothing into the "coming-to-be" of becoming. Becoming constitutes the mediated unity of "the unseparatedness of being and nothing" (*SL*, p. 105). Hegel shows how each mediation leads to a series of new immediates which pass over and cease to be as that which has passed over in its coming-to-be until these mediations collapse into the determinate being of *Dasein* – its new immediate. Being is a simple concept while Becoming is a highly dynamic and complex process. Similarly, *Dasein* or determinate being is a simple immediacy to begin with which gets increasingly more complicated as it transitions into Essence and Conceptual Understanding. It is in this early shift from becoming to determinate being that you have a genuine sublation, albeit as a new immediate, spirit has a new beginning.

In Hegel's treatment of consciousness as pure thought represented by the *Logic* (1812), as well as his treatment of history in the *Phenomenology of Spirit* (1807) and anthropology and psychology in the *Encyclopaedia* (1817/ 1830), spirit – whether it be the mind of each individual or the collective psyche of the human race – continues on this circular albeit progressive path conquering each opposition it encounters, elevating itself in the process. Each mediation leads to a new beginning, and spirit constantly finds itself confronting opposition and overcoming conflict as it is perennially engaged in the process of its own becoming. In the *Logic*, the whole process is what is important as reason is eventually able to understand its operations as pure self-consciousness; however, in its moments, each mediation begets a new starting point that continually re-institutes new obstacles and dialectical problems that need to be mediated, hence eliminated. But thought always devolves or collapses back into the immediate.

This dynamic is a fundamental structural constituent that offers systematic coherency to Hegel's overall philosophy of spirit which is furthermore germane to the specific issue at hand. The individual psyche – as well as culture itself – mediates opposition and conflict it generates from within its own evolutionary process and attempts to resolve earlier problems unto which new immediacy emerges. Mediation is therefore an activity performed from within the mind and between interpersonal forces that in turn make new experience possible. As we will see, projective identification becomes the basic structural process of dialectical progression that is responsible for the epigenesis of unconscious organization, consciousness, the ontology of the self, and civilization at large – a dynamic responsible for both maturation and psychic decay.

The structure of mind

Hegel's theory of mind is comprehensively outlined in the Philosophy of Spirit (*Philosophie des Geistes*) which is the third part of the *Encyclopaedia*.[6] Unbeknown to psychoanalysis, Hegel provides one of the first theories of the unconscious. He gives most of his attention to the unconscious within the stage of presentation (*Vorstellung*) in the context of his psychology, thus belonging to the development of theoretical spirit. Here Hegel refers to a "nocturnal abyss within which a world of infinitely numerous images and presentations is preserved without being in consciousness" (*EG* § 453). Hegel explains that the nightlike abyss is a necessary presupposition for imagination and for higher forms of intelligence.[7] While these more complex forms of the psychological would not be possible without the preservation of images within the unconscious mind, the unconscious is given developmental priority in Hegel's anthropological treatment of the soul (*Seele*).

For Hegel, the unconscious soul is the birth of spirit which developmentally proceeds from its archaic structure to the higher order activities of consciousness and self-conscious rational life. Like Freud (1926a) who shows that the ego is a differentiated portion of the id,[8] the conscious ego is the modification and expression of unconscious activity. For Hegel, the soul is not an immaterial entity (*EG* § 389), but rather the embodiment of its original corporeality, the locus of natural desire (*Begierde*) or drive (*Trieb*).[9] As the general object of anthropology, Hegel traces the dialectical emergence of the feeling soul from the abyss of its indeterminations; at first unseparated from its immediate universal simplicity, it then divides and rouses itself from its mere inward implicitness to explicit determinate being-for-self. Through a series of internal divisions, external projections, and re-internalizations, the soul gradually emerges from its immediate physical sentience (*EG* § 391) to the life of feeling (*EG* § 403) to the actual ego of consciousness (*EG* § 411), which further becomes more refined and sophisticated through perceptual understanding, ethical self-consciousness, and rational judgment, the proper subject matter of the *Phenomenology*.

For Hegel, spirit begins, like ego development for Freud,[10] as an original undifferentiated unity that emerges from its immediate self-enclosed universality to its mediated determinate singularity. This is initiated through a dialectical process of internal division, self-externalization, and introjection as the reincorporation of its projected qualities back into its interior. Here lies the basic process of projective identification: unconscious spirit splits off certain aspects of its interior, externalizes its Self, and then reconstitutes itself by identifying with its own negated qualities which it re-gathers and assimilates back into its unconscious framework. Through the complexities of mediation and sublation, spirit achieves higher levels of unification until it arrives at a full integration of itself as a complex whole, uniting earlier finite shapes within its mature universality.

Negativity, aggressivity, and conflict are essential forces to the thrust of the dialectic, a process Klein emphasizes in her characterization of ego development. The sleep of spirit is an undifferentiated void with the inner ambience of violence. It experiences the primeval chaos of an intense longing to fill its empty simplicity, desire being its form and content, the desire to fill the *lack*. Through the drive toward self-differentiation, unconscious spirit defines itself as a determinate being for itself and thus effects the passage from the universal to the particular, from a unity which lacks difference to differentiated plurality and singularity. There is an antediluvian cycle of negativity that we may say belongs to the prehistory of conscious spirit, a circular motion of the drives that constitute the dialectic of desire. Awakening as sensation from its nocturnal slumber, the feeling soul remains the birthplace of what is the substance of the "heart," for the abyss is the midwife of mind.

The dialectical structure of the unconscious

As we have seen, the dialectic informs both the inner organization and the content of the unconscious. It is the dialectic that provides the Self with intrapsychic structures and functional operations that can never be reduced or localized, only conceptualized as pure activity. This pure activity of the dialectic as Self is constantly evolving and redefining itself through such movement. The unconscious forms of spirit (initially as feeling soul and then as ego) are thereby necessarily organized around the dialectical activity of the abyss. These structural operations, however, are not mechanistic, reductionistic, or physical as in the natural science framework often attributed to traditional psychoanalysis.[11] They are mental, telic, and transcendental, always reshaping spirit's inner contours and the internalized representational world within the night of the mind. Therefore, as a general structure, the unconscious is *aufgehoben*.

For Hegel, the unconscious is pure *process*, a changing, flexible, and purposeful activity of becoming. As the very foundation, structure, and organizing principles of the unconscious are informed by the movement of the dialectic, the architecture of the abyss is continually being reshaped and exalted as each dialectical conflict is sublated by passing into a new form, that in turn restructures, reorganizes, and refurbishes the interior contours of the core self. Therefore, the structural foundations of the self are never static or inert, but always in dialectical movement – having its origin and source in the unconscious, revamping the texture in which spirit emanates. This self-generating dialectical movement of the unconscious is the evoking, responding, sustaining, and transcending matrix that is itself the very internal system of subjective spirit.

The concept of the self as subject in Hegel is of particular importance in understanding the unconscious nature of mind. Essentially, the stage-by-stage (phase) progression of the dialectic is expressed as an epigenetic theory of self development. Through sublation, Hegel's notion of the self encompasses a movement in which the subject is opposed to an object and comes to find itself in the object. This is exemplified by Hegel's treatment of the master–slave dialectic outlined in the *Phenomenology*. During the dialectical movement of spirit, the subject recognizes or discovers itself in the object. This entails the mediation of its becoming other to itself, with the reflection into otherness returning back to itself. The process of the development of the self is, like the soul, a process of differentiation and integration. As seen in the *Logic*, Being is characterized by an undifferentiated matrix which undergoes differentiation in the dialectical process of Becoming that in turn integrates into its being that which it differentiated through its projection, reclaiming it and making it part of its internal structure.[12] This is the very fabric of projective identification. The outcome of the integration is once again differentiated then reintegrated; unification is always reunification. Therefore, spirit comes to be what it already is, the process of its own becoming.[13]

Interfaces with Klein

Klein's theory of splitting has revolutionized the way we understand ego development. For Klein, the ego exists at birth plagued by anxieties characteristic of psychosis which it attempts to fend off and control through the primary defense mechanisms of splitting, projection, and introjection, giving rise to the paranoid-schizoid and depressive positions that mold object relations. While Klein refers to these defensive maneuvers as 'mechanisms,' they are not mechanistic. Ego activity is never fixed or static operations taking the forms of predetermined tropisms; rather psychic organization is the continuity of subjective temporal processes. It is more accurate to conceptualize these early mechanisms as defensive *process systems* comprised by the ego's intrapsychic relation to itself and its object environment, initially the maternal object. This makes ego development and object relations an intersubjective enterprise.

In her seminal essay, "Notes on Some Schizoid Mechanisms," Klein (1946) proclaims splitting as the original primordial defense, a process she started analyzing as early as 1929. Beset by the death drive (*Todestrieb*), the immature ego deflects the destructive impulse by turning it against the object accompanied by oral-sadistic attacks on the mother's body thus giving rise to persecutory anxiety. Splitting is the very first in a series of defenses that are never completely separate from one another, hence forming the dialectical cycle we have come to label as projective identification. While Klein cogently articulates the gradual evolution and strengthening of the ego, she concedes that "so far, we know nothing about the structure of the early ego" (1946, p. 4). Here Hegel is instructive for contributing to psychoanalytic theory.

As previously outlined, Hegel traces the dialectical course of the soul as a sentient feeling entity – at first a prenatal agent – only to gradually acquire more personal unity and organization as ego. It is important to note that both Klein and Hegel use the same word *Ich* to designate the personal agency of the ego – at first an unconscious constellation that later makes consciousness possible. Klein says very little about the prehistory of the ego prior to birth, yet she is suggestive. "The question arises whether some active splitting processes within the ego may not occur even at a very early age. As we assume, the early ego splits the object and the relation to it in an active way, and this may imply some active splitting of the ego itself" (1946, p. 5). Klein is correct in showing that splitting is the ego's original defensive activity despite the fact that she omits explaining how the ego is formed in the first place. This is presumably due to her scientific attitude guided by empirical considerations, but by way of Hegel's speculative metaphysics, the logical progression of the dialectic clarifies this process. Through Hegel's logic, we can reasonably conclude that the ego exists prior to birth and is prepared by the unconscious activity of the soul lending increasing order to intrapsychic structure. Because the ego cannot simply materialize *ex nihilo*, it must emanate from a prior unconscious ground or abyss (*Ungrund*). The ego has a prenatal life which is developmentally prepared prior to conscious perception: unconscious experience precedes consciousness.

Not only does Hegel situate splitting at the inception of the soul's development, he demonstrates that splitting is the earliest activity of mind. Splitting becomes the prototype of mental process and remains a fundamental operation in the normative as well as the pathological functions of the psyche. The unconscious soul first undergoes an internal division or separation of its interior which it projects as an external object *within its own internality*, only to re-gather and again make it part of its inner constitution. This primary splitting activity is architectonic, thus forming the foundation for psychic growth. Since splitting is identified as the initial movement of the dialectic thus effecting its transition into mediatory relations, it becomes easy to see how splitting becomes the archetype of later ego activity which Klein emphasizes in her developmental framework. But unlike Klein (1946, 1955) who repeatedly tells us that the ego's first object is the mother's breast, it would follow that the ego's first object is itself – its own internality. Hegel does not contradict Klein's main theses, he only substantiates her theoretical innovations. The ego must first posit and set itself over its initial immediacy which it does through splitting.

In "Splitting of the Ego in the Process of Defence," a posthumously published unfinished paper, Freud (1940 [1938]) addresses the notion of disavowal and the "alteration of the ego" that goes beyond his earlier treatment of splitting in cases of psychoses (*SE*, 19, pp. 152–153) and fetishism (*SE*, 21, pp. 155–156), which is now included within his general theory of neurosis. Freud, as does Klein, generally sees the conceptualization of splitting as a defensive process that is usually confined to the domains of conflict, while Hegel's emphasis on the internal divisibility of the soul makes splitting a generic process that may be applied to any mediatory aspect of division and negation within the mind. But in *New Introductory Lectures*, Freud (1933) is clear that splitting is a general ego operation: "the ego can be split; it splits itself during a number of its functions – temporarily at least. Its parts can come together again afterwards" (*SE*, 22, p. 58). Freud also alludes to an innate and normative function of splitting as it is applied to the synthetic processes of the ego. He states: "The synthetic function of the ego, though it is of such extraordinary importance, is subject to particular conditions and is liable to a whole number of disturbances" (*SE*, 23, p. 276). While Freud had emphasized the synthetic functions of ego unification in several places before (see *SE*, 20, pp. 97–100; 20, p. 196; 22, p. 76), and it had always been an implicit part of his theory, Hegel shows that splitting is a basic psychic operation that may take on more pathological configurations throughout development, such as in the cases of psychotic and schizoid disorders articulated by Klein and her followers, or in pathological narcissism and borderline personality, a topic that occupies much of the literature today.

For Hegel, the ego is unconsciously implicit within the sentient feeling soul and is already a prenatal form of self-awareness. Both a sensuous and cognizing agent, unconscious spirit intuits itself as an "intro-reflected" or pre-reflective, non-propositional self-conscious being – intro-reflection being the process of unconscious spirit's immediate self-awareness and self-identification. In Hegel's discussion of the ego's actual emergence from its natural embodiment as soul, the ego has to confront its corporeal confinement and inwardness. He states: "It is through this *intro-reflection* (*Reflexion-in-sich*) that spirit completes its liberation from the form of *being*, gives itself that of *essence*, and becomes *ego*" (*EG* § 412, *Zusätz*). In its alteration from mere immediacy to determinate mediate being, the soul *senses* its Self as an impression, already containing the rudiments of ego-awareness in its self-intuiting. In its ego explicitness, before the soul makes its final trajectory to consciousness, unconscious spirit has already undergone a splitting of its interior in manifold accounts by its own hands. In each incremental process of splitting that accompanies sublation there is an internal division, projection, and (re)introjection of its particularization back into its internality. Each introjective maneuver is a re-incorporation of its projected interior that takes place through an identification with its alienated shape(s) that it takes to be an exterior object although possessing its internal qualities. Such projective identification may be said to be the truncated recognition the soul has with itself through the process of intro-reflection – itself a preliminary form of unconscious self-consciousness – only that the ego has undergone a splitting as an element of defense against its unconsciously perceived conflict which subsists due to the negative tension of the dialectic.

As noted, this continual process of internal separation, projection, and introjection as re-incorporation is the general structural operation of projective identification. The ego projects its internality as alienation, comes to recognize and identify with its alienated qualities, then takes hold of and repossesses its earlier disavowed shapes. It is through this continual elevating process that both the content and the developmental hierarchy of the mind become more complex and sophisticated. Unconscious spirit comes to take itself as its own object through intro-reflection once it projects its interior as its exterior then "reflects upon it, takes back into its internality the externality of nature, idealizes [or cognizes] nature" (*EG* § 384, *Zusätz*), and thus effects a transition back into reunification. Spirit is continually engaged in this dialectical process in all its shapes; however at this level in the soul's development, unconscious spirit displays an early form of self-recognition through its projective identification as mediated intro-reflection.

This model of unconscious self-consciousness as self-recognition becomes the logical template for Hegel's theory of self-consciousness outlined in the dialectic of desire and recognition advanced in the *Phenomenology* (§§ 166–230). Although Hegel discusses desire and recognition in his phenomenological treatment of self-consciousness, it is already prepared in the anthropology as an ontological feature of unconscious spirit. The soul is desirous – the abyss is unconsciously self-aware, with drive (*Trieb*) and intro-reflection providing the logical prototype for desire and self-consciousness to emerge in conscious life. While both Freud and Klein see the ego as a more modified portion of the id, Hegel more clearly shows that consciousness is the manifestation of unconscious structure.

But why would the unconscious ego *need* to split itself in the first place? Here Klein and Hegel are on the same page. The ego's original activity is one of negation: it defines itself in opposition to what it is not. Following Freud (1920), Klein speculates that splitting mechanisms arise in an effort to subvert the death drive which threatens the ego with internal destruction. Splitting is a defense against felt or perceived annihilation. As too for Hegel, unconscious spirit first encounters an inner negativity, aggressivity, or conflict that becomes the impetus for dialectical intervention. In fact, splitting itself is a violent cleaving operation that divides subject from object. For Klein, splitting disperses the destructive impulse, while for Hegel splitting is destructive – it destroys as it negates. But the destruction incurred by the canceling function of the dialectic is also preserved in the same moment as the ego sublates itself to a higher state. Splitting and projection highlight the negative side of the dialectic while introjection serves a synthetic function. The repetitive process of projective identification may be applied toward the general ascending thrust of sublation or succumb to contentious dichotomies that are mired in chaos. While the relationship between the death impulse and negation still remains equivocal, destruction is nevertheless a key element in the progressive unification of the ego.

In several works, Klein (1946, 1952) underscores the point that the ego has an orienting principle toward higher degrees of unification. Elsewhere she states: "Together with the urge to split there is from the beginning of life a drive towards integration" (1963, p. 300). This is the affirmative and ongoing drive of the ego that forms the edifice of the Hegelian dialectic, a proclivity that inevitably strives for wholeness which Klein herself endorses. Hegel's emphasis on holism anticipates Klein's (1960) advocacy for a well-integrated personality, the goal of which is to master early developmental frictions that arise from persecutory anxiety and its vicissitudes.

But for Hegel and Klein, there is a dual tendency for both progression and regression, elevation and withdrawal back to previous points of fixation. As Klein (1946) puts it, "the early ego largely lacks cohesion, and a tendency towards integration alternates with a tendency towards disintegration, a falling into bits" (p. 4). Hegel refers to this disintegration as a fixation and/or regression to the form of feeling – the original self-enclosed simple unity of the feeling soul, a dynamic responsible for "madness" (see *EG* §§ 403–408).[14] Like Klein who stresses the primacy of developmentally working through the paranoid-schizoid and depressive positions, Hegel sees mental health as the ability to achieve holism through sublation: while feeling is never abandoned as such, it devolves into the higher instantiations of self-conscious rational thought. Even Klein (1963) herself says that "the urge towards integration, as well as the pain experienced in the process of integration, spring from internal sources which remain powerful throughout life" (p. 313). For Hegel, this would be tantamount to the labor of spirit, an arduous poignant crusade. If the subjective mind is not able to developmentally progress toward synthetic rational integration, then earlier primitive defensive constellations will persist unabated.

Bion on thinking, linking, and fantasy

While Klein (1946) first defined projective identification as a defensive process expressed through splitting and schizoid mechanisms, she later (1957) suggested that envy was intimately imbedded in projective identification, a process by which the ego forces itself into the psychic reality of the other in order to destroy its coveted attributes. Shortly after this theoretical modification, Bion (1959) distinguished normal from pathological forms of projective identification, which has further led revisionist Kleinians to articulate many distinct yet related modes of projective-identificatory processes (Hinshelwood 1991).

Bion, himself analyzed by Klein, was the first psychoanalyst to recognize normative functions of projective identification imbedded in normal thought processes. Bion (1959, 1962a, 1962b) distinguished between two alternative aims of projective identification marked by difference in the degree of violence attached to the mechanism. The first, *evacuation*, is characterized by its forceful entry into an object, in fantasy, as a means of controlling painful mental states directed toward relief and often aimed toward intimidating or manipulating the object. This is a pathological manifestation of projective identification. The second, *communication*, is a more benign attempt to communicate a certain mental content by introducing into the object a specific state of mind, a function often seen in the process of *containing* – a process in which one person contains some part of another. This is a normative function. It may be argued that evacuation is itself a form of communication, thereby the distinction becomes blurred; but for our purposes, evacuation highlights the thrust, intensity, and urgency of the need to expel psychic content. In all likelihood, evacuation and communication operate in confluence separated only by their motives and force of violence enacted through projection.

In his influential essay, "Attacks on Linking," Bion (1959) presents his mature view of projective identification as a form of communication taking on both normal and abnormal valences. Drawing on Klein, pathological forms fall within a range of *excess*, such as the degree of aggressivity of splitting, hatred, intrusion, omnipotent control and fusion with the object, the amount of loss or defusion of the ego, and the specific awareness of destructive intent. Normal projective-identificatory processes, however, play an adaptive role in social reality and are ordinary operations of communication and empathy which furthermore transpire within the process of thinking itself.

Bion's (1957) model of thinking, linking, and fantasy is preliminarily addressed in his effort to differentiate psychotic from non-psychotic personalities, with special emphasis on the awareness of psychic reality. For Bion (1954), drawing on Klein's (1930) and later Hanna Segal's (1957) work on symbol formation in the development of the early ego, the awareness of psychic reality is contingent upon the capacity for verbal thought derived from the depressive position; yet this process goes back even further. Linking – the capacity to form relations between objects or mental contents – serves a functional purpose, a process derived from the paranoid-schizoid position. Bion (1957, 1959) envisions psychotic organization to be largely plagued by violent attacks on the ego – particularly on the links between certain mental contents – and the awareness of inner reality itself. As a result, the schizophrenic lives in a fractured world of terror where mental links are "severed" or "never forged." Fantasy formation is fragmented, persecutory, and horrific. Attempts at linking conjunctions or making connections between objects are all but destroyed, and when minute links exist, they are impregnated with perversion and cruelty.

What is of importance in understanding the normative functions of projective identification is how Bion conceives of the phenomenology and evolution of thinking, a process that brings him in dialogue with Hegel. Bion (1957) informs us that "some kind of thought, related to what we should call ideographs and sight rather than to words and hearing exists at the outset," a capacity derived within the non-psychotic part of the embryonic psyche (p. 66). He continues to tell us that this crude level of thinking "depends on the capacity for balanced introjection and projection of objects and, *a forti-ori*, on awareness of them" (p. 66). Ultimately for Bion, both pre-verbal and verbal thought necessarily require an awareness of psychic reality.

Throughout the course of his theoretical contributions, Bion explicates three phases in the process of thinking. The first relies on the presumption of *a priori* knowledge whereby an innate *preconception* meets a *realization* in experience which results in a *conception*, the product of thought (Bion 1959, 1962a). Bion's notion of preconceptions is similar to Segal's (1964) notion of unconscious fantasy used as a means of generating hypotheses for testing reality. A preconception may be understood as a predisposed intuition of and expectancy for an object, such as a breast, which "mates" with the realization of the actual object in experience, thus forming a conception.

The second phase depends on the infant's capacity to tolerate frustration. A positive conception is generated when a preconception meets with a satisfying realization. When a preconception encounters a negative realiz-ation – absence – frustration ensues. Klein shows that when the immature ego encounters absence, it experiences the presence of a bad object, or per-haps more appropriately, a bad self-object experience. Bion, however, extends this idea further and posits that the experience of absence is transformed into a thought. The notion of absence, lack, or nothingness is conceptually retained. Yet this process is contingent on the infant's ability to modulate frustration. If frustration tolerance is high, the generation of absence into a thought serves the dialectical function that presence is possible, namely the absent object, such as the breast or bottle, may appear or re-present itself at some later time in the future. For Hegel, affirmation and negation are dialect-ically conjoined, separated only by their moments. With application to Bion, nothing stands in opposition to being which, once realized, is expected to return. If the capacity to manage frustration is low, the experience of noth-ingness does not advance to the thought of an absent good object, but rather remains at the immediate level of the concrete bad object experienced in the moment, which must be expelled through omnipotent evacuation. Bion (1962a) believes that if this process becomes arrested, advances in symbol formation and thinking are deleteriously obstructed.

The third phase of thinking involves more advanced levels of projective identification which Bion (1962b) describes as the container–contained rela-tionship. Here the infant has a sensory experience, feeling, or need which is perceived as bad which the infant wishes to banish. This type of projective identification evokes within the mother the same type of internal sensations experienced by the infant. If the mother is adequately well-balanced and capable of optimal responsiveness, what Bion calls *reverie*, she will be able to contain such feelings and transform them into acceptable forms which the infant can re-introject. Bion labels this process of transformation the *alpha function*. In normal development, the container–contained relationship allows the infant to re-introject the transformed object into something tolerable which eventually results in internalizing the function itself. If successful, this process aids in the increased capacity to modulate frustration and developmentally strengthens the infant's cognitive capabilities to conceptualize and generate symbolic functions, which generally leads to the fortification of the ego. Not only does Bion breach the sharp schism between feeling and thought that has dogged philosophical rationalism, he shows how emotions are made meaningful within the broader conceptual processes of thinking (Spillius 1988).

Hegel's philosophical psychology

Bion's theory of thinking is prefaced by Hegel's detailed analysis of the ontological processes of thought and the phenomenology of consciousness. In the *Science of Logic*, Hegel is concerned with articulating the ground, scope, and functional operations of thinking, reason, and the coming into being of pure self-consciousness, while the *Phenomenology of Spirit* comprehensively outlines the various appearances or shapes of individual and collective consciousness. Hegel's philosophical psychology is presented in his philosophy of subjective spirit outlined in the third division of his *Encyclopaedia*. Recall that Hegel discusses the role and function of the unconscious soul in the Anthropology which preludes the activities of conscious awareness. In the Psychology, he shows how the normative operations of thought, perception, attention, imagination, fantasy, memory, and concept formation are intimately associated with unconscious processes that are prepared by the soul or unconscious ego.

Subjective spirit expresses itself as cognition actively concerned with finding reason within itself (*EG* § 445). As the forms of theoretical spirit or intelligence unfold, the unconscious abyss is the primary domain of this activity. Hegel points out that intelligence follows a formal course of development to cognition beginning with (a) intuition or sensation of an immediate object (*EG* § 446), followed by (b) presentation (*EG* § 451) as a withdrawal into the unconscious from the relationship to the singularity of a presented object in consciousness and thus relating such object to a universal, leading to (c) thought (*EG* § 465) in which intelligence grasps the concrete universals of thinking and being as objectivity. In the stage of intuition as immediate cognizing, intelligence begins with the sensation of the immediate object, then alters itself by fixing attention on the object while differentiating itself from it, and then posits the material as external to itself which becomes intuition proper. The second main stage of intelligence as presentation is concerned with recollection, imagination, and memory; while the final stage in the unfolding of intelligence is thought, which has its content in understanding, judgment, and reason.

By Hegelian standards, Bion's model of thinking appears rather simplistic; but in his defense, Bion (1962a) himself admits his theoretical system "differs from philosophical theory in that it is intended, like all psychoanalytical theories, for use . . . composed in terms of empirically verifiable data" (p. 306). However, Hegel is very clear that his speculative outlook is not at odds with empiricism; instead "experience" becomes the standpoint of "*speculative thinking*" (*Encyclopaedia Logic*, §§ 7–9). In the *Philosophy of Nature* he also states: "Not only must philosophy be in agreement with our empirical knowledge of Nature, but the *origin* and *formation* of the Philosophy of Nature presupposes and is conditioned by empirical . . . science" (*Philosophy of Nature*, § 246). Like Bion, Hegel is concerned with articulating the inner meaning and ontology of thinking that applies to both normal development and disease.

Bion's scheme is remarkably compatible with Hegel's on many levels, emphasizing: (1) the awareness of inner reality, (2) the nature of pre-conceptual mental activity, and (3) the process of realization as conceptual thought. In our discussion of Hegel's theory of the soul, the unconscious ego attains for itself via *intro-reflection* a preliminary level of non-propositional, pre-reflective self-consciousness; that is, the nascent ego does not yet posit itself as a subject reflecting upon itself as an object, but rather is intuitively aware of its internal divisions and shapes that it sets over itself through its splitting activity. Such unconscious self-consciousness is the prototype for the process of consciousness. In fact, consciousness itself is a split off and projected instantiation of unconscious structure.

Unconscious intro-reflection corresponds to Bion's notion of innate *a priori* knowledge in the form of preconceptions, yet for Bion this gets explained through encounters with realized or non-realized objects resulting in positive (satisfying) or negative (frustrating, non-gratifying) conceptions. Hegel's epistemology derives from the logic of the dialectic, while Bion's is merely presupposed yet verified through the subjective encounter. In order for conceptualization to occur, certain mental pre-conditions or configurations must be thought to exist prior to experience which are mobilized from the beginning. Through the principle of sufficient reason, there must be a ground to psychic life that precedes conscious experience, and this assumption remains a cardinal pillar of psychoanalytic doctrine.

For Hegel, the process of conceiving or conceptual thought is a complex achievement, an activity attained very early from Bion's account. Bion's notion of preconceptions would be explained by Hegel as the implicit realization of ideas or the Concept (*Begriff*) within the deep internal abyss of spirit – a process fully actualized in Absolute Knowing. Put in more accessible language, the unconscious ego generates pre-conceptual, pre-linguistic ideas belonging to its innate natural constitution, what Klein and Bion would contend are drive derivatives. But Hegel also locates pre-conceptual mentation within the realm of unconscious feeling, a position closely allied with Bion's. Furthermore, both Hegel and Bion place primacy on the awareness of psychic reality – for Hegel, in the feeling soul, and for Bion, as a precondition for the process of thought and symbol formation to transpire. For both Hegel and Bion, awareness of inner reality is a necessary and universal condition for symbolization, fantasy, and language acquisition to occur.

Unconscious intelligence

Hegel is very specific in tracing the intellectual development of the subjective mind, a process that has further implications for Bion and Klein. For Hegel, intelligence moves from sensation of its immediate material to attention, whereby it fixes the object as well as separates it from itself, to intuition as positing the object externally. At this point, the presentation of a certain object thrusts intelligence into its second main movement which has three corresponding sub-stages: (a) recollection, (b) imagination, and (c) memory. Presentation (*Vorstellung*) is implicit within intuition because attention is paid to two moments, namely feeling and the attending act, whereby an object is isolated and related to externally. Attention now becomes introspective and must *re-collect* the content intuited within itself, "within its *own space* and its *own time*" (*EG* § 452). This content initially appears as an image (*Bild*) which is taken up by the ego and disassociated from its external context in which intuition had occurred. Abstracted from the concrete immediacy of intuition, the image becomes contingent or arbitrary and is but a fleeting moment since attention may focus on only one thing at a time.

Essentially, the ego internalizes its presented content by gathering up and separating the external image or impression and then making it part of its internal structure, but being only a transient impression it vanishes quickly from consciousness. "Intelligence is not, however, only the consciousness and the determinate being . . . recollected within it, the image is no longer existent, but is preserved unconsciously" (*EG* § 453). Here Hegel points to the underworld of spirit; intelligence is *not only* consciousness but is a "nocturnal abyss (*nachtlichen Schacht*) within which a world of infinitely numerous images and presentations is preserved without being in consciousness." Hegel specifically equates "intelligence as this unconscious abyss," thus forming the domains of two fundamental realities, the world of the deep and the world of consciousness.

This is the first textual mention of the unconscious within the Psychology (§ 453), thus pointing to its relationship with consciousness. Hegel explains how unconscious presentations are preserved within certain "fibers" and "localities" of the abyss, recalcitrant, as they were, to the tangibility of conscious processes, subsisting as intrinsically concrete yet simple universals.

Intelligence has "imperfect control of the images slumbering within the abyss" that cannot be recalled at will (*EG* § 453, *Zusätz*). Hegel himself even concedes that we have no means of knowing the full extent of all that which lies within the unconscious, suggesting that there are certain elements to psychic life that may resist incorporation into the dialectic. "No one knows what an infinite host of images of the past slumbers within him. Although they certainly awaken by chance on various occasions, one cannot, – as it is said, – call them to mind" (*EG* § 453, *Zusätz*). This concession on Hegel's part points to the inner autonomy of unconscious processes and organizations, presumably belonging to the soul – the unconscious ego – and how, from the standpoint of consciousness, they share a divided existence within spirit. This suggests that there is always an element of "chance," as Hegel says, and contingency that spirit can never completely overcome.

Imagination

What is of particular interest here is Bion's theory of ideographs in relation to Hegel's theory of imagination and fantasy. Bion (1957) postulates that something analogous to ideographs and sight is formed in the pre-verbal ego, presumably as early as the paranoid-schizoid position if not from birth onward. This would corroborate Hegel's theory of imagination and particularly his notion of symbolization. As noted before, unconscious images are preserved within the abyss of the mind, and due to the negative character of the dialectic as well as early developmental contingencies that mold ego development and object relations, they can take on many persecutory qualities and valences that are in need of evacuation. To recall an image is to repeat or re-present an intuition, and this is why it is free of immediate intuition because it is "preserved unconsciously." We recognize in immediate perception images we have experienced before. While consciousness isolates a specific feature, it relates it to the universality of unconscious recollection. Representation is therefore the synthesized product of relating an immediate intuition to an unconscious universal which becomes an object for consciousness. It is in imagination, however, that the process of relating one representation to others is intellectually carried out.

For Hegel, imagination mediates between intuition and thought. In imagination, representations are related to one another in the flow of consciousness which becomes linked with other images, affects, and thoughts as they are generated and manipulated by the ego's activity. Retrieved from the abyss, they are now technically under the ego's control, but with qualifications. Imagination also assumes three forms or sub-stages, namely: (a) reproductive imagination, (b) associative imagination, and (c) fantasy. First, representations are reproduced from the abyss but fall under the direction of the ego as "the issuing *forth* of images from the ego's own inwardness" which it now governs (*EG* § 455). The line of demarcation that divides the unconscious ego from the conscious ego is now breached: the ego vacillates between its unconscious and conscious counterparts.

Images are not only retrieved but issued forth from the ego itself, assuming that unconscious material is externalized into conscious apprehension, or as Hegel puts it, "excogitated . . . from the generality of the abyss." This process immediately initiates an association of variegated images and features that are related to further presentations which may be either abstract or concrete and varying in content and form; thereby the range of intellectual connections expands. However, if links are attacked, as Bion informs us, such connections would be attenuated. But normatively within this multiplicity of associations, the synthetic functions of intelligence are already operative as thought implicit within intelligence. Imagination in general determines images. As a formal activity, the reproduction of images occurs *"voluntarily"* (*EG* § 455, *Zusätz*); it does not require the aid of an immediate intuition to effect this process as in the case of recollection which is dependent upon the presence of an intuition. Distinguished from recollection, intelligence is now "self-activating."

Fantasy

Fantasy is the third movement of imagination where the ego fully manipulates its representations and images, drawing lines of interconnection where particulars are subsumed under universals and given the richer elaboration of symbols and signs which effect the ego's transition to memory, the third stage of presentation. Fantasy is a subjective bond the ego has with its contents, and with the introduction of symbolization, allegory, and sign, imagination gains increased synthetic mastery over its presentations that are imbued with "reason." Here the inwardness of intelligence "is *internally determined concrete subjectivity*, with *a capacity* of its own deriving" (*EG* § 456). Within fantasy, there is an imagined existence as hidden unconscious processes infiltrate the creative centers of subjectivity. This can be both monstrous and sublime.

While fantasy attains its most elaborate articulation in language and speech, it does not strictly require words in order to show itself. This may be achieved by the mind's manipulation of its own operations with respect to both content and cognitive functions, such as the confluence of certain feeling states attached to interrelated images. In fact, fantasy is the *a priori* condition for language, it is a pre-linguistic organization that precedes organized conceptual thought.[15] Here Hegel's position is Kleinian: fantasy precedes concept formation. While Klein, Bion, Segal, and others focus upon the content, motives, and qualitative attributes underlying the phenomenology of fantasy, Hegel clarifies the ontological processes that make fantasy possible.

Fantasy both symbolizes and engenders signs. Initially it subsumes singulars under a universal through symbolization, but because the immediate content is both a particularization and a universal, interpretation remains ambiguous. Fantasy becomes a central operation in unconscious production, a spewing forth of impulses and desires from the wishing well of the abyss. It may be suspended in space and time, conform to the abyss's will through regression or withdrawal irrespective of the ego's counter-intentions, and warp objective reality to the tone of the ego's own subjective caprice. This is why images may be either disturbing or pleasing. The "*symbolizing, allegorizing* or *poetical* power of the imagination" (*EG* § 456) is not confined to the mere subjective, however; it may take an external objective referent as the embodiment of its creativity. This move constitutes "the phantasy of sign making" (*EG* § 457).

Through signification, intelligence is concerned with unifying the relations between determinate content and what it signifies universally. The synthesis of fantasy is the unity of the sign with the universal and its self-relation. Hegel states, "in phantasy intelligence has being, for the first time, not as an indeterminate abyss and universal, but as a singularity, i.e. as concrete subjectivity, in which the self-relation is determined in respect of being as well as universality" (*EG* § 457). This statement suggests that universality itself is a sort of abyss, in that all particularity is lost in it, whether this be the soul's initial immersion with and undifferentiation from nature or its subsumption in universal spirit. Such unification of the sign with universality is seen by spirit as its own activity that is internal and proper to it. Here intelligence gives itself being which is now within its own capacity to do. Not to be underestimated in its importance, the sign "adds proper intuitability" to images as an objective existent (*EG* § 457). While the symbol refers to the intuition of the content and its relation to its essence and Concept, the sign *designates* meaning in which the content of intuition becomes dissociated to what it signifies (*EG* § 458). In symbolic fantasy, intelligence pays attention to the given content of images, but in sign fantasy it replaces imagined universality with objective affirmation – the presented universal is liberated from the content of images. Hegel tells us:

> The *sign* is a certain immediate intuition, presenting a content which is wholly distinct from that which it has for itself; – it is the *pyramid* in which the alien soul is ensconced and preserved.
>
> (*EG* § 458)

Hence intelligence proceeds from the pit to the pyramid, the soul sublated as intelligence gains more mastery over its self-designating operations. The content of intuition becomes "irrelevant" to what it signifies. Spirit may now focus on the signified universal rather than on the particular features of its intuited content. But before its final transition to memory, imagination must cancel its subjectivity, its internality, and give itself objective being. In this way it unifies "the universal and being, one's own and what is appropriated, inner and outer being, are given the completeness of a unit" (*EG* § 457). These operations belong to the mature liberated ego, a developmental progression from the primitive functions of unconscious fantasy guided by archaic forces.

Intelligence goes beyond the sign to understanding its meaning. With each new immediate intuition, intelligence moves from unconscious determinateness which transforms intuitions into images, images into representations, representations into associations, and is thus raised to the level of objective existence and self-determining being as sublatedness – a normative process conforming to the dialectic of projective identification. Intelligence is now presented (as presenting itself) with a "*tone*" from the unconscious soul "which intelligence furnishes from the anthropological resources of its own naturalness, the fulfillment of the expressiveness by which inwardness makes itself known" (*EG* § 459). Sound instantiates itself further in speech, and as the interrelations of words, in a system of language which endows the sensations, intuitions, and representations with a "second determinate being" that sublates the immediacy of the first. Spirit no longer needs the constant presence of external signs; when they vanish as ephemeral phenomena, intelligence draws upon its inner meaning and "inner symbolism" as it generates and relates to its own processes. Intelligence remains active, it confers meaning through sounds and words and as such becomes a sublated intuition for itself. Networks of meaningful relations are externalized as signs, and when they disappear the mind must reconstitute their significance through its own self-relating activity. Imagination first makes visible unconscious processes in the form of images, then manipulates their relations through fantasy, conferring symbolization and assigning meaning – the name, a word. When the name vanishes, imagination either must create a new name for its set of relations, or it must recollect a previous name and its meaning and attach it to new associations. This requires memory.

Intelligence has moved from its initial task of internalizing intuitions, to its externalization of the abyss through imagination, to which it takes its next shape as memory, the task of which is to integrate its previous two movements. While intelligence gains greater dynamic unity in verbal, reproductive, and mechanical memory, Hegel sees theoretical spirit through to its end, namely to thought as understanding, judgment, and formal reason. Thought knows itself, it *re-cognizes* itself which achieves its fullest logical elaboration as pure thinking: thought thinking about itself and its operations. While these are the greater faculties of spirit, they need not concern us here. Bion's model of ideographs is given richer articulation by Hegel's analysis of imagination which has further implications for understanding unconscious fantasy.

We may say that the types of thoughts and conceptions Bion speaks of during the ego's early development of thinking, linking, and fantasy are not the type of conceptualizing belonging to formal intelligence or reason, but are instead associated to the *functions* objects serve. I believe the pre-verbal ego constructs meaning not through concepts or words, but through images, impressions, and/or sensory-tactile sensations that are internally processed in relation to a felt referent and related to objects encountered in fantasy, either real or imagined. Thought is originally the succession of sensory impressions imbued with emotional mediacy linked to functional meaning associated with objects of experience. What becomes encoded or imprinted on the psyche is the functional qualities, properties, attributes, and consequences of the presence and experience of objects. Under the influence of internal drives and their derivatives – such as wishes and their vicissitudes – the nascent ego constructs meaningful relations to objects through the functional attributions of fantasy which are subject to the anxieties and/or pleasure associated with its own internal impulses and subjectively perceived object attachments. Images and sensory experience related to objects are imbued with functional meaning, linked to associative affect or corresponding feeling states, recorded, and laid down as memory traces in the deep abyss of the unconscious which are called up when fantasy is mobilized.

We are justified, I believe, in further saying that the nascent ego performs such mediatory operations by attaching functional meaning to objects in the form of qualities and their related expectations which take on the signification of the affects evoked corresponding to gratifying or anxiety-ridden associations. In effect, the ego assigns an object and the experience of such a task or job which is related to the quality and expectation it evokes, the represented meaning of which stands for the function the object serves. Thus sensory impressions become the original contents for the earliest modes of thought, first having their origins in the prenatal activity of the unconscious mind where the embryonic ego senses its own internality along with the predisposed preconceptions belonging to its various constitutional pressures. In the beginning moments of conscious life, the ego forms meaningful associations to objects based on the functional qualities and evoked affective states mediated through fantasy, a process that becomes more robust during language acquisition and formal concept formation. What Hegel refers to as the function of symbols and signs, or what Bion calls ideographs, we may speculate occurs at the crudest level of conscious life if not before. While the incipient ego does not think in concepts or words, the experience of objects is dialectically mediated through projective identification in fantasy which signifies various functional meanings. It is only when language is introduced that such mediatory relations acquire conceptual signification in the form of names and words.

We have seen the overwhelming presence and indispensable function of the nocturnal abyss throughout the stage of presentation, the necessary precondition for higher activities of mind to become manifest. Presentations are fleeting and much of memory fades, but it becomes imprinted within the soul and wells up from imagination. Hegel explains:

The power of memory is replaced by an unchanging tableau of a series of images fixed in the imagination. . . . Not only is spirit put to the torment of being pestered with a deranged subject matter, but whatever is learnt by rote in this manner is as a matter of course soon forgotten again. . . . What is mnemonically imprinted is as it were read off from the tableau of the imagination . . . and so really brought forth from within, rehearsed from the deep abyss of the ego.

(*EG* § 462)

As Hegel reminds us once again, intelligence is unconsciously constituted as ego. There can be no doubt about the importance of imagination and its relation to the abyss; spirit is as much dependent on imagination – especially fantasy – as it is on reason. In fact, their relationship is so intimate that it leads Hegel to say, even with stipulations, that "phantasy is reason" (*EG* § 457). Imagination therefore becomes the locus of the powers of the mind.

Toward process psychology

Hegel's anticipation of Klein's and Bion's theories of projective identification as the process of the self returning to itself due to its own self-estrangement adds to our understanding of both the normative and pathological processes of mind. In health and illness the ego projects certain aspects of the self onto the object world, which it then identifies with and finally re-introjects back into the subject. In effect, the self rediscovers itself in the product of its own projection and then reintegrates itself within itself as reunification. This is the generic structural movement of the Hegelian dialectic, whereby internal division, external projection, and re-incorporation function as a mediating and sublating dynamic.

With the introduction of the Hegelian dialectic, psychoanalysis may enjoy new vistas and advances in theory, application, and technique. There is a preponderance of evidence in traditional and contemporary psychoanalytic theory to conclude that the mind in general and the unconscious in particular is dialectical both in its structural organization and its internal content.[16] In general, psychoanalysis would contend that the dialectical modes of *Geist* are themselves differentiated and modified forms of the mind maintained through ego mechanisms of desire, intentionality, and defense.[17] Klein herself, as well as all post-Kleinians, constantly refer to the dialectical forces of splitting accompanied by projection and introjection that are responsible for both good and bad self-object representations as well as the general division between the ego and the object and the internal polarities that maintain rigid antitheses struggling for reconciliation. Hegel's emphasis on psychic holism mirrors the general consensus among Kleinians that the ego strives for wholeness guided by an orienting principle aimed toward increased synthetic integration – the primary motive of sublation. This is simply the dialectic of desire, the internal thrust of spirit that yearns for self-completion.

Although Klein discovered projective identification, which further led Bion to advance the distinction between its normal and pathological variants, Hegel was the first to articulate the formal structural processes of projective identification having its source and origins within the unconscious mind. Since Bion, a less pejorative attitude toward patients' use of projective identification has been adopted among clinicians, which has further initiated attempts to define different aspects and subtypes of this phenomenon differentiated by form and motive – such as the degree of control over the object, the attributes acquired, the need to protect certain positive qualities or to avoid separation, its relation to splitting, the force of evacuation, communication, etc. – all subsumed under a general rubric (see Spillius 1988).

As we have seen, Hegel's philosophical depiction of projective identification has implications for understanding psychic structure, psychosis and schizoid mechanisms, linking, thinking, symbol formation, fantasy, and containers and change. More recently this concept has been given special attention in its relation to countertransference and empathy (see Ogden 1982; Tansey and Burke 1989). Generally we may say that within the context of therapy, the patient projects onto the analyst certain disavowed and repudiated internal contents that the analyst unconsciously identifies with, such as the behavioral fantasies, attributions, or personal qualities that are the objects of splitting, which the analyst then introjects as a function of his or her own ego, thus leading to conflicted inner states that the analyst must manage. If the analyst's countertransference reactions are too strong and/or remain unrecognized as the internalized projected attributions of the patient, s/he may potentially act out such negative states within the therapeutic encounter, thus potentially leading to further internal disruptions in both parties negatively affecting the intersubjective field. Seeing how such a process is dialectically informed may auger well for further advancements in theory and intervention.

Hegel's philosophy may be especially significant for the future of psychoanalysis. His logic of the dialectic adds systematic coherency and philosophical rigor to the theoretical speculations and empirical verity governing psychoanalytic investigation. For Hegel, psychic life is a burgeoning process of becoming: the reality of the inner world as well as that of nature and culture is a dialectical enterprise. If we are to espouse Hegel's great insight that reality – including every intellectual discipline – is about *process*, evolution, and change, then his implications for psychoanalysis may bring about a new relation between wisdom and science. Dialectical psychoanalysis becomes an auspicious sign for realizing the value of process psychology.[18]

Notes

1 When Klein republished her 1946 paper, "Notes on Some Schizoid Mechanisms," in *Developments in Psycho-Analysis* (London: Hogarth Press, 1952), she added the term "projective identification" as a way of explaining the process of splitting in connection with projection and introjection (p. 300).

2 In his *Wissenschaftslehre* (§§ 1–3), Fichte discerns these three fundamental "principles" (*Grundsaetze*) or transcendental acts of the mind. Cf. Johann Gottlieb Fichte (1794).

3 For example, see Donald Carveth's (1994) incorrect assessment of Hegel's logic, p. 151.

4 Cf. Immanuel Kant (1781/1787), *Critique of Pure Reason*, Second Division: Transcendental Dialectic, Book II, chs I–II.

5 *Science of Logic*, trans. A.V. Miller (Atlantic Highlands, NJ: Humanities Press, 1812/1969). All references to Hegel's *Science of Logic* will refer to *SL* followed by the page number.

6 From the *Encyclopaedia*, M.J. Petry (ed.) outlines Hegel's Philosophy of Spirit in *Hegel's Philosophy of Subjective Spirit*, Vol. 1: Introductions; Vol. 2: Anthropology; and Vol. 3: Phenomenology and Psychology (Dordrecht: D. Reidel Publishing Company, 1978). Petry's edition provides a photographic reproduction of Hegel's original text published in 1830 along with the *Zusätze* added by Boumann when the material was republished in 1845. Petry's edition also indicates variations between the 1927 and 1830 editions of the *Encyclopaedia*. His edition has several decisive advantages over A.V. Miller's edition of the *Philosophie des Geistes* translated as the *Philosophy of Mind*. In addition to having the original German text and his notations of the variations between the 1827 and 1830 editions, Petry also provides notes from the *Griesheim* and *Kehler* manuscripts. He further provides an accurate translation of the word "unconscious" (*bewußtlos*) whereas Miller refers to the "subconscious." For these reasons Petry's edition is a superior text to the Miller translation. For comparison, I have also examined Hegel's 1827–28 lectures on the Philosophy of Spirit: *Vorlesungen über die Philosophie des Geistes* (Hamburg: Felix Meiner, 1994). I have mainly relied on Petry's translation but provide my own in places that warrant changes. Hereafter, references to the Philosophy of Spirit (*Die Philosophie des Geistes*), which is the third part of Hegel's *Enzyklopädia*, will refer to *EG* followed by the section number. References to the *Zusätze* are identified as such.

7 Cf. Petry, *Hegel's Philosophy of Subjective Spirit*, Notes to Vol. 3, p. 405.

8 Cf. *Inhibitions, Symptoms, and Anxiety, Standard Edition*, Vol. 20, p. 97. Hereafter all references to the *Standard Edition* will refer to *SE* followed by the volume and page number.

9 Compare to Freud, "The ego is first and foremost a bodily ego" (*The Ego and the Id, SE*, 19, p. 26).

10 For both Hegel and Freud, the inchoate ego is originally encased in a unity and is therefore modally undifferentiated from external forces – the inner and outer are fused in a symbiotic organization. Freud informs us, "originally the ego includes everything, later it separates off an external world from itself. Our present ego-feeling is, therefore, only a shrunken residue of a much more inclusive – indeed, an all embracing – feeling which corresponded to a more intimate bond between the ego and the world about it" (*Civilization and its Discontents, SE*, 21, p. 68). For Hegel, the natural soul moves from an undifferentiated unity to a differentiated determinate being; so too for Freud, ego boundaries gradually become more contrasted, constructed, and consolidated throughout its burgeoning activity. Freud notes that originally an infant is unable to distinguish between its own ego and the

external world as the source of stimulation and sensation. But eventually the infant comes to discern its own internal sources of excitation, such as its bodily organs or somatic processes, from external sources of sensation (e.g. mother's touch, breast, etc.), that become set apart and reintegrated within ego organization. It is not until this stage in ego formation that an object is set over against the ego as an existent entity that is outside of itself. Once the ego moves from primary to secondary narcissism, attachment to external cathected (love) objects forms the initial dynamics of object relations and character development.

11 Freud is often misunderstood to be a reductive materialist, relying on his unofficial and immature views espoused in the *Project for a Scientific Psychology* (*SE*, 1, p. 295). Freud realized that he could never offer an adequate theory of mind solely from a neurophysiological account and by 1900 had officially abandoned his earlier materialistic visions for a psychological corpus (cf. *The Interpretation of Dreams*, *SE*, 4–5, p. 536).

12 This point has also been discussed by Jerome Levin (1992), p. 51.

13 In the *Phenomenology*, Hegel tells us: "As Subject . . . the True . . . is the process of its own becoming, the circle that presupposes its end as its goal, having its end also as its beginning; and only by being worked out to its end, is it actual" (*PS* § 18). Later he says, "The realized purpose, or the existent actuality, is movement and unfolded becoming . . . the self is like that immediacy and simplicity of the beginning because it is the result, that which has returned into itself" (*PS* § 22). In the *Science of Logic*, Hegel further extends the development of the Self to that of the Concept: "The Concept, when it has developed into a *concrete existence* that is itself free, is none other than the *I* or pure self-consciousness" (*SL*, p. 583). For Hegel, the Self and the Concept are pure becoming: "The Idea is essentially *process*" (*Encyclopaedia Logic*, § 215).

14 Hegel offers a cursory description of thought disorder and insanity; however, a critical discussion of his contributions is beyond the scope of this immediate project. For a more detailed analysis of Hegel's theory of abnormal psychology, see Berthhold-Bond (1995) and Mills (2002) for a review.

15 For Hegel, fantasy developmentally and temporally precedes language or linguistic acquisition. In his discussion in the *Encyclopaedia*, §§ 456–457, fantasy occurs before symbolization and signification and "derives from what is furnished by intuition." It is not until § 458 that he introduces language proper.

16 Freud's conceptualization of the unconscious is organized by the dialectical exchange of psychic forces that seek to maintain some form of homeostasis. Within all psychoanalytic disciplines since Freud, there appears to be a universal dialectical interplay between the subject and the object. Historically, the post-classical movement in psychoanalysis emphasized the role of the ego as agent of unconscious activity and focused on the ego's motives toward mastery and adaptation of inner forces via defensive construction and transcendence over instinctual demands. While the classical position emphasized the pleasure-seeking aims of drives, object relations theories have emphasized the primacy of object relatedness as the central motive of unconscious activity oriented toward interpersonal involvement and relational attachment. Self psychology introduced the centrality of the self as agent motivated toward fulfilling "selfobject" needs of empathic attunement and validation from others, mirroring of self-worth, and the pursuit of idealized relationships all in the narcissistic service of the self. While the field of psychoanalysis has radically departed from Freud's metapsychology and presently focuses on relational theories, intersubjectivity, and contemporary selfobject theory, Freud's psychoanalytic theory remains subsumed as the theoretical foundation of contemporary thought. However, whether unconscious motivation emanates from the influence of

drives, the ego, object relations, or the self, all disciplines within the historical development of psychoanalysis observe the phenomenology of the dialectic.
17 See Freud's discussion, *SE*, 19, p. 24; 20, p. 97; 22, pp. 75–76. ·
18 This chapter was originally published in *The Psychoanalytic Review*, 2002, 87(6): 841–874, and is reproduced with permission by Guilford Publications.

References

Berthhold-Bond, Daniel (1995) *Hegel's Theory of Madness*. Albany, NY: SUNY Press.
Bion, W.R. (1954) Notes on the Theory of Schizophrenia. *International Journal of Psycho-Analysis*, 35: 113–118.
—— (1957) Differentiation of the Psychotic from the Non-Psychotic Personalities. In Spillius, E.B. (ed.) *Melanie Klein Today: Developments in Theory and Practice. Volume 1: Mainly Theory*. London: Routledge, 1988: 61–78.
—— (1959) Attacks on Linking. In Spillius, E.B. (ed.) *Melanie Klein Today: Developments in Theory and Practice. Volume 1: Mainly Theory*. London: Routledge, 1988: 87–101.
—— (1962a) A Theory of Thinking. In Spillius, E.B. (ed.) *Melanie Klein Today: Developments in Theory and Practice. Volume 1: Mainly Theory*. London: Routledge, 1988: 178–186.
—— (1962b) *Learning from Experience*. London: Heinemann.
Carveth, Donald. L. (1994) Selfobject and Intersubjective Theory: A Dialectical Critique. Part I: Monism, Dualism, Dialectic. *Canadian Journal of Psychoanalysis/ Revue Canadienne de Psychanalyse*, 2(2): 151–168.
Fichte, Johann Gottlieb (1794) *The Science of Knowledge*. Peter Heath and John Lachs (eds. and trans.) Cambridge: Cambridge University Press, 1970/1982.
Freud, Sigmund (1886–1940) *The Standard Edition of the Complete Psychological Works of Sigmund Freud*, 24 vols. James Strachey (trans.). London: Hogarth Press.
—— (1895) *Project for a Scientific Psychology*. (*Standard Edition*, Vol. 1).
—— (1900) *The Interpretation of Dreams*. (*Standard Edition*, Vols. 4–5).
—— (1920) *Beyond the Pleasure Principle*. (*Standard Edition*, Vol. 18).
—— (1923) *The Ego and the Id*. (*Standard Edition*, Vol. 19).
—— (1924 [1923]) Neurosis and Psychosis. (*Standard Edition*, Vol. 19).
—— (1926a) *Inhibitions, Symptoms and Anxiety*. (*Standard Edition*, Vol. 20).
—— (1926b) The Question of Lay Analysis. (*Standard Edition*, Vol. 20).
—— (1927) Fetishism. (*Standard Edition*, Vol. 21).
—— (1930) *Civilization and its Discontents*. (*Standard Edition*, Vol. 21).
—— (1933 [1932]) *New Introductory Lectures on Psycho-Analysis*. (*Standard Edition*, Vol. 22).
—— (1940 [1938]) Splitting of the Ego in the Process of Defence. (*Standard Edition*, Vol. 23).
Hegel, G.W.F. (1807/1977) *Phenomenology of Spirit*. A.V. Miller (trans.). Oxford: Oxford University Press.
—— (1812/1831/1969) *Science of Logic*. A.V. Miller (trans.). London: George Allen & Unwin.
—— (1817/1827/1830/1991) *The Encyclopaedia Logic*. Vol. 1 of the *Encyclopaedia of the Philosophical Sciences*. T.F. Geraets, W.A. Suchting, and H.S. Harris (trans.). Indianapolis: Hackett Publishing Company, Inc.

—— (1817/1827/1830/1970) *Philosophy of Nature*. Vol. 2 of the *Encyclopaedia of the Philosophical Sciences*. A.V. Miller (trans). Oxford: Clarendon Press.

—— (1817/1827/1830/1971) *Philosophy of Mind*. Vol. 3 of the *Encyclopaedia of the Philosophical Sciences*. William Wallace and A.V. Miller (trans.). Oxford: Clarendon Press.

—— (1978) *Hegel's Philosophy of Subjective Spirit*. Vol. 1: Introductions, Vol. 2: Anthropology, Vol. 3: Phenomenology and Psychology. M.J. Petry (ed.). (Dordrecht: D. Reidel Publishing Company).

—— (1827–1828/1994) *Vorlesungen über die Philosophie des Geistes*. Hamburg: Felix Meiner.

Hinshelwood, R.D. (1991) *A Dictionary of Kleinian Thought, 2nd edn*. Northvale, NJ: Jason Aronson.

Kant, I. (1781/1787) *Critique of Pure Reason*. N.K. Smith (trans.). New York: St Martin's Press, 1965.

Klein, Melanie (1929) Personification in the Play of Children. In *Love, Guilt and Reparation and Other Works, 1921–1945*. London: Hogarth Press, 1981.

—— (1930) The Importance of Symbol Formation in the Development of the Ego. In *Love, Guilt and Reparation and Other Works, 1921–1945*. London: Hogarth Press, 1981.

—— (1946) Notes on Some Schizoid Mechanisms. *International Journal of Psycho-Analysis*, 27: 99–110; In *Envy and Gratitude and Other Works, 1946–1963*. London: Virago Press, 1988: 1–24.

—— (1952) The Mutual Influences in the Development of the Ego and Id. In *Envy and Gratitude and Other Works, 1946–1963*. London: Virago Press, 1988: 57–60.

—— (1955) On Identification. In *Envy and Gratitude and Other Works, 1946–1963*. London: Virago Press, 1988: 141–175.

—— (1957) Envy and Gratitude. In *Envy and Gratitude and Other Works, 1946–1963*. London: Virago Press, 1988: 176–235.

—— (1958) On the Development of Mental Functioning. In *Envy and Gratitude and Other Works, 1946–1963*. London: Virago Press, 1988: 236–246.

—— (1960) On Mental Health. In *Envy and Gratitude and Other Works, 1946–1963*. London: Virago Press, 1988: 268–274.

—— (1963) On the Sense of Loneliness. In *Envy and Gratitude and Other Works, 1946–1963*. London: Virago Press, 1988: 300–313.

Klein, M., Heinmann, P., Isaacs, S., and Riviere, J. (1952) *Developments in Psycho-Analysis*. London: Hogarth Press.

Levin, Jerome D. (1992) *Theories of the Self*. Washington, DC: Hemisphere.

Mills, Jon (1996) Hegel on the Unconscious Abyss: Implications for Psychoanalysis. *The Owl of Minerva*, 28(1): 59–75.

—— (2002) *The Unconscious Abyss: Hegel's Anticipation of Psychoanalysis*. Albany, NY: SUNY Press.

Ogden, Thomas G. (1982) *Projective Identification and Psychotherapeutic Technique*. New York: Jason Aronson.

Segal, Hanna (1957) Notes on Symbol Formation. *International Journal of Psycho-Analysis*, 38: 391–397.

—— (1964) Phantasy and Other Mental Processes. *International Journal of Psycho-Analysis*, 45: 191–194.

Spillius, E.B. (ed.) (1988) *Melanie Klein Today: Developments in Theory and Practice. Volume 1: Mainly Theory*. London: Routledge.

Tansey, Michael J. and Burke, Walter F. (1989) *Understanding Countertransference: From Projective Identification to Empathy* Hillsdale,. NJ: Analytic Press.

Chapter 8

Childhood play as tragic drama

Walter A. Davis

For my Mother, Lu Davis (1914–2004)

Introduction

> You must become as little children.
>
> Matthew 18: 3

Recovering the tragic

My purpose is to restore the claims of the tragic and illustrate its powers as a way to think about childhood.

Heidegger speaks of the forgetting of Being as the central problem of metaphysics. I want here to recall another forgetting, which may be of equal significance, especially when our concern is with the psyche. Freud's deepest discovery was our self-division. There is in us something that demands our destruction. And there is something in us that radically opposes itself to that demand. Psyche is the battle between these forces.[1] Recapturing the tragic requires keeping one's eye focused at all times on that primary fact. We exist on the horns of a dilemma. If through compliance one violates oneself in order to attain the love of the super-ego, one creates a "false self system" to conceal an inner deadening. If one rejects the demands imposed on us by the other, one suffers an assault by a malevolent, punitive force that demands our destruction. The result: self-torture is the primary condition of the psyche. We try to flee awareness of that condition, however, and such flight character- izes the way the tragic has been theorized in the West since Aristotle. Freud constitutes a reversal of that tradition. What Freud shows, contra Aristotle, is that the tragic is not an avoidable event that befalls some subjects as a result of a flaw in their character, thus serving as a lesson of what happens when one loses contact with human nature (i.e. normalcy, rationality, social adapta- tion). Rather, the tragic is the situation that all subjects face, the condition implicit in being a subject.

Next to Freud no one has contributed more toward a tragic understanding than Melanie Klein. But even more than with Freud, constituting her contribution requires liberating her insights from her metapsychological framework. Klein's thought is vitiated by a central contradiction. Klein thinks she is developing a theory of life and death *instincts* that are innate and biologically grounded in the child when what she actually reveals is a condition that for personal reasons she is intent on denying: that childhood is the effort to deal with the effects that the imposition of another's Unconscious has on the struggle of the emerging psyche to preserve itself.

One of Klein's greatest discoveries takes the form of the following axiom: whatever conflicts a child is undergoing invariably turn up directly in their play. Childhood play, so understood, is not only adaptation, ego development, or discharge of tension. Nor is it merely a transitional experience. Childhood play is primal drama, the attempt of the child to mediate the traumatic emotional experiences and emotional conflicts that define it. The child's world is one of primary emotions joined in a life-and-death struggle. Meaning and meaninglessness, ego and narcissistic self-cohesion, these come later. For as Klein shows, children's play is a world of catastrophic anxiety, driven by the child's effort to preserve itself from destructive forces of a persecutory character. To enter our first world is to confront the agons of a psyche trying to maintain what Winnicott calls its "ability to go on being" through intense emotional reactions to the forces that prey on it.

Klein, unfortunately, explains that drama in abstract metapsychological terms, as if the child's task were to master instincts, that is, as if all the sources of difficulty have their origin within the child. The complex dramas she uncovers point toward something of far greater complexity, which exceeds and cannot be explained within the metapsychological framework of her thought. *Childhood is the experience in which one finds oneself invaded by the desires and unconscious conflicts of others.* Such is the condition one tries to mediate through play. Play is thus one of the most serious acts we will ever perform. For we are the result. The primary coherence and integrity we have as psychological beings is not a result of the development of perceptual, cognitive, linguistic, and social skills. It is a result of the dramas we create for ourselves through the act of playing. Such is the understanding of childhood that Melanie Klein makes possible. I will attempt to constitute it through a revisionary reinterpretation of the themes that are central to Klein's study of childhood. Such a reinterpretation will make no attempt to repeat or summarize her thought. Its purpose, rather, will be to articulate an understanding of childhood and childhood play that cannot be found in Klein but that she, more than any other psychoanalyst, makes possible.

Artistic self-mediation: between psychosis and neurosis/normalcy

My purpose in this chapter is to articulate the understanding of childhood play that can be derived from a critical reading of Klein's work and thereby recapture some of the more revolutionary ideas we can derive from her thought. What Klein saw (and couldn't explain) is that play, like art, is a form of self-mediation that is distinct from logical, conceptual, cognitive, adaptational mediation. That is so because it has for its subject the traumatic condition of the psyche. Moreover, play offers us a way of mediating that condition that is distinct both from instinctual drive-discharge and from those subsequent forms of conceptual, cognitive, and linguistic mediation that structure ego development. Unfortunately those alternatives control current conceptions of psyche – and with disastrous results. For what is thereby lost sight of is a mode of self-mediation that is beyond instinct and prior to the concept, with distinct capacities which are, as we will see, precisely those needed to shape the inner world and internal constitution of the psyche. To understand this possibility we need to develop a new category that identifies a way of being distinct from psychosis, neurosis, and normalcy and that provides principles of psychic development capable of mediating precisely what those ways of being are unable to mediate. Such processes, as we will see, offer the psyche the only way to deal with the tragic conflicts at the center of its being. That category is art or artistic self-mediation. Childhood play, I will show, is the key to its comprehension. Play founds a mode of self-mediation that is distinct both from psychosis and from neurosis/normalcy. Like the former it preserves the primary conflicts of the psyche. But whereas psychosis shows a psyche fragmenting and dissolving under their force, artistic self-mediation establishes our ability to work within them. It thereby also avoids the act that defines neurosis/normalcy: the effort of the ego to prosecute a vigorous fear and hatred of inner reality.[2] Mediation through the ego depends on superimposing the order of the ratio and the mechanisms of defense upon inner conflicts. The effect is a progressive estrangement from one's inner world. Artistic activity, in contrast, takes those conflicts as its subject matter. As such it constitutes our foremost and deepest way of acting upon ourselves. Sometimes such self-referring activity results in the production of artifacts. But the primary work of art even then is the one performed upon oneself. Childhood is our first effort to engage that task and through it to give form to our inner world. Indoctrinated in the rational and adaptational ways of mediation provided by the ego, most of us have lost contact with this way of being. One expression of that loss is the theoretical frameworks we impose upon the study of childhood so that it will develop according to the cognitive principles that only come to control us when we are firmly ensconced in that later world. To put it another way, we are estranged from self-knowledge because we have lost the ability to be as we once were when, as a child, we found in play a way to mediate what Tustin calls the heartbreak at the center of our being. Regaining an understanding of play constitutes, as we will see, the possibility of calling into question and reformulating many concepts central to psychoanalysis.

Psyche as agonistic self-mediation

> A child, through intercourse of touch
> I held mute dialogues with my mother's heart.
> Wordsworth, *The Prelude*

The reality of emotion

Here is one way to conceive the origin and internal structure of the Psyche. Psyche is what happens when the spontaneous vitality of the child is assaulted by the impositions of the m/other's Unconscious; that is, when the repressed conflicts and desires of another are transmitted to the child as demands on the child to be a certain way in order to fulfill the other's needs. *A child is a mother's unconscious.* The psychological birth of the human infant is the process whereby the unconscious conflicts of the m/other become the psychic condition of the child. The result I term the catastrophic condition. I will say more about this concept shortly. What I want to note here is the function of a similar awareness in the radically new concept Klein develops of the ego. Ego for Klein is neither a biological principle seeking the discharge of instinctual tensions nor a cognitive, developmental principle seeking the adaptations that define the defense ego. It is the struggle to stay alive, to maintain one's integrity as psyche in the face of experiences that threaten one's annihilation. The effort to go on being, to persist in its being, is the reality that defines the psyche.[3] As Klein shows, the core situation of the psyche is the anxiety of being destroyed from within. Psyche, as opposed to instinct, ego, mind, and brain is what arises when one is overwhelmed by another and wounded in one's very being. As a result, psyche is, in its inner constitution, the effort to maintain one's existence in the face of experiences that threaten one's annihilation. Life and death are not biological instincts. They are the fundamental terms of the agon or drama that defines the psyche.

The storm of primitive affects and actions that result from this condition create the terrifying world of infancy Klein describes. It is not, contra Klein, a world of instincts seeking discharge. It is a world of intense and inherently tragic intersubjective conflicts. Childhood is not about what happens when instincts are frustrated. It is about what happens when the other acts upon us in a way that threatens our annihilation. The inner world is first and foremost a fight for one's life, a battle between an internalized force that demands submission and what comes into being through opposition to that force. We exist *qua* psyche insofar as we are able to mediate ourselves within the register of what Bion and Winnicott call catastrophic anxiety. Such is the burden of primitive emotion and conflict in the development of the child's psyche.

As Klein sees, the first objects have only *emotional attributes*. That is so for two primary reasons: the radical openness of the child to the other and the depth of anxiety that is felt whenever that openness is appropriated for the other's emotional and psychological needs. Once again Klein foreshadows a revolutionary understanding that shatters the limits of the metapsychological framework in which she casts it. For emotion here is not instinct craving discharge nor a confused way of being opposed to and later supplanted by cognitive, rational control. *Emotion is the effort of the psyche to preserve itself by engaging in agon the forces threatening its destruction.* In short, emotion is here *cognition*. It is the way one knows the truth of one's condition and the way one expresses that truth. Or, to put it in a more telling way, it is how children reveal to their parents everything those parents deny. Childhood is that time when we have being and know solely through our emotions, that time when we have not yet learned how to lie. Tragically it is also the time when we face perhaps the deepest emotional conflict we ever will: the recognition that to be true to one's emotions is to risk persecution from those to whom one is, in one's emotions, intimately bound.

Childhood can profitably be viewed as essentially the battle over what emotions will be tolerated, rewarded, forbidden, made terrifying, etc. That agon is a function of how the child reacts to the demands of the m/other's psyche and how the mother in turn reacts to the child's efforts to defy or oppose her conscious and unconscious demands. Affect, feeling, emotion compose an order of psychic formation that is more primitive than language can express and more fundamental than the subsequent world of ego defenses and conceptual mediations that we superimpose upon our feelings in order to protect ourselves from them. Regaining contact with psyche requires a theory of emotion adequate to the task that defines childhood. That task may be defined as the effort to turn traumatic affect into agonized act. That is, to create tragic emotions where before there were psychotic states. Under the impact of the m/other's unconscious, the inner world of the child is defined by the attempt to find some way to act in a situation that will otherwise result in the dissolution and fragmentation of the psyche. Such is the function of emotions when emotion is all one has and when to feel is to be burdened with oneself in a fundamental way. For the child there is no alternative to emotion. To refuse to feel is to die within. Whereas to feel is to cognize one's situation as prelude to the necessity of agon.

To understand such a process we need a theory of emotion quite different from the reductive ways affect and emotion have thus far been conceptualized in psychoanalysis.[4] The theory I propose, which I can only sketch briefly here, is based on a fundamental distinction between primary and secondary emotion. Primary emotions burden the subject with the anxiety of conflicts that put it at issue and at risk. *Such emotions are defined by the absence of any inner distance between what one feels and who one is.* One is assaulted from within by the wound at the origin of the psyche. Secondary emotions, in contrast, provide the defense ego with ways to displace and discharge anxiety. The motives the ego requires for its maintenance – safety and self-esteem – find in secondary emotions the means to resolve conflict in a way that distances and protects the ego from the threat of disruptive experiences. In toning down and deadening experience, such emotions restore and reinforce the ego's phantom identity and its adaptational adherence to a world of consensual validations and reflected appraisals.

Let me illustrate the difference by offering definitions of two secondary emotions: *Pity* is the effort to short-circuit anxiety by turning suffering into something one can only experience passively as that undeserved misfortune that comes as a result of factors over which one has no control and thus limited responsibility. *Fear* is the effort to externalize anxiety by displacing inner conflict into concern over matters outside the psyche.

And definitions of two primary emotions: *Anxiety* is that existential awareness of one's responsibility to reverse the control that the other (parents, social and ideological forces) has over one's psyche. *Envy* is the need to destroy anything that makes one feel contempt for oneself or that activates a memory of possibilities squandered.

Primary and secondary emotions stand in a necessary, agonistic relationship. All secondary emotions are modifications derived from primary emotions, their function being to tranquilize the psyche by displacing anxiety into those discharge mechanisms that make us feel good. Secondary emotion is thus the main way in which the force of traumatic experience is indefinitely postponed. Our dependence on such emotions is another sign of the rift that separates us from the world of the child. For the child has not yet developed such abilities. It lives wholly within the world of primary emotions. Emotion is here the very being of the subject. As we will see, the movement of childhood is from the chaos of primitive affect to the binding of oneself to the force of those primary emotions one chooses because they are alone adequate to one's situation. As our original mode of cognition, primary emotion is the effort of the psyche to know its condition and to radicalize the way of feeling that most empowers it within that condition.

Such an understanding of emotion purges the psyche of all substantialism. The inner world is not a world of objects; it is a world of actions. All here is existential process. Psyche is action through and through, a process devoid of any principles that could eventuate in a substantial, essentialized identity.[5] We exist *qua* psyche insofar as we are able to create dramas out of the catastrophic experiences that put us at issue. As emotional self-mediation the psyche is beyond biology, prior to ego development, and independent of what those frameworks can comprehend. The understanding of primary emotion is the key to a truly concrete phenomenology of the human subject.[6]

Qua psyche the only development is self-overcoming through agonistic self-mediation. This is the life of the psyche we have lost contact with and must regain if psychoanalysis is to be true to its mission.

Intercourse of touch: psyche in its origin

In attaining the condition that requires play for its development the psyche in the course of infancy goes through five distinct dramas or developments that bring it to the tragic exigencies of its condition. (1) *Subjectivity* has its origin in an affirmative flow of vital energies that derive from prolonged experiences of joyful interaction in mutual loving recognition. Psyche here is a *spontaneous vitality* that is awakened by the nurturing presence of another. In this its first form *I am* is an *elan conatus* – a desire to sustain intense experiences of expanding well-being – that seeks neither discharge nor quiescence. (2) The first transformation of psyche comes with the rupturing of this desire. The *subject* experiences the assault of a destructiveness that attacks the ability to go on being. The *I am* drifts toward extinction as it fragments in states of pure catastrophic anxiety. (3) The tension between its first two experiences makes the subject ripe for the next transformation. It comes in abrupt shifts from eroticized pleasure to hysterical anxiety as the other projects their unconscious conflicts and desires into the child. Subjectivity becomes the turmoil of negative intensities: rejection, disgust, prohibition, and fear experienced as the conditions of embodiment. (4) The *I am* has become a fundamental confusion about one's body-psyche and the damage its expression does to the other. *Qua* subject one oscillates between a tidal wave of aggression in which one drowns and the panic anxiety of an incessant self-unraveling. The resulting condition is a desperate effort to clutch at opposition as the only way to preserve one's being. (5) The inner condition of psyche is now that of a being emptied of everything save abandonment and an abjection that is terrified by itself. The *I am* has become a being assaulted by the *call of its own freedom, thrown into existential dread over the contingencies it must assume. Such, in depth, is the process of transformation that takes place during childhood.*[7] The outcome is the burden that makes us human: the need to reverse one's condition, supported in that effort by nothing save the principles of self-mediation that have arisen in the course of the experiences outlined above.

This account, of course, presents the pivotal events of childhood in the later language of concepts. For the child it all happens in a much more immediate way. Through touch. Touch is, as Wordsworth knew, that process in which the body becomes body-ego through intercourse with another's psyche.[8] What follows is an attempt through vignettes drawn from my own childhood to offer one picture of the course of that experience. In effect these vignettes are the empirical illustration of my argument. They are not so, however, in the manner of observational science (as in Bowlby say) or child case material. In an attempt to articulate something these methods cannot know I follow a very different method. My hope is that the vignettes will operate like a dream or a day residue to activate processes in the reader's unconscious that will restore contact with those experiences of childhood that we have lost contact with in psychoanalysis precisely because they cannot be measured or known by behavioristic examination. To state the contrast in terms of an obvious objection to my approach: it will be said that children are incapable of the kinds of experience recorded in the vignettes. My reply: we can't yet say what the child can or cannot know because we don't know all the ways that the child does know; the ways that the traumatized body, for example, knows and sustains that knowledge as a future bequest to consciousness. The recovery of such experiences, of course, activates strenuous defenses in the adult ego. Those defenses form the other side of the contract I offer the reader in what follows. Understanding the theory will in some ways be a function of what the reader is willing to open up in his or her psyche.

(1) First born, my father away in the military, I am alone with my mother for prolonged periods of silence and slow time, at the breast or in her arms while she hums and sings to me snatches of old lauds or coos smiling on me like the sun. In prolonged intimacy, after the satisfaction of physical need, in the tenderness and caressing that accompanies that intimacy a new process, beyond or more than the biological, begins. In the pure affirmation of my being by another I bloom in the outpouring of an affirmative energy that is unbounded, an ecstatic flow of affect that seeks neither discharge nor quiescence but the continuance of heightened sensations which are sought and prolonged as pure ends in themselves. My mother's loving attention brings about my second birth: the emergence of an *elan conatus* that is immediate and ex-timate and that holds nothing back in opening and extending itself toward the other in an embrace that is total and unreserved. William Blake's energy is eternal delight is here experienced as the genesis of an *I am*, a *Sum* that is prior to and beyond all cogitos. I here co-incide with myself in the sheer, unbounded joy of being alive.

Touch is here the soothing caress that flows into an affirmation of being that pours forth toward an unhindered embrace of life in all its forms. *Psyche* as spontaneous vitality is the effort to preserve and expand a condition of ecstatic joy.

(II) Another experience persists alongside the ecstatic one. My mother and I live with my grandfather and grandmother. The latter I will later learn is the key to my mother's psyche. All I know now, because I experience it directly, is the force of one of my grandmother's many fixed beliefs. Babies should not be allowed to cry. Belief for her is always backed by practice. Whenever I cry she hurries to where I am and shoves a bottle of milk into my mouth while berating my mother for her inability to know how to care for her child. In her anxiety my mother too sometimes uses this method when my noises threaten to bring on another of her mother's outbursts. I thus experience a way of being antithetical to the one I love. Often, crying, I am grabbed, lifted quickly from the crib and turned violently by fingers that press down hard on me. Thrashing, the bottle is shoved in my mouth and held down there. Sometimes the rubber nipple becomes a hard, intrusive point rubbed aggressively against my gums. I gag, unable to swallow. But the more I thrash about the harder the pressure becomes. It is bearing down on me, suffocating me. *I am* now no more than a phantasmagoria of wheeling motion in slivers of bright light dwarfed by huge, looming shadows. I choke on the rancid taste in my mouth. And then I become it, the pressure that is bearing down on me. My being concentrates into a dense point that shatters, crushed in the grip that holds me. What Winnicott calls "the ability to go on being" dissolves in a drift toward inner death. The only way to stop it is to stop crying. But I can't. And then I do. It becomes something else: it bleeds inward in a self-laceration that weds panic and rage to a state of self-torment.

Touch is here an abrupt force that insists on bending me to its will. Psychological birth proper comes with this experience. Spontaneous vitality recoils under the assault of a destructiveness that ruptures the continuity of being and threatens the ability to go on being. The *I am* fragments into states of pure catastrophic anxiety.

Yes, reader, your initial experiences might have been quite different than what I have presented in the first two vignettes. But what were they and what did they do to you?

(III) I am alone with her, with the source of warmth and comfort – at the breast – once again restored to a prolonged state of caress and sensual sucking that is after and independent of the satisfaction of hunger. My mother is calm. Restoration hangs upon her lips. All that was broken can be repaired. And so she lets herself go, relaxing as in a warm bath to the sensations that cascade through her. She swells in the wellness of being and I am one with her in this, in the interchange of quickening sensations. And then, as if to the ringing of an inner alarm, anxiety seizes her. The swelling nipple is abruptly withdrawn. Attempts to retrieve it are met by a refusal mixed with panic. Everything that has happened between us must now be turned into its opposite and with an equal intensity. My mother is in inner turmoil. Her breath is heavy, forced. Her voice broken, high-pitched. Her eyes dart about. Her face which a moment before smiled from within collapses in on itself, Picassoed in a constriction that wells up in tears choked back by the guilt that has seized pleasure and turned it into shame and shame's duty – inversion. Desire must become disgust; permission, prohibition; mutuality, abandonment; with all this communicated in the immediacy of a touch that has become cruel and insistent in its demands. I am held in an embrace that is claustrophobic then abruptly pushed away, a being given over to the anxiety of a fundamental confusion. Intercourse of touch has become a self-division at the heart of intersubjectivity.

Touch is here the abrupt shift from erotic pleasure to hysterical anxiety. Caught in that turmoil, one internalizes and becomes a fundamental confusion about one's body psyche and the damage its expression does to the other. Shame and guilt are born, empowered with the ability to withstand all attempts to overcome them.

Do you have analogous experiences, unremembered, that persist in another way: as emotions you feel toward yourself that you can't get rid of?

(IV) When I am 15 months old my mother and I take a long trip by train to visit my father at a naval base where he is stationed. The first night there my mother decides to solve the problem of my frequent crying that has made her life at home a nightmare. Asleep, I am put in a crib in a room alone. My parents retire to an adjoining room. In the night I wake and cry, anticipating the quick soothing comfort that always comes then to quiet me. Nothing happens. Now in panic anxiety I anticipate the angry hands pressing the bottle down into my gums, tumbling me into the dark suspiration of breath in which I expire. And so I cry out for her to come first and save me from this. Nothing happens. Time passes. The cry becomes something else: louder, frantic as I thrash about. It is everything now. I feel it on me in the hot, sticky plastic of a mattress that has become one with my own sweating skin. I'm burning in it, on fire in my own crying. Somehow thrashing about I hit on something hard, grab onto it, and work my way up and over the bars of the crib onto something hard and cold. I crouch there in the dark, screaming, my fists clenched in an effort to hold myself together – to stop myself from becoming nothing but the scream. How long this lasts I'll never know. Time is contracted to a point of rage and I am one with it in the dark spiraling into the dark nothing. Eventually they come of course and find me there like that, on top of a dresser, my red face bathed in sweat, my fists balled in a rage, screaming.

Touch is here the absence of anything within that can stem the inner panic of endless falling into an abyss, an engulfing nothingness. Subjectivity is the tidal wave of an aggression in which one drowns, a panic become rage. In its desperation the *I am* clutches at opposition as the only way to sustain a remnant of its being.

Could experiences like this be more common than we realize and more central to the constitution of the psyche than we want to admit? Can you know again how it was for you when spontaneity and basic trust confronted an absolute No? When, perhaps, you held yourself together in the only way you could – through some mode of anger?

(V) Three months later, on the precise day that I am 18 months old, I am weaned and, by account, reach out of my own volition for milk that is in a metal cup before me. I take the cup to my mouth and drink. Something happens in my throat then. I gag, unable to swallow what curdles within me. I'm choking but I can't swallow. My throat constricts. Then everything becomes the effort to turn myself inside out. I vomit up the milk and dash the cup to the ground. How many times this experiment is repeated I can only imagine. What I know is that the result is always the same. The moment milk enters my mouth I retch within, gag, choke, then vomit what I am powerless to swallow. (I have never been able to drink a glass of milk my entire life.) The moment I first feel free – the moment the bottle is no longer forced upon me – I experience what has been happening inside me for a long time. Only now I act from that place. I am the upsurge of a negativity that expresses itself in an absolute expenditure without reserve. Freedom here does not derive from an autonomous Sartrean spontaneity. It rises out of abrupt reversal within a terrifying passivity. My first action is a violent effort to evacuate what was shoved down my throat.

Touch is here an uproar from within, an abrupt and violent reversal, a nausea that acts. Deracinating itself from within, subjectivity is the demand for an active reversal that is lived long before it is cognized. A *subject* has emerged. This happens when natural, biological processes are blocked then transformed into something else: symbolic action as self-definition. But with no relief, resolution, or catharsis. One is the anxiety one becomes as a result of one's action.

And for you, reader, what was your first experience of freedom? Did it come naturally as the fruition of natural developmental processes or was there something in excess and traumatic in its genesis?

The experiences evoked in these five vignettes present the origin and first form of what I will term, with a bow toward Kant, *the psychological imperative*. That is, they trace the *existentializing* modifications in its self-reference that necessarily occur if psyche maintains its awareness of what it means to live with one's being at issue. Psyche is the issue of traumatic experiences, experiences that are not products of natural frustration or of biological instincts and their maturation. They are the result of ruptures within intersubjective relating, of what happens in the child as a result of the m/other's projection of her unconscious conflicts as demands that affect the very form and emergent identity of the infant's psyche. As psychological birth, childhood is the process whereby the parent's psychological conflicts are transmitted so that they become the conflicts, the self-division, and the self-torture of the child. To put it more concretely, this is the dilemma that defines the inner world of the child *qua* psyche: *the desire to restore a way of being one has lost in order to escape an inner torment one cannot bear*.

The psychotic core

A final concretization of the child's condition completes the foundation we need in order to understand play. Thanks to Klein and her followers we now have a complex understanding of the psychotic condition – and its origin in the child's experience.

The psychotic lives in the world of a nameless dread that cannot be mediated. No boundaries separate the self from the destructive other. The only response, accordingly, is rigidity or chaos – schizoid withdrawal into affective numbing or an endless Munchian howl. One is bound in a self-mutilating identification to an inner persecutor from which one is unable to separate oneself. All one can do is shift rapidly and mechanically, back and forth, between hypervigilance and hyperactivity. One has found no way to symbolize or verbalize one's conflicts. The result: whenever the brittle defenses that enshroud the psyche are shattered the psyche unravels in the return of fragmented, meaningless visual images of a violent, intrusive, and terrifying nature. They are what haunts one, the terror one has been unable to survive except by severing it off from the brittle shell in which one trembles, awaiting their inevitable return. Dissociation is the only relationship that maintains in the phantom psyche's inner world. Consequently, any troubling experience can only activate a self-paralyzing trinity: fright, flight, freeze. For such is the basic relationship that the psyche has to itself. An artificial core of sanity covers over the sense of inner pollution. The split between the two is of necessity harsh and unremitting. Surface calm and practiced adaptation conceal an inner world frozen in the following conditions: a pervading sense of betrayal and abuse at the hands of hostile forces; an absence of trust, especially in oneself; an oscillation between emotional flooding and a ceaseless effort to maintain a precarious control over emotions that are so overpowering and so chaotic that they leave nothing in their wake save the scorched earth of the psyche they ravage. Beneath it all, this: a hostile super-ego presides over a persecutory realm in which the tortured subject ceaselessly bows in a submission that leaves nothing save the head permanently bowed in anticipation of the blow. Such is the psychotic condition.[9] Self-mutilation, the eroticization of fear, compulsive self-abuse, the courting of danger, the equating of pleasure with shame and humiliation are the dominant signs of the underlying psychic economy – a personality in permanent capitulation to the forces that destroy it. As Bion argues, the psychotic world is defined by a ceaseless attack upon linking. That, as we will see, is why play is so important. Play forges the only links that enable us to mediate that condition.

Play

> I prayed to rediscover my childhood, and it has come back, and I feel that it is just as difficult as it used to be, and that growing older has served no purpose at all.
>
> Rilke

If we are lucky most of us spent most of our waking hours between ages 2 and 7 engaged in a single occupation – playing. But working one's way back into a knowledge of how one was then is a redoubtable enterprise. The most important thing to remember when studying childhood is that the way we were then is something we have forgotten. We were once in our being very different from the way we are now and operated by principles that follow a radically different logic. That fact sets our task: to feel our way back into a way of being we have lost, to become again as a child and experience the world the way we did then.

Art as existentializing cognition

My purpose in what follows is not to study play in all its forms but to apprehend its innermost, most significant possibility, and thereby integrate

Klein's essential contribution by describing the structure of self-mediation through which play confers on our subjectivity an identity we can attain no other way. Here is a general formula defining the nature of play. Play is the activity whereby the child takes the catastrophic anxieties of its condition and transforms them through the power of symbolic actions to create those primary emotions that give order to the child's inner world by actively reversing the force of inner destructiveness thereby bringing about a psychological identity that is inherently tragic and engaged in the effort of active reversal.[10] What follows develops each key concept in this definition.

From catastrophic anxiety to symbolic action

Play is the way children symbolize the conflicts and the emotional truth of their situation. It is an attempt to say what one is not allowed to speak, to represent what can be represented in no other way. As such it is the founding moment in the movement from passivity to active reversal. Play is an attempt to mediate the catastrophic condition that defines psyche at the end of infancy. It takes overpowering affect and turns it into primary emotion through the construction of symbolically self-liberating agons. Such is the act through which the psyche gives form to itself by imposing order on the chaos and conflicts that define its inner world. As drama, play is the effort of the child to take the anxieties of its primary condition and form from them symbolic actions that address the wound and the heartbreak at the core of the psyche. So understood, play is not primarily discharge, pleasure, adaptation, or wish-fulfillment. It is conflict mediated in the only way it can be – by taking action within oneself. Play is not the escape from anxiety.[11] It is the child's way of working on and within anxiety. And as such it is the act whereby we lift ourselves beyond instinct by finding another way to relate to conflict, a way that sustains and works upon it rather than taking flight from it. Psyche, as distinct from behavior, matures through that act.

From affect to primary emotion

Thereby traumatic experiences become primary emotions of an I who is capable of self-representation and who acts – even if only upon itself – on the basis of the self-knowledge given through one's feelings. Play is an attempt to fathom, discover, and create the truth of what one feels. Thereby play enacts an irreversible transformation of psyche's relationship to the anxiety that defines it. Symbolic action is the process of taking action on and within one's heart in the crucible of those searing experiences in which one feels the catastrophic force of the m/other's psyche. Thus through play the heart's abiding affections are formed through an *inquiry* into the heartbreaking nature of one's condition. Bion says inquiry begins when love is doubted. Play is the sign that that process has begun. As such it is not the evacuation of feelings.

It is, rather, the operation one performs on what one externalizes. Getting one's feelings out is merely the first moment of the process. The determinative operation is what one subsequently does with them in the action one creates out of them. Play is the true "labor of the negative": a dynamic rejoinder to the other's imposition of their unconscious conflicts and desires on us. For play binds the overpowering affects of our subjection to images that memorialize trauma. In so doing play creates the permanent record of what will become the dynamic unconscious, that buried register which preserves in image those experiences in which our being was existentially at issue.[12] Ego development covers over this register of the psyche. Repression crypts it. Art attempts to recover and explore it by reawakening the distinct cognitive power of the principles of mediation that play introduces into experience.

From inner chaos to inner world

Play is the effort to give order to the conflicts of one's internal world by turning passive suffering into articulate drama. That movement constitutes its inherent direction. Through play the psyche transforms itself from the initial chaos of an inner world ruled by overpowering forces to a realm defined by definite conflicts that reveal to the psyche the actions it must take in order to reverse the power that the other, as destructive super-ego, has over its being. To put it in correct terms, play does not reflect the inner world; it creates it. Through play one discovers the ability to impose form on oneself by creating rules that follow no dictate other than a logic of feeling. That logic is the inner principle that structures dramatic engagement and through it a mediation of experience prior to the conceptual order and beyond its organizing abilities. As the first and primary way in which the psyche mediates itself, play makes possible the movement from evacuation and projective identification to the creation of agons whereby *conflicts* are *bound* to the possibility of *actions* capable of bringing about irreversible changes in the very structure of the psyche.

Play as active reversal

In effecting that transformation play is the origin and first form of active *reversal*, the act whereby we take what passively overwhelms us and turn it into an opportunity to mediate ourselves. Through such action within and upon oneself psyche moves toward the only kind of freedom and autonomy we can hope to attain, one that depends on the overcoming of those internal forces that originally render us powerless. As such, play is the first realization of tragic integrity. We possess inner coherence and integrity *qua* psyche insofar as we are able to mediate ourselves artistically at the register of our most traumatic experiences. Other subsequent forms of mediation have little to do with this, the most important act we perform, except as props that help the ego flee the inner world. In play the psyche discovers the one method adequate to its condition. We are the conflicts that define us. The construction of symbolic actions represents the original and deepest ordering activity whereby the psyche acts on itself. That activity is prior to rationality and beyond the capacities of conceptual mediation. Drama is our primary mode of being, the activity whereby we give form to ourselves by mediating the conflicts that define us. The child lives in the immediacy of that destiny. That is why the way one plays as a child is of such overwhelming importance to one's future life.[13] It is through play that each child forms the principles, the competency that will control their emotional response to experience. That is the enormous and inescapable task of childhood. The child is called to the act that has the greatest consequences: the creation of the emotional conditions that will regulate all of one's subsequent perceptions, cognitions, and actions in *matters of the heart*. This is the deepest way in which the child is father to the man. As adults we often discover, shockingly, that what we are now able to feel, confront, and engage is a function of what we felt when, as a child, in playing we worked upon our heart and gave it form. For that is what psyche is: one's ability in situations of conflict to feel and act from one's primary emotions.

The most important theoretical implication of the above is the fundamental difference between the forms of self-mediation found in play and those that structure ego development and cognitive psychology. Play reveals that the true life of the psyche is prior to them and beyond their powers and thus that the paradigms current in psychoanalysis are inadequate to the understanding we seek. The world of play is a world of traumatic tasks that have little to do with the tasks of cognitive development and ego adaptation. Such operations are of little use when one is faced with those situations that threaten the extinction of one's ability to go on being. Moving that issue to the center of theorizing is the task facing a science of the psyche, if by that we mean a discipline that refuses to resolve psyche into something else: mind, brain, behavior, cognitive development, ego adaptation, linguistic competence, or social adaptation.

The Unconscious as form-giving power

> A man's [*sic*] work is nothing but a slow trek to rediscover, through the detours of art, those two or three great and simple images in whose presence his heart first opened.
>
> Camus

What is it about play that enables it to do all these things? That is the question. Answering it necessarily begins with a reflection on creativity in general.

Formlessness, reverie, and unintegration are essential to the onset of play.[14] It is only then that one feels free in that freedom where being lost is the condition for discovery. Bertrand Russell speaks of the joy of not knowing the solution as the condition for mathematical and scientific discovery. Only when one doesn't know is one free to explore. Such freedom is the primary condition of play. All must be *sui generis*, ruthless, unbounded by rules. For the creative person, not knowing does not cause anxiety; it quickens the recovery of inner resources that are non-analytic. Genuine creativity is one with the feeling that one is creating totally out of oneself, finding in oneself what was unfound before. The surprise of unexpected discoveries is one with the sense of recovering one's deepest feelings and impulses. Each advance accordingly requires deepening one's contact with those things one has buried in oneself. Creativity is regained access to one's original contingencies.[15] The freedom one feels is not just freedom from rules and restraints; it comes from the sense that one has tapped an inner spring of infinite expansiveness which is sharply opposed to the limitations that analytic processes place on thought and awareness. To search is here a joy that transcends insistence on a solution. Moreover, anxiety and suffering are welcomed as integral to the activity. That is why genuine creativity is a source of great anxiety for most people: it requires that one live for long periods of time in a state of unintegration and formlessness and then sustain the anxiety of what rises up in one's consciousness once one has broken with the defenses that structure the ego. Tolerance of anxiety and willed suffering are not incidental to creativity; they are essential. One is free to explore only when one refuses to abridge or interfere with that process. From one point of view creativity can be seen as a shattering of the ego and a loss of the principles on which it depends. For the creative person, however, this loss is felt to be a source of immense power since it entails the recovery of everything that the ego represses and denies. In creativity we recover not only an abandoned way of functioning but also those things buried in ourselves which have that way of functioning as their subject matter.

The freedom one feels is the possibility of a new edition; that is, the possibility of relating to one's deepest crypts in a transformative way. One need not collapse in nameless dread before one's inner world for one has recovered a way to work within the space of one's deepest anxieties. But only if one abides in the anxious joy of knowing that being lost, without a solution, searching in ways that make no sense, appalled by frightening discoveries, leaps of imagination, unexpected connections, and a true ruthlessness in relating to oneself is the path to discovery. The creative person knows that search is only authentic when freed of the need for an answer, especially those answers imposed by the world. True creativity is one with a joyful embracing of anxiety as the source of self-discovery. By the same token, creativity is blocked for most human beings not because they lack talent but because the rigidity of their ego boundaries makes it impossible for them to experience the states out of which creativity flows as anything but sources of an anxiety that must be arrested. The greatest wrong done to creativity, especially in terms of the child, is the phobic belief that one can only create when one is free of anxiety. Creative joy, in contrast, is the feeling that one has finally found a way to work within the space of one's primary experiences and anxieties, that one need not repress or despair because one has finally embarked on the task of recovering a "self" or inner world one never knew or only knew long ago when one was a child, before one lost or sacrificed it to the claims of everything that it renders meaningless. Creativity embraces suffering and turns it to account because it has found that within which is equal to it.

For most of us (sadly) little of the above can be recovered or endured for long. For the child, however, there is nothing else. Faced with the deepest anxieties, under the threat of psychotic dissolution, the child finds in the act of playing a power equal to its condition. What poses a threat to the ego and is rendered unintelligible by the attainment of rationality has a different being for the child. And fortunately the child has not yet developed these ways of being. The split between consciousness and the unconscious, between what one knows and its repression, has not yet taken place. The child lives in the immediacy of the Unconscious. In play its principles of operation freely express their powers to order experience. (There is, of course, one remnant of this in all of us: in dream we enter again a world and a way of functioning we once lived.) Play is the process through which the forms of ordering that define the Unconscious develop and achieve determination. That movement may be schematized as follows. Through play the Unconscious develops from that primary process which knows no no in the expression of desire to the development of modes of binding, of image making, whereby the psyche regulates its relationship to itself.[16] To renew Coleridge's insight into the nature of the imagination, the Unconscious is that which "dissolves, diffuses, and dissipates" all that is fixed and determined in order to create an order that is one with our power to evolve form out of that which is chaotic and overwhelming. For example, the making of images that epiphanize the tragic impact of our most traumatic experiences is the creation by and of a self that only exists through the construction of that dynamic Unconscious that stores those images as the permanent record one must access in order to confront who one is and how one feels. Art is an attempt to restore our contact with that register of our being, the register we lived in when as a child we played.

While it is our purpose to praise play as an activity informed by the ordering principles of the Unconscious, it is important to take note of how often play falls short of its *telos*. Otherwise we will confuse the true article with the many things that can overtake the child on the way to it. Play has its pitfalls and inherent limitations. Some of these have to do with the limits of externalization, as when the study of play is limited to the study of the child's use of toys and objects. One thereby fails to see all the ways in which drawing, painting, and storytelling are crucial forms of play. Other limitations derive from the seductive power of easy solutions. Play can easily become mechanical and repetitive. The simplest, most brutal solutions often triumph. Too often play stays too close to bodily processes of discharge. The symbolic capacity is shrunken before it can develop when all one has been given to play with are war toys or barbie dolls. But the greatest dangers are within. Omnipotence strives to arrest complex symbolizing of internal conflicts. Play can easily become manic, with triumph, contempt, and dismissal substituting for more complex engagements. The release of aggression can become an end in itself, as can a masochistic wallowing in the repetition of self-punitive rituals based on identification with the aggressor. Prodded in the wrong direction, play can also become too safe, too far removed from anxiety; an artificial way to make oneself feel good by displacing an anxiety into repetitive, self-soothing gestures. And, of course, there is the danger from the culture: one can become Disneyfied and find the creative possibilities of play colonized by infantalization, i.e. by the child's internalization as conditions of its pleasure the infantile desires that adult culture imposes on children in order to indulge pretty beliefs that have nothing to do with childhood. The only way to overcome all these dangers is by sustaining the trick of true play: to suffer so that one's suffering becomes creative. For unless creativity remains one with the massive problem that defines it, a formalism of pleasure will overtake its vital function in the psyche.

(VI) At age 2½ I am given stuffed toy dolls of Mary and her Little Lamb. I loved the lamb ("whose fleece was white as snow") and did my best to keep it from getting dirty. But every chance I got I took Mary and threw her in the toilet. Sometimes I simply left her there. Other times I tried to climb up on the toilet seat to reach the chain and flush her away. Sometimes I'd be caught, like that. Other times Mary was returned to me – clean, dry, pristine, saved. Later, in response to my repeated efforts, she was often returned to me wet, soiled. I'd grab her then and run toward the toilet, arrested by the clap of my mother's hand on my butt, my upraised fist held in the gesture of throwing away the one toy I was destined never to lose. For this little drama always has the same end. Gently, sometimes jokingly, but always in a clear insistence on its truth, my mother presses Mary into my hands, telling me once again: "Look. I found her. Mary. You don't want to hurt her. You love Mary." It is as if my mother and I have set out together to rewrite the *fort/da* game of Freud's precocious grandson, Ernst. My entry into language is into the art of lying so that I'll learn to lie to myself about what I feel.

> And you, what was the experience like for you when the word
> became the bearer of messages that hollowed out a new space
> within you?

The pictures one draws and the stories one invents when one first learns to play
are not finally the most important thing. Much of children's art is forgettable,
though one also finds here many remarkable abilities that are lost around age 8
and seldom regained: a bold use of color to endow objects and people with
symbolic meaning; a freely experimental search for expressive, surreal forms; a
self-contained world in which everything is symbolically connected; patterns
of repeated images that rework persistent concerns in strikingly new ways.
Children's stories too are often heartbreaking in their loneliness, their singular
acts of courage, the nakedness with which lovelessness and the overpowering
need for love are expressed, the willingness to lay bare the terms of one's
despair. And also often something else: the ability to represent what can't be
put into words or what one is soon taught one dare not talk about: violation,
abuse, cruelty, dark secrets of the family brought into the uncompromising
light of day. If we had before us the full body of artistic work of a 3- or 4-year-
old child it would tell a complex story. But the deeper story would remain
the one told through it: that of a psyche striving to give form to itself by
developing the creative powers needed to sustain that struggle.

(VII) My efforts were dominated by Chicken Little. Chicken Little, a
simple story with a happy ending provided by a paternal *deus ex
machina*. But that's not what I remember, nor what I saw each time
my mother read it to me. I keep seeing an upturned and frighted face,
gawking: then the paralyzed motion of one frozen in the posture of
running. A mad scurrying about, a frenzied tale, and a parade of
terrified listeners huddled together in tight circles, oblivious to the
natural beauty all around them. I drew that story and colored it and
painted it again and again. Finally I got it right. Chicken Little's horri-
fied face looking backward as he ran furiously without moving under
the pressure of dark clouds of great mass and weight. And then the
terrible breaking up of the sky into huge jagged planes of slate blue
descending on us like shattered glass, descending toward the silence
of a wide open mouth screaming without sound. Unseen by Chicken
Little in his desperate passage, strewn at the side of his path, are
flowers banked in sunlight. Their stalks are broken, one and all, and
yet the flowers continue to bloom. The sun shines down on them
like honey then disperses itself in gentle showers upon their eager
smiling faces. But Chicken Little never sees this reality. Someone
else does. For the first time however he is not only the one in the

picture but outside it also. He has painted it and stands apart –
beyond the picture frame – viewing the scene as a whole. The stories we hear become the stories we retell in an attempt to fathom
what it is in them that arrests the imagination and astonishes the
heart.

Which ones had that effect on you? What story did you tell and
retell yourself until you got it right?

The truth of play is the complex inner adjustment that is effected through it.
In discovering the power to create one discovers the power to impose form on
oneself. One is no longer trapped in the need to discharge painful feelings.
One has found a way to take what one feels, withdraw deep into oneself and
there work on it until it comes out in a new form – one revealing one's power
to master experience not by denying it but by giving it expressive form. One
has found that the place within us to which we can always retire is a place of
immense power fitted with the ability to internalize experience in a new way.
One no longer has to fear one's inner world for one has found a way to create
images that arrest horror, submitting it to the ability to give form to oneself
through an activity that is bounded by nothing save the scope of the imagination. Which is to say that it is bounded by nothing save the limits we impose
on ourselves in confronting the limits imposed on us by those experiences that
are universal because they alter the very terms of the relationship that the
psyche has to itself. Their study constitutes the next step in understanding play.

Mood, death, the melancholic position

Who shows a child as he [sic] really is? Who sets him
in his constellation and puts the measuring-rod
of distance in his hand? Who makes his death
out of gray bread, which hardens – or leaves it there
inside his round mouth, jagged as the core
of a sweet apple? . . . Murderers are easy
to understand. But this: that one can contain death, even before
life has begun, can hold it to one's heart
gently, and not refuse to go on living,
is inexpressible.

Rilke

Klein's discovery of the depressive position reveals that there are certain
times when we enter into ourselves in a prolonged state of contentless
brooding. Nothing definite is thought about. The world of practical activities
and concerns drops away. We are arrested by the claims of something else,
something that cannot be represented, that gives us no information, nothing

to know and nothing to do. And yet we feel in us the movement of something profound which transforms and deepens our relationship to ourselves. We have entered the world of Mood. To attain what it offers we must sustain the long delay through which that which is fundamental announces itself in the very indeterminacy through which it works within us. Mood, as Bollas argues, is non-representational knowing.[17] Its mode of development is soliloquy: that speaking to oneself about oneself in a language of feeling that is dark to itself yet uniquely compelling. One feels oneself held in the grip of a movement toward one's own unexamined depths. Mood attunes us to a process that operates by a logic radically different from that which informs all ways of thinking and acting that are grounded in the ratio.[18] In mood a different order of awareness and of reflection announces itself through questions that are themselves radically indeterminate: who am I? what does it mean to be a human being? what should I do? what may I hope? why am I unable to break the hold that such questions have over me? Mood is the ability to sustain these questions as questions so that they can work upon us. Here insistence on an answer shows that one has not understood the question. Equally absurd is the later demonstration – dear to those philosophers intent on dismissing the experience from which philosophy derives – that such questions are metaphysical and therefore meaningless. Common sense also proves of little use here. Such questions cannot be clarified or limited by confining them to a particular field of inquiry or discipline. Their scope is comprehensive. One only begins to understand them and why mood is the necessary medium of their development when one sees that they have two ineffable realities as their referent: (1) the fact of being alive, and (2) subjectivity as the relationship one has to oneself in terms of the responsibilities that being alive imposes on us. Accordingly, comprehension here is a matter solely of feeling and of deepening the claims of what one feels. Mood is the self-transformation of psyche through the deepening of a relationship to our ontological situatedness. Such is the transformation that enters the child when it discovers death. For death is what I've been talking about in the foregoing, mood the experience whereby it becomes a fundamental regulator of the psyche.

(VIII) A window seat filled the bay window at the front of my grandfather's house where we lived until I was 7. This is where I play. Crayons, pencils, coloring-books, blank tablets are everywhere, at my fingertips. I am surrounded by books, which my mother reads to me as I draw. My mother and I are alone here, in long hours of slow time. Nothing intrudes on the solitude of a play made sacred by all the ways she encourages the development of my imagination: freedom in the drawing and coloring of pictures, delight in the memorization of nursery rhymes, the enchanted reading of stories bathed in the music of her voice and the comfort of her smile. This is the timeless space in which I play, dreaming on things to come.

But this day is different. I sit at the window and look out, waiting for my mother. The long afternoon becomes evening before she returns. Someone had come to sit with me, but soon retreated to another part of the house. What I remember most about this day is being alone, the whole day, looking out at a world receding from me. All the treasured objects around me that made this space the hallowed place of play also recede. I drew no pictures, imagined no stories. Something else was happening now in the long hush of another kind of time. I felt it in the cold pressure at my forehead each time I leaned against the window and gazed, in mute reverie, at something I knew and did not know and was calling on myself to know. No pictures formed; no words came. I was free of memory and desire. Something new was entering me, pure and entire, and I was held in its spell. I felt no fear, no anxiety, no effort to escape, no craving for expression. Everything had become strange in a discovery that was awesome and singularly compelling long before it became terrifying. I collected myself in silence, waiting within the change I felt taking place in me. And then I took it into myself fully and became one with it in the simple acceptance of an ineradicable fact. And in that fact the world was new made. Everything had become tremulous, like the unsubstantial realm outside the window, glistening with an unspeakable beauty that was one with the question that now spread itself across the twilight sky.

The evening too was uncanny. It was like I wasn't there, like all the relatives and neighbors who gathered had formed a silent conspiracy to take no notice of a child wandering around in a room full of adults. I'm sure my mother came and hugged me, but I can't remember that. What I remember is the look of something frightened in her eyes and something forbidding in her manner. She sat with my grandmother and my aunt in a corner at one end of the room, in three chairs propped together. The others stood in groups, in hushed conversations, a striking contrast to the alcoholic boisterousness and rich laughter of most family gatherings. Each group would move, as if on silent cues, to sit for a time with the three women in the corner. I wandered among them, undetected. And so the evening too entered me purely. It was as if what had held me the long afternoon had passed unaltered into its formality permitting me to see the adult world in a new way. It had lost its bright solidity and become as strange and forbidding as the things I now saw in the faces of those I thought I knew so well. They no longer formed a charmed circle. They were bound together by something else.

But this circle could be broken into only by knowledge. How long I waited, summoning myself in what I didn't know was courage, I'll never know because the moment was timeless. I saw my Uncle Don, standing alone in the hallway, on his way back from the kitchen, a drink in his hand. Why I chose him I'll never know. He was the most formal of my mother's brothers and had in him a smugness and a stiff superiority. There he stood, motionless, unable to move forward, halted by a child blocking his passage. I'll never forget the trapped, fearful look on his reddening face, the attempt to turn away, and the coughing as he cleared his throat. "How's grandpa?" I asked him. "Not so good," he mumbled forcing his way past me. It's a sentence I've never forgotten, my entry into a new experience of language. Language is what we use to avoid the truth; to keep everything at a distance.

It didn't matter. I knew already. What he couldn't tell me. It's what I'd been knowing the whole day, seated at my window. It started with a scream that woke us early in the morning. "My God Sarah." That was all he said, to my grandmother. The stroke seized him as he sat on the edge of the bed. There was a dull thud then, but all we heard was the scream as she rushed into the room and grabbed at my mother. Often in sleep (and without waking) my grandmother would make a howling noise like a fire-engine. She kept making it now, trembling as my mother sobbed into the phone. I'm told I never saw him. That I was kept in another room until long after the ambulance came and took him away. It didn't matter. I had all I needed for death to do its work in me as I sat all the long day and took it into myself and remade myself in its image.

All playing is preparation for what Rilke calls the pure event that defines childhood. That event is the internalization of death, the experience that totally transforms the subject's relationship both to itself and to experience. Play is thereby deprived of the circumstance that prevents it from becoming truly serious – the sense of limitless possibility bounded by nothing but the free play of our imagination. Death puts an end to that. That which absolutely resists desire brings about a transformation of desire. Play is now projection of possibility submitted to an awareness of our eventual non-being. Through the internalization of death, play binds itself and is bound to the fundamental contingencies. In discovering death we are born into that finitude that makes us human: mood, or inner brooding, as that attunement to the eternal questions through which a subject now at issue to itself gives itself self-representation as *who/why*, that is, as a subjectivity forever bereft of any substantial identity, a *who* defined by the act of bringing the question *why* to every experience. Mood is that transformation of our emotional being that is pivotal in the development of the psyche. Through it *who am I?* becomes a question that is lived as the heart of one's inwardness.[19] So understood, death is not the end of childhood. It is childhood's deepest experience, where everything in one's opening of oneself to experience is measured by the reality one must internalize in order to live. Through death the *elan conatus* becomes existential subjectivity. Art, or play, is thereby assigned a new task, the sustaining of melancholic awareness as the inner space in which one must play, not in order to make reparation but in order to complete childhood's journey to self knowledge through the creation of what I term the fundamental fantasy.[20]

The fundamental fantasy

Work of the eyes is done, now
go and do heart-work
on all the images imprisoned within you; for you
overpowered them: but even now you don't know them.
Learn, inner man, to look on your inner woman,
the one attained from a thousand
natures, the merely attained but
not yet beloved form.

Rilke, "Turning Point"

The fundamental fantasy is the effort to compose an *image* or *symbolic act* whereby we picture to ourselves the fundamental terms of our condition, the possibilities of our identity. There is no greater, more complex artistic effort. Everything that composes play here receives its fullest actualization in the creation of an image that fuses and epiphanizes all that one has internalized in the long labor that is one's childhood. Fantasy for the child is radically different from the trivial affair it becomes for most of us. For the child it is, quite literally, a matter of life and death, a true confrontation with the force of thanatos in the psyche. The drama of childhood play is the ability to dream and in dream to construct those fantasies that image the truth of one's inner condition.

(**IX**) I must have dreamt it, countless times, in bits and pieces before it all came together and entered my waking consciousness with a force that made everything else unreal, a film dissolving into a single image at the center of a single room. Still a child, dressed in the little blue Navy suit modeled on the one my father wore, I lie in a casket in a dim room lighted only by candles. All the family is there, hushed, seated in a circle, like mannequins frozen in formal poses and ritual gestures. I am calm. All struggle is gone, all protest. I accept what has happened in a spirit of love and equanimity. Only one thing remains. A request. Without moving I ask them to make an exception to a rule that I already know cannot be broken. But it is the thing I need more than anything. And so I ask them again to bring Brownie, the teddy bear I love, and place him next to me so I won't be alone. It is a plea but there is no panic in it, yet no hope that it will be heeded. And so finally in the great rush of what must be love I accept it all. It is what they've been waiting for, the thing that enables them to cry. The cry grows. It is the bond that unites them, giving them the identity they need to be a family. This knowledge is the central reality of the fantasy. It frees me to what I now know I must do. I'm alone then, down in a crypt, in a cold stone place, a realm of shadows in a dim twilight. I go forward, toward a casket. I see myself lying there, in it — and I become what I see. A child is sleeping, beautiful and resigned. The beginnings of a smile are frozen on his lips. But no one will come to kiss them back to life. He will stay like this forever. He is sleeping but he will not awaken.

And for you, what is the fantasy buried deep in your unconscious that you must recover if you are to begin to fathom the truth of your childhood?

The fundamental fantasy is an attempt to represent one's identity in terms of *who* one is for the Other and what it means to be a function of their desire. In completing the task of play the fundamental fantasy thereby performs the following functions in the self-mediation of the psyche:

1   It pictures the true terms of one's inner world in terms of its impossibilities and tragic contradictions.
2   The question *who am I?* receives the answer that one dreads.
3   The psyche poses to itself the two key Lacanian questions: (a) am I alive or dead? (b) who am I for the other?
4   It reveals that the core problem of the psyche is not to secure the good object but to expel the bad object.
5   It pictures the fading or dissolution of the subject under the force of thanatos, thereby staging what Winnicott sees as the question that defines the depressive position: the fear that hate will be stronger than love. In the fundamental fantasy this fear is confronted, represented, suffered.

6   The terror that haunts the psyche is represented as something that has already occurred.

7   And yet, in the teeth of it, one takes action and sanctifies that action. In the fundamental fantasy a lacerated heart has the courage to find agency even if the agency is only to picture the worst.

That is why the fundamental fantasy constitutes an irreversible act of self-mediation. In it one represents the truth of one's condition in an image to which one binds one's psyche at the very moment one represses that awareness. Crypted, that image remains the deathless cry of what is most vital in us, what we must recover in order to initiate the long and arduous process of coming back to life.[21] The conscious fantasies that preoccupy the adult mind are displacements of all the above. That is their reason for being and the unconscious significance that we place on making them as trivial and self-indulgent as we can. Once again the child knows better. And suffers that knowledge in the only way one can – through the agon of articulate art.

Conclusion

> Genius is the ability to re-enter one's childhood at will.
>
> Baudelaire

My effort has been to trace the self-mediation of the psyche from the traumatic condition that exists at the end of infancy to the darkly compelling condition that marks the end of childhood. That movement is one with the development of *play* as the activity through which the psyche attains the ability to represent itself to itself and thereby achieve the coherence of an I, a subject that knows and experiences itself as who/why, a being endowed with an inwardness that is attuned to the conflicts and the emotional energies of the inner world and their sharp opposition to the principles of flight that shape the development of the ego. Perhaps that is why genuine art is so radically destabilizing. It wants to take all that claims to be solid and that is often no more than a tissue of lies and submit it to the creative violence that takes place whenever one begins to play.

Notes

1   There are many other ways to conceive the human being – and to study the child – than the one attempted here: in terms of mind, behavior, cognition, social adaptation, language acquisition, etc. But in terms of a psychoanalytic understanding of the conflicts that make us human they constitute perhaps so many displacements, revealing ways in which we flee our subject. Overcoming naturalism and substantialism remains, however, the philosophic task facing psycho-

analysis. On this see my *Inwardness and Existence* (Madison: University of Wisconsin Press, 1989). The current effort to ground psychoanalysis in biology and neurophysiology moves in the antithetical direction. As a result it finds no way to know the ways that psyche differs from mind, brain, and behavior. The method of the present chapter offers one way to recapture that difference.

2 This is one of Winnicott's greatest and least understood ideas.

3 The allusion here is to Spinoza's conatus rethought along vitalist and existentialist lines.

4 For a seminal sorting out of theories of affect and emotion that have been developed in psychoanalysis, see Ruth Stein, *Psychoanalytic Theories of Affect* (New York: Praeger, 1991).

5 The finest effort to develop such a position remains Sartre's *Being and Nothingness*. My attempt, however, is to ground existence in a way quite different from Sartre's quasi-Cartesian method and, of more importance, at a point in experience prior to and beyond both the preflexive order and the cogito.

6 That is, to a study of the human being that would be truly concrete where Hegel's necessarily remains abstract, tied to the ratio and the imposition of logic and the order of the concept upon experience.

7 And thus to an actual genesis of the existential, a grounding of its emergence in experiences that are prior to the more abstract ways in which Sartre and Heidegger posit it.

8 There is one experience in which some of us regain contact with this way of being – the experience of sexual intercourse as intersubjective touch.

9 One purpose of this description is to suggest that much of what we call neurosis is a concealed psychosis and much that calls itself normalcy but a further attempt to delay or flee that underlying psychosis.

10 For Bion's seminal articles on this see *Second Thoughts* (New York: Jason Aronson, 1983).

11 For a discussion of the pivotal concept of active reversal, see *Inwardness and Existence*, pp. 259–265.

12 The weakness in Winnicott's otherwise remarkable understanding of childhood is his insistence on focusing on the good enough mother and splitting her off from the other (and perhaps dominant) experience of the mother. As with Klein, personal factors were determinative here: the mother Winnicott sought and the one he had were quite different. Unfortunately, the weakness in Winnicott's approach has become the dogma of his followers, especially in the argument that creativity in the child comes only when the child is free of anxiety.

13 For the theory of the Unconscious introduced here, see my *Deracination: Historicity, Hiroshima, and the Tragic Imperative* (Madison: University of Wisconsin Press, 2001), pp. 133–150.

14 To allude to one of Freud's most famous statements: with respect to play even more than with respect to neurosis one must listen to the details of one's illness in order to derive from them much of value for one's future life; namely, the principles that will enable one to give order to one's psyche.

15 All who attempt to develop a psychoanalytic theory of art are indebted to the pioneering work of Anton Ehrenzweig, *The Hidden Order of Art* (Berkeley: University of California Press, 1967). What follows draws on several of his formulations but places them in a context quite different from his metapsychology.

16 On art as concern with one's original contingencies, see Otto Rank, *Art and the Artist* (New York: Knopf, 1932), and the first volume of Sartre's *The Family Idiot* (Chicago: University of Chicago Press, 1981).

17 I develop this theory of the image and its connection to the dynamic Unconscious in *Deracination*, pp. 203–212.

18 See Christopher Bollas, *The Shadow of the Object* (New York: Columbia University Press, 1987), pp. 99–117.
19 Heidegger is the philosopher who, in *Being and Time*, first brings mood (*Befindlichkeit*) to the center of thought. In this, as he knew, he followed Rilke.
20 This view is antithetical to the concept of reparation which controls Klein's understanding of the depressive position. Perhaps reparation is, as Glover suggested, a reaction formation. Or, perhaps, the final prop needed to assure the absolute status Klein insists on giving to the wholly good mother in the structuring of the psyche. In reparation we purge ourselves of any doubts we may have had about her goodness; and confess that our untamed instincts have been the sole source of trouble. Melancholic consciousness is an attempt to sustain a more tragic understanding of one's psyche. Lacan used the term fundamental fantasy. As will become apparent, however, while the concept performs an *a priori* structuring function in Lacan, it refers in my theory to an existentializing act.
21 I allude here to the concepts of the crypt image and the thanatoptic image, which form the culmination of the theory of psyche and the Unconscious developed in *Deracination* (see pp. 222–235). In closing I want to indicate here that the present chapter constitutes a theoretical supplement to my recent book *An Evening With JonBenét Ramsey* (Nebraska: Universe, 2003). I there attempt to dramatize the tragic understanding of childhood that I have here theorized.

Chapter 9

Attachment, metaphor and the relationality of meaning

Keith Haartman

In affectionate remembrance of David Bakan, teacher and friend.

The basic semiological concepts of "meaning" and "signification" shape how we depict "the bonds of affection" (Bowlby 1988, p. 73) – the emotions that accompany attachment. We speak of "meaningful relationships" and "significant others." Put simply, meaning is an object relation and object relations generate meaning. Melanie Klein made the groundbreaking claim that symbolism, consciousness and relationality form an indivisible whole. The ego's relation to its objects, both internal and external, dictates the scope of symbolic awareness and reality testing. Many of Klein's followers refined her psychoanalytic legacy precisely by finessing her semiological insight and broadening the clinical and theoretical implications.

This chapter reviews Kleinian works on the relationality of meaning and suggests that the bonds of affection in attachment represent the same emotional bonds that wed the signifier to the signified in metaphoric thinking. Love binds the symbol to the symbolized. I hold that because metaphor and attachment are themselves mutually dependent, the traumatic disruption of attachment to primary objects impedes the intrapsychic attachment between unformulated affects and ideational signifiers. Psychic integration, affect regulation, and mentalization – all core constituents of the depressive position – occur when the ego remains open to the psyche's unconscious and spontaneous creation of metaphors.

Also, by prioritizing the role of metaphor, I argue that we make a significant error if we view symbolic equations and beta elements as nothing more than regressive or degraded forms of thought. "Dead metaphors," to use Don Carveth's (1984) evocative term, remain dead only to the ego. Unconsciously, a sophisticated intelligence – a covert mentalization rooted in attachment affects – continues to work in the service of the depressive position.

The relationality of meaning

A host of psychoanalytic thinkers recognize the relationality of meaning. Mary Main's Adult Attachment Interview (Main *et al.* 1985) assumes that narrative competency – the ability to "make meanings out of the inchoate flow of an 'unstoried' life" (Holmes 1993, p. 146) – correlates with secure attachment. Stephen Mitchell, the most influential spokesperson for relationality in psychoanalysis, also defines the treatment principally as a "method for generating meaning" (1997, p. 24). Similarly, James Grotstein holds that in lieu of a one-person drive model, postmodern psychoanalysis has witnessed the rise of a new duo: intersubjectivity and "semiotic meaning" (1995a, p. 287).

Among the schools of psychoanalysis, nowhere is the idea of meaning as an object relation more apparent than in Kleinian thought. Klein (1988) argued that the phantasied relations between self and other determine the vicissitudes of representational thought and conscious experience. Klein made the simple, momentous discovery that the link between ego and object mirrors the link between symbol and symbolized.

Kleinians implicitly view meaning as an object relation by (a) emphasizing, in their own idiom, the intrapsychic dimension of attachment through concepts of linking and integration, and by (b) showing how the state of the link, whether acknowledged and accepted *or* denied and destroyed, directly affects symbolism and thought.

For Hanna Segal, "problems of symbol formation must always be examined in the context of the ego's relation with its objects" (1988, pp. 163–164).

> Disturbances in the ego's relation to objects are reflected in disturbances of symbol formation. In particular, disturbances in differentiation between ego and object lead to disturbances in differentiation between the symbol and the object symbolized and therefore to concrete thinking characteristic of the psychoses.
>
> (p. 163)

Segal's notion of "symbolic equations" belongs to the paranoid-schizoid position where boundaries between ego and object remain blurred due to projective identification. Here, blurred relational boundaries create blurred semiotic boundaries; the symbol merges with the symbolized so that fiddling on a violin literally equates to masturbation. With an awareness of the object's separateness in the depressive position, the ego maintains a distinction between symbols proper and symbolized objects. Fiddling now becomes a metaphor for masturbation and not masturbation proper.

Segal defines symbolism as a "three-term *relation*" (emphasis added; p. 163) between the symbol, the ego, and the thing symbolized. She cites Klein's 1930 paper, *The Importance of Symbol Formation in the Development of the Ego*, where Klein briefly describes her analytic work with Dick, a "psychotic" 4-year-old on the autistic spectrum. According to Klein, Dick's terror of his aggression forced him to obliterate his attachment to the object, along with his capacity to symbolize and his ability to think:

> The defense against the sadistic impulses directed against the mother's body and its contents – impulses connected with phantasies of coitus – had resulted in the cessation of the phantasies and the standstill of symbol formation.
>
> (Klein 1988, p. 224)

Dick's mental development stalled because his anxiety kept him from symbolizing his aggression. Without symbolism, Dick failed to relate to his aggression and regulate it through fantasy. He was "devoid of affects" (p. 221). Klein and Segal stress Dick's lack of "interest" in the external world. The term "interest" hints at something crucial. Dick radically detached himself by withdrawing his emotional investment, his "libidinal interest" (p. 220), as Klein puts it. Because he severs his "affectional bonds" (Bowlby 1988, p. 73) and forsakes his attachment, Dick fails to symbolize the world and to see it as anything more than a sensorial chamber of surfaces and pulsations.

With Segal's three-termed relation in mind, I suggest that an emotional decision to attach to other humans is intrinsically tied to symbolism. The primary libidinal bonds of attachment between ego and object are identical to those that attach symbols to what they symbolize. When the ego cathects a valued object upon which it depends, it simultaneously propels symbol and symbolized into a relation. As Segal points out, the Greek term *symbol* means "bringing together, integrating" (1988, p. 171). Yet note the symbols that Segal includes in her paper: a violin that stands for a genital; pencil shavings for bits of mother's body; a gluttonous witch for greedy impulses and so on. Each of these embodies a particular type of symbol – a metaphor. Symbolic equations refer to reified or "dead metaphors" (Carveth 1984).

Consider Thomas Ogden's account of the schizophrenic conflict (1980). Schizophrenia involves a "conflict between wishes to maintain a psychological state in which meaning can exist, and wishes to destroy meaning and thought . . ." (p. 513). Ogden's model consists of four stages each distinguished by an increased sophistication in symbolism, thought and meaning.

The initial phase of "non-experience" (pp. 519–522) amounts to a state of meaninglessness: no feelings or thoughts, no curiosity, and no emotional differentiation between experiences. The patient treats the therapist like an inanimate object indistinguishable from other objects. Gradually, from out of the blankness, comes a nascent yet meaningful comprehension of the therapist. In this second phase of diffuse "projective identification" (pp. 522–524), patients become fleetingly aware of feelings of deadness and meaninglessness.

But by attacking the frame and mocking the therapy, they violently project these feelings into the therapist. Yet most importantly, the therapist acquires emotional value as a discernible object available for projective relief. A greater degree of "object relatedness" accords with an improved capacity to link thoughts together (p. 523).

Patients in the third "psychotic" phase (pp. 524–527) permit themselves even greater degrees of mental freedom. While they regularly fragment their emotional realizations, their thinking relies more heavily on the phantasmagoric, on the widening scope of metaphoric associations (albeit the bizarre sort that correspond to symbolic equations). Ogden views the florid quality of psychotic thought as an emotional breakthrough that occurs as the therapeutic relationship deepens: "Here the therapist is valued, not simply as a partially separate container for [the patient's] projective identifications, but increasingly as a separate person whose loss can be feared and to a small extent mourned" (p. 526). In the final stage of "symbolic thought" (pp. 527–529), patients discover or recover an ability to play, to communicate coherently, and to reflect on their thoughts and experiences.

Because Ogden intends mainly to establish the conflict between meaning and non-meaning in schizophrenia, he alludes to, but pays less attention to, a point I want to underscore. *Gains in symbolism dovetail with gains in attachment while conflicts between preserving and negating meaning dovetail with conflicts between preserving and negating object ties.* In Ogden's model, meaning and relationality are like synchronized watches. They behave like alternate frequencies on an identical spectrum.

Ogden claims that as the schizophrenic conflict subsides, the patient "attaches meaning to his perceptions" (1980, p. 529). Ogden's use of the term attachment may represent more than a linguistic coincidence. The semiological "attachment of meaning" between signifiers and signifieds increases as patients gradually come to value (e.g. Klein's "libidinal interest") and attach to the analyst.

But how does the patient actually attach meaning to perception? The linking properties of metaphor may provide the answer.

Patients first emerge out of the void of non-experience by bonding to the therapist. Although primitive and based on projective identification, the bond as an "object cathexis" is real and marks the patient's tentative entry into meaning. Because projective identification provides the blueprint for the attachment, we can say that the object cathexis – the awareness of the therapist as meaningful and as something more than a mere perceptual trace – is a product of metaphor. The therapist-object first acquires meaning and value in the form of an "orientational" metaphor (Lakoff and Johnson 1980, pp. 14–21), that is, as a spatial container that "houses" another metaphor, the patient's corporealized emotions. Intolerable feelings gain expression through an "ontological" metaphor (pp. 25–32) that "attaches" the inarticulate quality of affects to concepts of physical substance. Portrayed perhaps as feces or "shitty feelings," the patient transmits his substances across an imagined trajectory, displacing them into the hollow repository of the therapist.

Ogden implicitly reveals how metaphor orchestrates relationality. The external object of attachment comes into focus through an intrapsychic attachment, through a conceptualization that relates a perceptual schema to a pre-existing ideational schema. A virtually meaningless, sensorial representation of the therapist attaches, via metaphor, to a simple, usable concept – a spatial container with an inside–outside boundary. With this linkage a cathexis occurs. The patient becomes aware of the analyst because the analyst morphs into an actual concept. A fledgling part–object relation now ensues. The point I want to make here is deceptively simple. The spontaneous appearance of a metaphor that differentiates and separates the therapist from the background mist of non-experience is intrinsically linked *and therefore a necessary outcome* of the patient's emotional decision to attach to the therapist.

In stage three, the patient's awareness of the therapist's separateness becomes more apparent and the emotional relationship grows more complex. Meanwhile, thanks to a simultaneous and dramatic disinhibition of metaphor, imaginative capacities gain complexity, producing innovative forms of psychotic fantasy.

While these metaphors appear as symbolic equations, such equations are better than no equations. Ogden describes a patient who smoked cigarettes and equated the burnt ashes with valuable bits of himself. He wanted to eat the ashes to help his body "put them back together" (1980, p. 524). Symbolic equations depict thoughts and feelings as literal objects inside the body. "Psychological processes," writes Ogden, "are felt to be methods of physically handling these objects" (p. 525). Again we see an unformulated affect, a painful sensory perception, attach to a consolidated concept of cigarette ash.

Even though the metaphor appears irrational and concrete, it seems to condense a host of possible experiences all in dire need of mental representation (e.g., burning rages and desires; the anality of ashes; the genitality of cigarettes). Also, the ontological metaphor of *substantive* feelings helps the patient to stop ejecting his experiences and to claim them *as his* via the primitive and figurative contiguity of swallowing. We even detect a reparative urge, a wish to put the ashes back together. Ogden states that in stage three, the patient begins to observe and think about the psychosis; he "dimly recognizes himself as the author and container of his terrifying feelings and thoughts" (1980, p. 526).

Grotstein's work on primitive mental disorders also epitomizes meaning as an object relation (1990a, 1990b, 1995a, 1995b, 2000). Grotstein views objects and thoughts as "interchangeable" (1977, p. 435); meaning arises when sense impressions "link up" with objects (1990b, p. 148). Like Ogden, Grotstein claims that a dialectic between meaningfulness and meaninglessness (1990a, pp. 30–31) shapes the psychotic and borderline conditions. For such individuals the dialectic of meaning follows the dialectic of ambivalence – the conflict between holding on to and getting rid of ties to other people. Psychotics and borderlines cannot "determine the meaningfulness of the self or of the self's relationships – and, for that matter, of experiences generally" (1990b, p. 140).

Disruptions of the bond between baby and mother account for states of severe meaninglessness. "These individuals," writes Grotstein, "have subtle to profound difficulties in engaging or being engaged (attached) to and by (bonded by) their mothers" (1995a, p. 301). "Orphans of the real" (1995a, 1995b), or infants exposed prematurely to unsymbolized experience, endure unfathomable horrors of black hole nothingness, of sheer absence and primal indifference. Conversely, maternal attunement weaves a protective fabric of innocence whose "fantasmal underpinnings" of symbol, illusion and fantasy "make sense" (1995a, p. 305) of raw sensory impressions.

Grotstein singles out randomness and chaos as qualities that best capture the nature of meaninglessness. The term "random" aptly expresses the worldview that often accompanies serious depression. Clinically depressed individuals frequently show an acute awareness of the blind and arbitrary forces that dictate the flow of events in life. Depressive meaninglessness refers to an emotional conviction – a pervasive cynicism – that no underlying pattern of connections, or "grand scheme of things," provides a sense of purpose or a response to the *why?* of existence. For Grotstein, the *because* first emerges out of the mother's loving acceptance of, and careful attunement to, her baby.

The legacy of early bonding inheres in what Grotstein calls "the background object of primary identification" (2000, pp. 17–22, 164–165), a Maya-like, myth-making object that, like Winnicott's environmental mother, "holds" the entire sensorium together by symbolizing it. The background object works as an anti-depressive psychological immune system. It crystallizes out of primary identification with the mother, especially her alpha-producing reveries that offer living proof that she accepts her baby and that the baby truly belongs in the world. For Bion (1983), a mother's openness to her infant's joys, rages, and agonies conveys her willingness to attach. She therefore invites her baby to attach in turn. This relational pact also has a semiological dimension. The mother's reverie transforms her baby's inchoate bodily states into alpha elements, or, comprehensible units of signified feeling.

When difficulties in early bonding compromise attachment, and one remains unable to commune intimately with others, deficits hamper the background object. Often, a depression sets in that features themes of existential meaninglessness. The deficits stem from trauma, the "quintessence" of which is "the presence of randomness and chaos" (Grotstein 1990a, p. 36), and the "terror of the objectlessness" (Grotstein 1995b, p. 330). For the baby, black holes form in emotional spaces left undiscovered by the mother.

When traumatic pain reaches an unbearable pitch, "the patient disappears emotionally from his or her body-self-representation" (Grotstein 1990a, p. 41). I hold that, as with Dick, Klein's 4-year-old analysand, such *emotional disappearances* occur first and foremost as retreats from other people (cf. Symington 1993, 1994). When traumatized individuals attack the affective links to their objects, their world becomes drained of meaning.

Why is this? I suggest that states of schizoid detachment – indifference, insulation, depersonalization, derealization, autism – rely on a dissociation, a destruction of object cathexes constituted by metaphorical linkages. For Grotstein, the psyche "makes sense" by linking sense impressions with objects; the background object (i.e. internalization of mother's holding and thinking) attaches conceptual images (alpha-signifiers) to somatic perceptions (beta-signifieds). Emotional detachment from others flicks a switch that disengages the background object, so that it fails to achieve its purpose of creating "purpose" and meaning – securing a libidinal tie between the symbol and the symbolized. Randomness and chaos represent states without coherent links between causes (unformulated emotions in need of symbols) and effects (symbolic images). When a traumatized psyche fails to attach raw emotional experiences to meaningfully attuned metaphors, the conscious texture of experience veers more and more towards randomness. If we call an event random, we view it as haphazard and imply that it has no "object" or purpose, and, therefore, no invisible yet inferable background of connectedness. This portrays the dilemma of severely depressed individuals. They too cannot discern an emotional background of causation. Depression specializes in posing the question, "what is the *object* and the purpose of my existence?"

By stressing how randomness characterizes the orphanage of pre-oedipal pathologies, Grotstein's model offers up an implicit equation: because the libidinal bond between the symbol and the symbolized harnesses the same emotions that establish love relations, every quanta of emotional detachment from primary object(s) introduces an equal quanta of randomness into the symbolic perception of the world.

Let me put it yet another way. When one allows oneself to attach, one's ego remains in contact with both its attachment affects *and* the internal object of attachment. *The psyche then unconsciously applies this emotionally laden attachment schema, a metaphor of a meaningful relationship, to the representation of the external world. Objects in the external world (along with the self) now appear attached to each other in a coherent background network of relations that generate meaning and, from an existential point of view, make sense.* Emotional detachment removes the possibility of applying the experientially based metaphor and leaves one's *conscious* picture of the world defined primarily by disconnection and randomness, and therefore denuded of meaning. I will continually return to this idea throughout the chapter.

We find existential meaning by believing in things, and, as Ronald Britton

(1998) holds, we unconsciously experience beliefs as internal objects with whom we establish vital relationships. Britton's perspective lines up with Pruyser's, who observes that ego ideals are love objects that command our "loyalty" and "commitment"; we "cherish," "love," "defend" and "cling" to our ideals (1974, p. 254). Britton writes,

> A belief is a phantasy invested with the qualities of a psychic object and believing is a form of object relating. I think belief, as an act, is in the realm of knowledge what attachment is in the realm of love. The language of belief is clearly cast in the language of a relationship. We embrace or surrender to them; we hold beliefs and abandon them; sometimes we feel that we betray them. There are times when we are in the grip of a belief, held captive by it, feel persecuted by it or are possessed by it.
>
> (1998, p. 12)

Like relationships, we relinquish beliefs "only through a process of mourning" (p. 12). Also, "the mental apparatus of belief" may be "dismantled or destroyed to abolish any *attachment to ideas*" (emphasis added; p. 15).

> I think this dismantling is analogous to abolishing emotional ties to all objects, thereby producing a loss of a sense of reality; similarly, abolition of the capacity to believe produces a loss of a sense of psychic reality.
>
> (p. 15)

I propose a slight modification of Britton's view. Like the destruction of meaning, the abolition of psychic reality – the loss of the feeling of truth – *not only resembles, but results from an actual decision (usually unconscious) to retreat from external and internal objects.*

Britton describes a patient who tried to empty her mind of thoughts by "flushing them down the lavatory" (1998, p. 19). Later, she "complained of feeling unreal." But when she sat in Britton's waiting room she grew calmer, imagining that he now held her safely in his mind. Contained in the analytic "sanctuary," the patient, during her sessions, immediately sought understanding by "reiterating 'What does it mean? What does it mean?' " (p. 20). By draping herself in the security of her attachment, the patient's mind turns directly to questions of meaning. Britton writes, "a sense of being in safely bounded space, is one function of containment; the other is providing meaning" (p. 21).

In reflecting on "psychic retreats," Steiner describes a "withdrawn" patient who, at the start of her analysis, suffered "attacks of incapacitating anxiety" (1993, pp. 14–25).

> [The attacks also occurred] when she got involved in long discussions on existential themes, which resulted in panic when she realized that she saw

no meaning in life. She would find herself trembling, would feel her surroundings recede and become distant, and found that she could not make contact with people because a diffuse barrier came between them . . . she had terrifying dreams in which . . . radioactivity produced a kind of living death and people became automata.

(p. 16)

Case scenarios such as these appear regularly in psychoanalytic literature. We regularly see a kind of two-way traffic: an approach towards human intimacy and meaning, or a retreat away from intimacy into a denuded, mechanical, lonely world.

In my own practice, Karen, a philosophy student in her late twenties, repeatedly "gets close" and "pulls back" in our analytic sessions. Karen has spent a great deal of her life in "exile." She knows that, to some degree, she imposes the exile to distance herself from the rest of the world – frenetic ants scrambling to "work, work, work" and to lose themselves in the dismal vacuity of consumer-culture. For Karen, analysis also feels sometimes like a de-humanized workplace or a ritualized, go-nowhere drill; as analyst I am Spock, an affectless engineer who demands, in the name of science, a steady robotic supply of un-free associations.

Karen's sense of exile and her transferential experience of me stems, in part, from a defensive reaction to her mother's unpredictable behavior. Although at times playful, loving and attentive, Karen's mother habitually and abruptly "withdrew into a cloud," and she sometimes spanked her child for "getting too excited." Now, the specter of sudden endings haunts the analysis. At the end of every session and every week, and at the cusp of every holiday, Karen struggles with humiliation; she berates herself for relaxing into pleasurable and exciting feelings of closeness. She has again been duped. Karen remains forever "stuck in the middle," uncertain whether to value and hold on to the analysis, or to devalue me as a useless babysitter and simply quit.

From time to time Karen experiences "gentle waves of joy" that sometimes last several days. When the waves come and the world "opens up," Karen also "opens up" and gets a little closer to me in the sessions. She senses a kind of music in things and feels more "grounded." Maybe she *does* belong – in the world and in the analysis.

Invariably, as the music returns and Karen risks experiencing intimacy, she says that "things make sense." The ideas she reads in philosophy and existential literature, ideas that normally only seem to apply to others and not to herself, now resonate *for her* and "string together" beautifully and playfully in her thoughts. Invariably too, when she withdraws out of fear and the music fades, Karen anxiously marvels at how everybody in the world has an opinion – a thousand different opinions – while she knows "fuck all." Karen's heightened sensitivity to the clamor of opinions almost always comes with a "floaty" feeling of drifting aimlessly in space. In distancing herself, she creates a "barrier" or a "brick wall" that divides us. And even when things do make sense, Karen notices that she pulls back a little from the experience of meaning, both living in it and yet vaguely standing outside, fretting and wondering *"when will it stop?"*

In a couple of sessions before a long weekend, during a period when Karen rode the waves and felt buoyant, she said, "In the evenings I entertain my thoughts and I enjoy them. They string together and flow so nicely. They make sense, hopefully. I imagined you there talking to me about them. I do want to tell you my ideas about life and existence, but if I do, will they stop?" Karen's thoughts, along with her intensified attachment feelings, contained integrative and reparative themes. "Right now," she said, "even the ideas I don't like so much make more sense." A few moments later she said, "Maybe philosophy needs psychoanalysis and psychoanalysis needs philosophy." For Karen, a temporary *rapprochement* between psychoanalysis and philosophy meant that the analysis had, for the time being, lost its quality of profane, mechanical work.

On the Friday before the long weekend, the prospect of a curt separation loomed again. With rejection and humiliation closing in, Karen drew back and the music stopped. "I'm in a lousy mood," she said. "I don't know. The sadness and the anger are just soaring back. I'm going to drive out of the city tonight. I want to be someplace else, not around people. I don't hear the music today. And I'm questioning myself too. How often should I hear the music? Always? Sometimes? When it goes, do I bring it on? What we spoke of yesterday seems fraudulent today. I know the long weekend has something to do with it. I wondered where *you* might be going this weekend."

Karen's experience of meaning comes with a desire to commune. Outside sessions, she conjures me in her mind and imagines us conversing about ideas that make sense. In sessions, Karen worries that sharing her ideas with the real, unconjured me will silence her music and erase her meaning. When will it stop? When will mother drop her again? Fear of abandonment quashes her attachment affects, and so too her excitement and joy. By severing her bonds of affection, the links that bind her thoughts separate and her beautiful string of ideas unravels. Karen's detachment disengages the background object of primary identification, and with a disappearing back*ground*, she becomes un*grounded*, floating aimlessly (randomly) away into solipsistic space. As maternal trauma repeats, Karen projects her now painful feelings of closeness and her fragmented ideas into an anonymous throng who espouse opinions, or scattered bits of pseudo-meaning. Opinions amount to shit, and Karen's own are no exception. Her capacity for belief, her subjective sense of truth, falters: she knows "fuck all." The overall dynamic fits in well with Segal's "three term relation" (1988, p. 163) between ego, symbol and symbolized. In this instance, instead of a fusion with the analyst that produces symbolic equations, the ego attacks the link to the object and the link between symbol and symbolized recedes. When Karen detaches emotionally and withdraws from the other, meaning fades.

Now let me complicate matters by adding another layer to the above formulation. Meaning fades, *but only in consciousness*. So long as the ego actively dissociates itself from its attachment affects, these feelings, along with the potential meanings they create, become unconscious. The relationality of meaning persists outside of awareness. In other words, Karen generates the illusion of meaninglessness because, while painful and confusing, she finds it preferable to the painful meanings of rejection and abandonment.

Meaning is an object relation. Confusions between ego and object coincide with confusions between symbol and symbolized. Gains in relationality coincide with gains in meaning. Retreats from the object compromise the process of symbol formation. Emotional detachment sabotages one's capacity for belief, dampens one's immediate sense of reality and, in the wake of these impairments, imbues experience with randomness and chaos.

In exploring these ideas I have emphasized metaphor and alluded to its role in attachment. Alan Schore's (2003) work on the relation between neurobiology and psychoanalysis draws a similar connection. He states that the right hemisphere, the seat of "social cognition," not only oversees "social, emotional, moral and empathic functions," but also reasons *analogically* by invoking familiar situations (p. 146). Also, in his book on unconscious wisdom, Merkur claims that the interpersonal function of the psyche employs metaphor for the "inborn task of representing the perspective of the object" (2001, p. 126). I suggest that the relationality of meaning, a decisive theme in Kleinian thought, hinges on the ubiquity of metaphor in intersubjective and intrapsychic domains.

The relationality of metaphor

In his introduction to semiotics Danesi refers to metaphor as a "relational process" (1994, p. 107). Metaphors "relate concepts to the world of experience" via analogy, through explanation by comparison. A metaphor takes something that is partly or wholly elusive – perhaps due to its novelty, abstraction, complexity or obscurity – and likens or "relates" it to some other thing – a concept, an object, an experience – already familiar to us.

Jacob Arlow, who claims that psychoanalysis "is essentially a metaphoric enterprise" (1991, p. 297), points out that the term derives from Greek usage and means "to carry over." He writes,

> [Metaphor] refers to a set of linguistic processes whereby aspects of one object are carried over or transferred to another object so that the second object is spoken of as if it were the first. Substitution is not arbitrary but is based on a point of resemblance between the substituted word or

phrase and its referent, which is stated or implied by the sentence as a whole or by the context of the communication.

(p. 292)

Arlow points out that metaphor "typifies how perception and memory are integrated in terms of *similarity and difference*" (emphasis added; p. 296).

Note that Arlow views metaphor as a linguistic process. While metaphor certainly operates at a linguistic level, I want to stress its crucial prelinguistic role in early object relations, and the way metaphoric processes continue to straddle non-linguistic spheres of experience both in infancy and in adulthood (cf. Schore 2003, pp. 96, 102, 145–146).

Lakoff and Johnson hold that we find metaphor not only in language, but also in thought and action: "human thought processes are largely metaphorical" (1980, pp. 5–6). Even simple concepts that seem unadorned by figurative trappings acquire their meaning by way of metaphors that crop up repeatedly in everyday patterns of speech. For example, "structural metaphors" structure one concept in terms of another: time is money ("how do you spend your time these days?"; "I've invested a lot of time in her") (p. 8). "Orientational" metaphors give concepts spatial dimensions: happy is up while sad is down ("that boosted my spirits"; "I fell into a depression") (p. 14). "Ontological" metaphors ontologize via entities or substances: the mind is a brittle object ("her ego is very fragile"; "I'm going to pieces") (p. 28).

Lakoff and Johnson demonstrate how metaphors mediate our conceptions of reality. Because it permits us to challenge and "see beyond the 'truths' of our culture," this position has a radical and liberating edge (1980, p. 239). Yet we never pull ourselves out of metaphor into some transcendent, positivist objectivity; we always replace old metaphors with newer ones. Lakoff and Johnson write,

It is as though the ability to comprehend experience through metaphor were a sense, like seeing or touching or hearing, with metaphors providing the only ways to perceive and experience much of the world. Metaphor is as much a part of our functioning as our sense of touch, and as precious.

(1980, p. 239)

With this passage, the authors elegantly dispel the view that metaphor is nothing more than a poetic embellishment, a linguistic device separate from ordinary thought. By invoking the idea of a sixth sense, Lakoff and Johnson highlight how metaphor does not simply modify or enhance literal meanings the way a spice might accentuate the flavor of food. Metaphor creates meaning *in the first place* and, like a sensory organ, serves as an *a priori* requirement for consciousness and conscious experience.

Time is money. The average westerner grows up in an economically driven world that organizes duration by dividing it into standard units measured by clocks. Seconds, minutes, and hours expedite the labor process, and in the process, turn time into a commodity. The mercurial quality of temporal duration as a felt sense becomes, in our culture, subjectively encoded as a quantity and then experienced in consciousness as a resource that, like money, runs out. Similar to experiences in the realms of love, sex, gender, aesthetics and so on, we only develop a proper representational awareness of time through metaphor. As a comparative process, metaphor borrows from the familiar to ground the intangible and make it knowable.

As in Ogden's description of schizophrenic non-experience (1980, pp. 519–522), the therapist, at first little more than a cloudy percept, barely appears on the patient's mental radar. The therapist fails to attract attention – a *meaning cathexis* – because, for the patient, the therapist-percept has not yet "linked up with an object" (Grotstein 1990b, p. 148), or a metaphorical companion that bestows semantic boundaries and qualities. The orientational metaphor of container – a step forward in the humanization of the relationship – attracts attention because it offers (a) an irreducibly meaningful schema and (b) a novel option for managing unconscious pain. Here, the metaphor works like a sense organ because the patient begins to sense the therapist *and* the previously unconscious pain. By developing an imaginative ability to place pain in the therapist, the metaphor achieves a breakthrough. Psychic pain, even if disowned, finds itself at last on the experiential map of consciousness.

Daniel Stern (1985) and Peter Fonagy (1991, 1995; Fonagy *et al.* 2002; Fonagy *et al.* 1993; Fonagy and Target 1995, 1996, 2000; Target and Fonagy 1996) show, in their respective writings, how affect regulation, intersubjectivity and attachment emerge directly through metaphor.

Stern demonstrates how attunements between infant and mother occur through cross-modal communication. In cross-modal exchanges, instead of miming the baby, the mother matches the baby's feeling state through alternate yet parallel forms of expression. She might match the excitement and rhythm of her baby's voice with her body. Perhaps she claps and nods in tandem with her baby's "ba!-ba!-ba!"'s, reflecting her child's exuberance with a smile and a wide-eyed look. A great variety of cross-modal translations occur because each of the five senses shares the abstract qualities of intensity, time and shape.

The "vehicles of transfer" in cross-modal attunement "are metaphor and analogue" (Stern 1985, p. 142). The hardwired capacities of cross-modal intelligence "permit mother and infant to engage in affect attunement to achieve affective intersubjectivity" (p. 156).

Metaphors presuppose the "underlying capacity" to transpose amodal information: "Most poetry could not work without the tacit assumption that cross-sensory analogies and metaphors are immediately apparent to everyone" (p. 155).

And thus attunement recasts behaviors by way of nonverbal metaphor and analogue. If one imagines a developmental progression from imitation through analogue and metaphor to symbols, this period of the formation of the sense of a subjective self provides the experience with analogue in the form of attunements.

(Stern 1985, p. 161)

Stern's work on the emergence of the subjective self shows how attachment and meaning blend together seamlessly. His discussion of attunement and intersubjectivity employs semiological terms like "sign," "referent," "symbol," and "metaphor"; with intersubjectivity "mental states between people can now be 'read' " (p. 27). When a mother empathically mirrors her baby with cross-modal responses, her analogs help label and make sense of the baby's emotional experience and lay the groundwork for self-reflection, affect regulation, and the awareness of other minds. The following quote reveals how metaphor lies at the heart of attachment and object relations:

Affect attunement . . . is the performance of behaviors that express the quality of feeling of a shared affect state without imitating the exact behavioral expression of the inner state . . . imitation does not permit the partners to refer to the internal state. . . . Attunement behaviors . . . recast the event and shift the focus of attention to what is behind the behavior, to the quality of feeling that is being shared.

(Stern 1985, p. 142)

Attuning metaphors go beyond mere imitation to show the child that she has been understood. Metaphor facilitates attachment by providing irrefutable proof of an animate presence beyond and yet with the baby, a presence that feels and thinks in unison, letting the baby know that she has been reached and understood. Mere imitation remains external. *Precisely because cross-modality embodies the dialectic between sameness and difference*, the infant is not just mimicked; she is inwardly recognized and loved. Metaphors promote attachment because they simultaneously reflect and yet differ from the child's expression. This mixture of congruity and incongruity carries the trace of mother's thoughtfulness, both signifying and announcing the existence of her mind, *and* thereby granting the baby access to it. It is as though metaphors say to the child, "Hello, I know you're in there"; they give birth to subjective mind-states, one's own as well as others'.

Over time, cross-modal attunements awaken the infant to intersubjectivity. Somewhere near the middle of the first year, children "discover" other minds and the "feelings, motives and intentions" that "lie behind the physical happenings"; they realize that people "'hold in mind' unseen but inferable mental states . . . that guide overt behavior" (Stern 1985, p. 27). Here, Stern depicts intentionality as something that "lies behind" and goes "unseen," implying that metaphoric sentience ushers in an invisible world that both envelops and lies within the visible world. In Kleinian terms, invisibility marks the domain of whole object relations. The objects' physical body and physical actions serve as symbols for a hidden symbolized, an unseen mental state. Intentionality provides the link between hidden causes and observed effects.

This brings us back to Grotstein. Randomness and chaos represent meaningless, objectless states where apparent effects occur haphazardly without hidden causes. Maternal attunement, on the other hand, enchants the world, animating it with symbol, illusion and fantasy. In Stern's terms, a mother mirrors her baby's feelings states by offering her metaphoric body – her expressions, voice, gestures, caresses – as a readable text that signifies her mind and conveys that her observable behaviors (apparent effects of action) are not random but deliberate and meaningful (invisible causes of intentionality). In the depressive position, the baby again and again discovers the hidden realm of mother's empathic awareness thanks to her cross-modal attunements. Such experiences become a further facet of the background object of primary identification. Later, they sublimate into an unseen "grand scheme of things," a transitional space where things signify beyond themselves and feel as though they line up and make sense.

I suggest that if and when we view the world as meaningful, we project on to its geography an image of the attuning (m)other. We unconsciously endow the world with intentionality and subjectivity when, as mentioned earlier, we apply the metaphor of attachment (that is, a metaphor based on actual affective experiences of attachment) to our representation of the external world.

Peter Fonagy and his research colleagues' work on attachment and reflective function also portrays metaphor as central to the development of self-awareness, affect regulation and intersubjectivity. The early representational mapping of affects occurs when the mother "mirrors," or reflects back to the baby the meaning of his emotional experiences (Fonagy et al. 2002, p. 35). Anxiety manifests initially as a "confusing mixture of physiological changes, ideas and behaviors." After the mother thoughtfully mirrors the affect, the baby " 'knows' what he is feeling." For the representation to work as an affect regulator, as a symbol that affords self-reflection and meaning, the mother must introduce a "discrepancy" that both complements and offsets the mirroring. The authors write,

> If the mirroring is too accurate, the perception itself can become a source of fear, and it loses its symbolic potential. . . . We may presume that individuals for whom the symptoms of anxiety signify catastrophes . . . have metarepresentations of their emotional responses which cannot limit their intensity through symbolization, perhaps because the original mirroring by the primary caregiver exaggerated the infant's emotions.
>
> (Fonagy et al. 2002, p. 35)

By "smiling, questioning, mocking display" (p. 36) the mother "contaminates" her mirroring with "incompatible" displays, and the baby recognizes mother's emotion as "analogous, but not identical." The *analogy* catalyzes symbol formation. As with Stern, the mother reflects *and* contrasts; over time the metaphorical dialectic of sameness and difference promotes reflective function (a conscious awareness of the meaning of one's own and others' emotions). And as with Stern, intersubjectivity expands the baby's universe by introducing a further dimension of invisibility. The child now goes "beyond observable phenomena" (p. 27) and steps "beyond appearance" (p. 288) to "grasp the distinction between [apparent behavior] and the mental state that might underpin it."

Stern and Fonagy's work intersects with the most prominent neo-Kleinian theorist, Wilfred Bion (1970, 1983). Grotstein states that Bion "propelled" Klein's work "into the post-modern age of intersubjectivity" (1995b, p. 321). With his concept of maternal reverie and containment, Bion stressed the importance of a mother's permeability. She must offer emotional access to her mind so that her baby can learn to think. The baby identifies with and internalizes the mother's containing function. Put differently, the baby takes in the metaphorizing mother who promotes "alpha function," the ideational awareness of emotion (Bion 1983; Symington and Symington 1996, pp. 59–72). In fact, I hold that alpha function represents unconscious metaphorical capacity and that alpha elements *are* primarily metaphors. Clinical material helps us to explore this idea further.

Metaphor and trauma

Currently in her early twenties, Darlene, the elder of two sisters, was raised by a disturbed, frantic mother and a narcissistic, sexually abusive father. Darlene's only sibling, a sister younger by two years, committed suicide in her teens. For some time Darlene has worked as a dancer in strip clubs. She entered treatment because she felt "trapped" in her job, and because she cannot have a close sexual relationship with a man. For Darlene, all penises are indistinguishable from her father's. In our second session she said, "I can't tell the difference between what's crazy and what's not."

Darlene depicts her mother as an indecipherable, "crazy-making" woman who catastrophized her daughters' lives. In Darlene's earliest memories, her mother chases her children and whaps them with wooden spoons and rulers. Darlene always offers the same impersonation, one that draws attention to her mother's mindlessness. A spurt of whiny complaints and reprimands lapses into meaningless expulsions – "na-na-na-na-na!" Darlene's mother projected her rage and confusion by ceaselessly warning her children of omnipresent dangers (e.g. the threat of disease and drowning at summer camp, the possibility of car accidents and city violence). Obese and intrusive, and paying special attention to the size of her daughters' behinds, the mother obsessed over her children's bodies, pitting the sisters against each other in rivalrous pageants of weight loss.

Darlene's father, a narcissistic businessman, regularly assaulted his eldest daughter. Darlene recalls a recurring scene in which she serves her father snacks, while he traps her between his legs and forces her to touch his penis. When the father made a business deal, he went on lavish sprees, buying clothes and sugary junk food for himself and his family. While normally neglectful, successful business ventures injected the father with manic enthusiasm; he exuded a playfulness that offset the unpredictable threat of his assaults. Darlene felt that her father, even as an abuser, supported her more than her mother because he occasionally offered desperately needed scraps of paternal attention and care.

Darlene experiences a host of somatic symptoms. For years she has suffered from migraines triggered by the glare of fluorescent lights. She claims that her susceptibility to the effects of fluorescent lighting eliminates the possibility of her returning to school to pursue a new career. Darlene often panics inexplicably and she soothes herself by binging and purging on sugary junk foods – "comfort foods" – familiar to her from her childhood. Her mother's jealous attack on her daughters' sexuality involved anal themes. She repeatedly commented on the size of her daughters' buttocks and regarded her daughters' teenage masturbation as a rectal itch due to worms. Because she identified with her mother's analization of sexuality, Darlene's dread of genital arousal led to chronic constipation as well as olfactory hallucinations in which she believed that her feet and mouth gave off a foul stench.

Darlene claims she "doesn't know the first thing about holding a baby." Her phrasing alludes to a dissociative split: Darlene cannot contain her internal child terrified and dumbstruck by precocious sexual arousal, overstimulation and oedipal guilt. She tries to soothe the child with sugary food but finally relinquishes the link by vomiting. Darlene also purges her ability to discern danger. When once a man in a convenience store made masturbatory gestures at her, a decision to inform the store clerk gave way to doubt and derealization. *Is he being sexual? Is this really happening?* And like many strippers with a history of sexual abuse, Darlene cannot see how her job retraumatizes her each time she performs. She has uncannily found herself "trapped" over and over by sexually predatorial males and has twice unwittingly taken jobs that lured her into the sex industry. During holidays and long breaks in our work, Darlene fails to experience the anxiety and rage that manifests somatically or gets displaced onto other relationships.

Darlene's rejection of her internal baby created a psychic fissure responsible for a series of splits between, for example, the good and bad father, the good virgin girl and the counter-phobic stripper, a clean, fashionable public presentation and a private "dirty" apartment. She explains that different "behaviors" and "parts of herself" connect to different people: "I can't share all of myself at once."

Recently Darlene visited a chiropractic clinic to treat a sore leg. One of the chiropractors, Michael, also worked as a personal trainer at Darlene's gym and she had developed a "huge crush" on him. Michael, on shift when Darlene entered the clinic, offered to examine her. Because of her secret feelings, Darlene felt uncomfortable. But she decided not to voice her reluctance explicitly for fear that Michael would discover her crush. She feebly suggested that their friendship at the gym represented a conflict of interest, but Michael insisted that she had nothing to worry about. In his office, when Michael handed her a waiver to sign, Darlene burst into tears.

To my surprise, Darlene explained that she cried not because she felt trapped, but because the overhead fluorescents prevented her from reading the waiver. The sexual vulnerability she felt so acutely in the waiting room had strangely vanished. She spoke now of the painful toxicity of the lights, how they give her headaches, scramble her mind and make her puke. If not for the fluorescents she might have gone to school and, like Michael, trained as a chiropractor.

Traumatized by her father's assaults, Darlene's ability to cope was already undermined by an impenetrable mother who refused to process her daughters' projections, who forced her calamitous dread into her children, and whose sexual jealousy only sharpened Darlene's guilt. External detachment from inscrutable, dangerous parents produced an internal detachment between metaphors and emotion. When Darlene attacks the links that affectionately bind her to her objects, the bonds between symbol and symbolized breakdown. By withdrawing from primary objects, our first "meaningful relationships," the internal object that links emotional experiences to sense-making metaphors – Grotstein's background object – switches off. Deficits emerge in the metaphoric capacities that sponsor thinking because a variety of raw emotions lose access to sectors of the mind that offer analogies for conscious mentalization. Yet, as I will clarify in a moment, this detachment and the deficits that emerge *occur in the ego only*.

Darlene's obliviousness suggests that detachment aims primarily to obliterate the awareness of psychic pain (cf. Bowlby's notion of "defensive exclusion," 1988, pp. 70–71). In the extreme, detachment corresponds to Ogden's description of "non-experience." A censorship that works in the service of detachment limits the supply of workable metaphors that reacquaint the ego with its emotions. Now, intense affects pushing towards consciousness get shoehorned into vague analogies and cryptic symbols. Although compromised by far-fetched resemblances, symbolic equations, and somatizations, these signifiers carry the burden of memory by smuggling vital emotions back into awareness.

The process stems from a dissociated sector that remains stubbornly attached to the object despite the trauma. The attachment affects that make life meaningful – affects that constitute what Symington (1993, 1994) calls the "lifegiver" – persist in overcoming defensive barriers in the hope of re-finding an actual attachment. Thanks to this covert process, affects retain some degree of proximity to awareness. Appearing more like symptoms than meanings, these fractured metaphors *are* metaphors just the same. But the relative absence of poetic precision leaves one less able to dialogue and integrate *intrasubjectively* – Darlene cannot hold her anxious baby self – and *intersubjectively* – she reveals different parts of herself to different people (cf. Segal 1988, p. 169).

The collapse of the dialectic of sameness and difference represents one of the most important ways in which detachment disturbs metaphor. While unconsciously the psyche continues to abide by this opposition, the conscious ego splits the dialectic by taking sides. Experiences that resemble the original trauma appear either as isolated fragments lacking associative depth (absolute difference) or as indistinguishable duplicates over-endowed with painful significance (absolute sameness). Interferences in the comparative function hamper the ability to differentiate between danger and safety: Darlene "can't tell the difference between what's crazy and what's not."

Sometimes Darlene's repetition compulsion stems from splitting off registrations of sameness. She fails to recognize the paternal resemblance in certain exploitative men and so finds herself repeatedly trapped. She fails to appreciate the resemblance between her work and the original abuse and so fails to symbolize her persistent distress. In the convenience store and in the chiropractic clinic, the dialectic remains momentarily intact. But anxiety and guilt lead her to detach and relinquish her awareness by eliminating the recognition of similitude or sameness. She then views the events as wholly different and completely unrelated. In the convenience store, as Darlene succeeds in splitting off all awareness of sameness, her affects disappear so completely that her subjective sense of realness also drops out (presumably the man's masturbatory gestures traumatically reminded Darlene of her father's request that she masturbate him). In the clinic she maintains a tentative link to the affect by displacing it into a remote and concretized metaphor: the intrusive, phallus-shaped fluorescent bulbs. As metaphor, the lights faintly preserve the sameness function, but the resemblance to the incest is less obvious than the symbolic resemblance of an intrusive, boundary-crossing, and therefore, inappropriate consultation. Because Darlene switches off the attachment affects that provide the "nerves," or the alarm system that heralds danger, the guiding metaphors that register pain cannot properly perform their task.

In other instances, the repetition compulsion occurs due to a splitting off of differences. Here, all penises represent her father's. If before she could not discern danger, now Darlene cannot discover the safety (and excitement) of sexual intimacy with non-exploitative males. She fails to realize that she need not flee as usual.

Darlene cannot take responsibility for her protection or her happiness. In line with Ogden's depiction of the paranoid-schizoid position we see "reactions as opposed to responses": "there is no interpreting subject mediating between perception of danger and response to it" (1990, p. 45). I hold that the "interpreting subject" subjectivizes experience through the *creative* application of metaphor. Selecting a metaphor from the archives of personal memory marks the uniqueness of the subject as an individual. The personal distinctiveness, as well as the freedom inherent in the act of choosing, turns the impersonal rawness of unformulated emotions into subjective meanings that one can own, think about, and respond to.

Recall Britton's claim that beliefs represent attachments. Abolishing emotional ties to the object issues in a loss of reality sense and an inability to believe. Darlene's difficulty in discerning craziness from sanity, as well as her derealization in the convenience store (*"is this really happening?"*), compare to the decline in Karen's feeling of truth and her anxiety about the multiplicity of opinions. The prospect of traumatic repetition leads both Darlene and Karen to detach emotionally. They both experience losses in the emotionally based sense of reality and they both pose ontological questions about truth: *What exists and what is real?* Reality sense and rudimentary beliefs about the existence or nonexistence of things rely on the conjunction of attachment affects *and* the meaning cathexes provided by metaphor.

I have argued that detachment leads to an impairment and loss of metaphor. Although in severe instances a wholesale disappearance of metaphor may, in theory, ensue, *most cases reveal a loss in consciousness of metaphorical awareness*. The distinction has real importance. Consider the phallic shape of fluorescent lights, and the harsh luminosity that assaults the eye and leaves Darlene paralyzed, headachy and nauseous (cf. Greenacre's "Vision, Headache, and Halo," 1952, pp. 133–148). Darlene says that the lights keep her from attending school and finding a new career. Such a concretization appears as a regressive movement into degraded thinking, into what Bion (1970, 1983) deems a "beta-element." But this fluorescent "hysteria" metaphorizes not only the bodily characteristics of the incest (penile penetration, seminal whiteness, physical revulsion), it also offers a somber and valuable commentary – a lucid analogical insight about the tragic implications of the incest. Like the *psychological* scars of trauma, the *physical* properties of the lights keep Darlene from moving forward with her life.

We need to disentangle the defensive and the integrative aspects of the symbolism. The defense constitutes *only* the obliteration of meaning, the withdrawal of metaphorical cathexes that, for example, makes Darlene forfeit the resemblance between Michael's inappropriate consultation and her father's inappropriate seductions. As in Ogden's paper on the schizophrenic conflict, the return of emotional ideation parceled into strange, concrete metaphors represents an attempt to restore meaning and insight. The lights and their effects point to a persistence of healthy mentalization, not to a regressive degradation of thought. The *apparent* primitivity stems from the dissociative measures taken by the ego in reaction to suffering. The decreased quotient of sameness or resemblance in the metaphor betrays an intelligence that empathically respects the self-protective censorship (cf. Grotstein 2000, p. xxviii). In the clinic, Darlene's sudden preoccupation with the fluorescents maintained a link to her terrified, abused child, a way of holding the baby, and maintaining, even if barely, the metaphoric dialectic that recognizes the distinction between safety and craziness.

Impelled by guilt to comply with her mother's denial of genital sexuality, Darlene identified with her mother's anal substitutions. Genital arousal fell prey to anal metaphors whose degree of difference was too great to adequately regulate the sensations and the affects they represent. How can Darlene be responsible to her sexual urges when her mother forbade her to play a role in choosing her own metaphors? The rectal clamping down of constipation offers no real control. Yet the constipation and the somatic hallucinations of a foul odor keep her sexual feelings from disappearing altogether. Dread, shame and discomfort remain preferable to the potential emptiness that accompanies a total rejection of sexual feeling. When in therapy Darlene found that she could speak to a man about her sexual feelings and her ambivalence, the hallucinations evaporated. Our conversations offered her better attuned verbal metaphors. Still, the hallucinations and the constipation contained at least two insights: Darlene unconsciously craved sexual intimacy *and* she viewed her longings as smelly and ugly. In contrast to regression, these anal-somatic metaphors served in our therapy as messengers, as stepping stones towards a higher level of self-awareness – a linguistic articulation of subjective states of revulsion, disgust and guilt.

Affects are intrinsically elusive. Whether through the introspections of psychoanalysis, psychotherapy, and contemplative meditation, or the expressions of visual art, poetry, literature and music, we are forever engaged in truly difficult work – apprehending, clarifying and finally representing the intricate abstractions of human feeling, the "inarticulate speech of the heart." The very nature of affect requires metaphor for mentalization. In fact, mentalization *is* metaphor. The degree of fit between metaphor and affect determines the degree of refinement in conscious mentalization. For example, while crucial as an attempt to restore self-awareness, anal metaphors introduce too much semantic and experiential difference to sufficiently represent and contain the emotions that surround genital arousal. As a result of what we might deem an "analogical misattunement" or a "non-empathic metaphor," Darlene's experiences in the realm of sexuality remain inherently alien, lodged in the non-reflective, non-subjective realm of the paranoid-schizoid position.

This leads us to Bion. Grotstein summarizes Bion's concept of alpha function:

> A normal, receptive mother in reverie employs her alpha function . . . to receive, sustain, defuse, tolerate, and translate (decode) her infant's raw

emotional experiences and therefore behaves as an auxiliary thinking, processing ego for the infant. The latter normally introjects this maternal function and is able to tolerate his or her own feelings long enough to feel them, think about them, process them, and internalize them.

(1995b, p. 321)

Bion describes alpha function as an "unknown process" (1984, pp. 38–39). Stern's notion of cross-modality, as well as Fonagy's discrepancy-based mirroring, shed light on the mystery of alpha by operationalizing it (Fonagy *et al.* portray their contributions as such (2002, p. 28)). Bion himself portrays alpha as synonymous with metaphor and analogue. Alpha elements refer to consolidated parts of the self available to encode and contain unmetabolized emotions on the basis of resemblance. They "comprise visual images, auditory patterns, olfactory patterns, and are suitable for employment in dream thoughts, unconscious waking thinking, dreams, contact barrier, memory" (1983, p. 26).

Elements are removed from mental storage to provide a model that is an approximation to the event it is to illuminate. The personality abstracts from experience the elements expected to recur and forms from these elements the model that will preserve something of the original experience but with enough flexibility to permit adaptation to new but supposedly similar experiences.

(p. 75)

Here, the term "flexibility" coincides with the metaphorical dialectic of sameness and difference. And similar to the idea that metaphor works as a sixth sense that renders percepts conscious, Bion holds that alpha function promotes "a capacity for awareness of sense data," especially the data and "psychic quality" of emotion (p. 52).

Due to the absence of "mental visual images" (Bion 1970, p. 10), beta elements – the opposite of alpha – refer to concrete sense impressions or "things-in-themselves" devoid of representational signifiers. Because they lack images that facilitate thinking (p. 12), beta elements "evade" rather than "modify" frustration (Bion 1983, p. 29). And because the mind experiences beta elements as mere accretions of physical stimuli, they lend themselves to projective evacuation and "discharge" (p. 83). Bion holds that hallucinations conform to beta elements, not thought representations (1970, p. 18): "In the domain of hallucinosis the mental event is transformed into a sense impression and sense impressions in this domain do not have meaning" (p. 37).

By Bionian standards, many of Darlene's experiences – the effect of the fluorescents, the hallucinations of smell – qualify as beta elements. The "psychic quality" of emotion has seemingly devolved into physical objects, into impersonal lights and odors whose externality gives clear evidence of projective identification. The content of the experiences represents things-in-themselves because Darlene views them, initially at least, as concrete entities that simply *are what they are*. But what if we assume that the meaninglessness of beta applies only to consciousness and that unconsciously the metaphorical dialectic remains operative? If we view concretized projections and somatizations such as Darlene's as mindless accretions of stimuli, we may foreclose on opportunities to mine the implicit insights that push for, and therefore await, recognition.

I suggest that we take Bion at his word and rigorously apply the definition he provides. We gain theoretic clarity when we view beta as a defensive process that opposes mental visual images. Beta proper strips emotional experiences of meaning by transforming them into vague sensorial registrations that lack semantic and psychological significance. Again, I view this as the conscious withdrawal of meaning cathexes due to the ego's splitting of the metaphorical dialectic.

Bion "follows the Platonic concept of thoughts existing without the necessity of a thinker" (Symington and Symington, 1996, p. 82). Instead of the platonic notion of unthought thoughts, I recommend an alternate model that opts for the repression of an ever-present thinker. This thinker continues to think unconsciously, patiently directing thoughts towards an ever-recalcitrant ego. With this model we may regard any return of ideation, whether impersonal, concretized, projected, somatic, or hallucinatory, as implicit or impaired alpha elements, as compromised metaphors disguised to satisfy the requirements of the ego's censorship. The level of potential pain for the ego matches the strictness of the censorship. And the strictness of the censorship is proportional to the degree of difference or obscurity in the metaphor. Even in psychotic extremes of the paranoid-schizoid position, the symbolic equations of poison, radiation, bad smells, extra-terrestrial and divine communications, maintain crucial unconscious links to alpha function, the depressive position, and mentalization. Darlene's fluorescent lights and her somatic hallucinations do not represent disintegrative evacuations "out of" or "away from" consciousness. They represent an integrative movement "towards" the ego, a resumption of mental images *despite the regressive constraints of beta*. In fact, we may regard Darlene's symptomatic experiences as a subjectivity in search of consciousness (Grotstein 2000, pp. 143–188).

Metaphor and sublimation

A 40-year-old man whom I will call Richard sought treatment with a colleague for obsessive thoughts and anxiety. After his mother died of cancer shortly after his first birthday, Richard's aunt and uncle adopted him. They removed Richard from the city, and brought him home to their small rural town. The couple, unable to bear children of their own, had previously adopted a girl who, by the time Richard arrived, was in her early teens. Richard's new parents, conservative Christians already in their early fifties, clearly loved their children. But they also parented with a stern, over-protective hand. The uncle forced Richard to attend a religious school that Richard hated. With much struggle, he finally switched out of the school in his teens. At 18, he returned to the city to study journalism. When Richard completed his degree, his parents pressured him to return to the country to look after them. Richard refused. When a few years later both of his parents passed away, Richard grew guilty and reproached himself for not moving back and tending to their needs.

Soon after the clinical work commenced and Richard became more comfortable in the therapeutic relationship, his guilt returned. Or, more precisely, as the attachment deepened, Richard allowed himself to re-experience his remorse and sorrow. He began to have a recurring dream in which he throws his arms around his deceased uncle and, weeping, apologizes for his decision. The appearance of the dream coincided with indications of his growing attachment and dependency – he now expressed concern about the possibility of the therapist departing to another city. His worry left him feeling depressed.

In the first session that he reported the dream, Richard, after describing it, felt short of breath. He hyperventilated and said he knew it was "psychological," not "medical." He reported tingling sensations and dizziness. Aware that the therapist was a physician as well, Richard inquired about the physiology of his symptoms. The therapist explained that by hyperventilating, carbon dioxide levels drop, pH levels become alkaline, and, as a result, free calcium also drops and causes the tingling.

"Wow," said Richard, "everything is connected! Fascinating!" His excitement swelled. Richard explained that lately he had been thinking a lot about existence and the interrelatedness of things. He found himself staring at flowers and thinking, "I am part of the universe just like these daisies." He said that he had never before thought of life in this way and that now he felt "connected."

This vignette illustrates how attachment affects promote symbolism by attaching the symbol to the symbolized. Richard's growing bond to the therapist brought him deeper into the depressive position. Through the relationship, he acquired enough positive feeling to confront the depressive anxieties that arise with greater integration. Richard's panic attack reflects a heightened sensitivity to emotional meanings: his guilt as well as his appreciation of separateness and dependence. We may also speculate that the daisies symbolize the early mother and her nipple-breast. Via the flower metaphor, Richard experienced feelings – wonderment and awe – that arose from a preverbal recollection in which he and his mother existed together in the same time and place.

Richard's realizations flow from a metaphoric apprehension of unity.

He intuits a web of interlocking relations that represents the opposite of randomness and meaninglessness. The world, now suffused with significance, becomes emotionally and existentially compelling. Why and how has this come about? I propose that Richard's attachment to his therapist served as a primary metaphor, one that reorganized Richard's conceptual schema of the external world. With the sublimation or abstraction of one attachment into many attachments, Richard contemplates a multiplicity of dependency relations in the universe. Captivated by his epiphany, Richard recognizes a pattern, a "grand scheme."

Because of the therapist's ability to hold and contain, Richard mustered the courage to imagine or mentalize the object's mind. As his dream shows, he safely mentalized the hurt he inflicted not only as an adult, but also as a child who presumably felt responsible for his mother's disappearance. As Richard unconsciously applies or "attaches" the notion of intersubjectivity to his external world schema, the cosmos becomes a metaphoric text that signifies beyond itself.

Richard imaginatively discovers something he had not seen before: the *invisible* intelligibility of the cosmos. Richard's perception of the world's intelligibility, that is, his exhilarating reflections on the empirical interrelatedness of things, is grounded in an unconscious phantasy or attribution of intentionality. His attachment feelings bring an awareness and appreciation of the "incorporeal intelligibles" (Bakan 2001) much expounded upon by both Plato and Aristotle. Bakan writes,

> The essential feature of this Greek thought was that the world was comprehensible by the mind. The Greeks presumed that the world was intelligible. They presumed that the intelligibility was *there*, objectively existent, to be grasped by the human being. The objectively existent intelligibility was that which was understood when a person understood something. It allowed, essentially, that insight was precisely outsight.
>
> (p. 533)

Imaginative insights about the world's invisible comprehensibility – whether it be inspirations of truth, beauty or value – stir feelings of wonder because they presuppose an unconscious "intentional stance" (Dennet 1987), a phantasy of cosmic subjectivity. In phantasy, what Bakan deems "objectively existent intelligibility" (i.e. Richard's ontological realization about interdependence) confronts the mind as a signifier of subjectivity, as evidence of an intelligible and comprehensible mind.

The meaning cathexis of metaphor generates a fascination about the universe as a concept, and it promotes a heightened consciousness, a greater awareness of the "reality" of the external world. Like the intersubjective epiphanies of the infant who, during the first year of life, moves beyond appearances and observable phenomena to grasp the abstract intelligibility of minds, Richard discovers the invisible world that envelops and lies within the physical world.

The phantasy-based, metaphoric attribution of intentionality to the external world is an unconscious feature of every depressive position. During mystical and peak experiences (Maslow 1970) these unitive fantasies (Merkur 1998, 1999; Haartman 2004, pp. 89–131), produced by the background object, flow into conscious awareness with exhilarating clarity. Like the depressive crises that sometimes erupt prior to unitive ecstasies – crises that occur cross-culturally (Haartman 2004, pp. 40–45) – Richard suffers a mild panic attack moments before a unitive inspiration captures his attention. My colleague, Richard's therapist, told me that he viewed Richard's panic as an "existential" crisis.

I agree. The emergence of an incorporeal intelligible (in Richard's case, an unseen metaphoric network of existential connections and dependency relations) heralds the conscious integration of an attachment affect in relation to an object. Acknowledging attachment occasions the frightening vulnerability that, as Kleinians point out, comes with a clear awareness of one's dependence and separateness (Rosenfeld 1987, pp. 87–88, 162–164). Richard's realization (and fear) of his dependence upon his therapist quickly spawned a realization about his embodied participation in a meaningful and valued, yet uncontrollable world.

The invisible intentionality of the depressive position serves as a matrix that endows the world with *value*. First, Richard bonded to his therapist. Then he *unconsciously* applied (i.e. "attached") the concept of intersubjectivity as a metaphor to his representation of the world and *consciously* discovered the intangible realm of value, the core of human conscience. Conversely, when we detach from the object, we obliterate the fantasy of the object's mind and separate ourselves from the very wellspring of metaphor. The two-dimensionality of value as a readable text then collapses into the one-dimensionality of impersonal, mechanical things that stand only for themselves.

Conclusion

Meaning is an object relationship. Metaphors secure the attachment between infant and mother *and* secure attachment grants the ego optimal access to the unconscious production of metaphors. In normal development, the background object of primary identification crystallizes out of the infant's internalization of the reflective mother who symbolizes and regulates emotional experience. The internalization of the background object hinges on the child's identification with mother's mind and her loving intentionality. Proof of mother's mind lies in her metaphorical mirroring. Very possibly, the infant's identification with the object's subjectivity acts as a species-specific cue for the instinctual, hardwired production of metaphors.

Metaphors play a fundamental role in psychic life. Meaning cathexes focus attention on bare perceptions and render them conscious. Experiences of elation and depression, for example, become less diffuse and incrementally more coherent and meaningful when assimilated by the basic orientational metaphors of "up" (happy) and "down" (sad) (Lakoff and Johnson 1980, p. 15). Metaphors serve as vehicles of the depressive position: they facilitate intrapsychic communication, affect regulation, and mentalization.

With trauma and emotional detachment, the poetic flexibility of metaphor deteriorates and the dialectic of sameness and difference collapses. An unconscious censorship that protects the ego imposes limits on the degree of analogical precision. Metaphors become concretized and cryptic.

I have suggested that emotional detachment destroys the ego's link to the mythopoeic background object. How might we formulate this more specifically? Anxiety and rage transform the other into a bad or persecutory object. As the object's subjectivity grows too terrible to comprehend through empathic fantasy, the comprehending subject denies or "repudiates" (Fonagy *et al.* 2002, pp. 13, 198) the very existence of the object's mind. Since mother's subjectivity first appears through metaphor, the *conscious* denial of the object's mind, *the main mechanism of detachment*, impairs the ego's ability to recognize usable metaphors and encourages symbolic equations. The literalist veil of the paranoid-schizoid position eclipses the invisible world of value: subjects become objects, events become random, and affects become symptoms.

Bibliography

Arlow, J. (1991) *Psychoanalysis: Clinical Theory and Practice*. Madison, Conn.: International Universities Press.

Bakan, D. (2001) On the Reality of the Incorporeal Intelligibles: A Reflection on the Metaphysics of Psychology. *Perceptual and Motor Skills* 93: 531–540.

Bion, W.R. (1970) *Attention and Interpretation*. London: Karnac.

—— (1983) *Learning from Experience*. Northvale, NJ: Jason Aronson.

Bowlby, J. (1988) *A Secure Base: Parent–Child Attachment and Healthy Human Development*. New York: Basic Books.

Britton, R. (1998) *Belief and Imagination: Explorations in Psychoanalysis*. New York: Routledge.

Carveth, D. (1984) The Analyst's Metaphors: A Deconstructive Perspective. *Psychoanalysis and Contemporary Thought* 7(4): 491–560.

Danesi, M. (1994) *Messages and Meanings: An Introduction to Semiotics*. Toronto: Canadian Scholar's Press.

Dennet, D. (1987) *The Intentional Stance*. Cambridge, Mass.: MIT Press.

Fonagy, P. (1991) Thinking about Thinking: Some Clinical and Theoretical Considerations in the Treatment of a Borderline Patient. *International Journal of Psychoanalysis* 72: 639–656.

—— (1995) Playing with Reality: The Development of Psychic Reality and Its Malfunction in Borderline Patients. *International Journal of Psychoanalysis* 76: 39–44.

Fonagy, P. and Target, M. (1995) Understanding the Violent Parent: The Use of the Body and the Role of the Father. *International Journal of Psychoanalysis* 76: 487–501.

—— (1996) Playing with Reality: I. Theory of Mind and the Normal Development of Psychic Reality. *International Journal of Psychoanalysis* 77: 217–233.

—— (2000) Playing with Reality: III. The Persistence of Dual Psychic Reality in Borderline Patients. *International Journal of Psychoanalysis* 81: 853–873.

Fonagy, P., Moran, G.S., and Target, M. (1993) Aggression and the Psychological Self. *International Journal of Psychoanalysis* 74: 471–485.

Fonagy, P., Gergely, G., Jurist, E.L., and Target M. (2002) *Affect Regulation, Mentalization, and the Development of the Self*. New York: Other Press.

Greenacre, P. (1947) *Trauma, Growth, and Personality*. New York: W.W. Norton.

Grostein, J.S. (1977) The Psychoanalytic Concept of Schizophrenia: II. Reconciliation. *International Journal of Psychoanalysis* 58: 427–452.

—— (1990a) The Black Hole as the Basic Psychotic Experience: Some Newer Psychoanalytic and Neuroscience Perspectives on Psychosis. *Journal of the American Academy of Psychoanalysis* 18: 29–46.

—— (1990b) Invariants in Primitive Emotional Disorders. In L. Bryce Boyer and P. Giovacchini (eds) *Master Clinicians on Treating the Regressed Patients*. Northvale, NJ: Jason Aronson.

—— (1995a) Orphans of the Real: I. Some Modern and Post-modern Perspectives on the Neurobiological and Psychosocial Dimensions of Psychosis and Primitive Mental Disorders. *Bulletin of the Menninger Clinic* 59: 287–311.

—— (1995b) Orphans of the Real: II. The Future of Object Relations Theory in the Treatment of Psychoses and Other Primitive Mental Disorders. *Bulletin of the Menninger Clinic* 59: 312–332.

—— (2000) *Who is the Dreamer Who Dreams the Dream?* Hillsdale, NJ: Analytic Press.

Haartman, K. (2004) *Watching and Praying: Personality Transformation in Eighteenth Century British Methodism*. Amsterdam: Rodopi.

Holmes, J. (1993) *John Bowlby and Attachment Theory*. New York: Routledge.

Klein, M. (1988) *Love, Guilt and Reparation*. London: Virago Press.

Lakoff, G. and Johnson, M. (1980) *Metaphors We Live By*. Chicago: University of Chicago Press.

Laplanche, J. and Pontalis, J.-B. (1988) *The Language of Psychoanalysis*. London: Karnac.

Main, M., Kaplan, K., and Cassidy, J. (1985) Security in Infancy, Childhood and Adulthood. A Move to the Level of Representation. In I. Bretherton and E. Waters (eds) *Monographs of the Society for Research in Child Development* 50: 66–104.

Maslow, A. (1970) *Religions, Values and Peak Experiences*. New York: Viking Press.

Merkur, D. (1998) *The Ecstatic Imagination: Psychedelic Experiences and the Psychoanalysis of Self-Actualization*. Albany: State University of New York Press.

—— (1999) *Mystical Moments and Unitive Thinking*. Albany: State University of New York Press.

—— (2001) *Unconscious Wisdom: A Superego Function in Dreams, Conscience, and Inspiration*. Albany: State University of New York Press.

Mitchell, S. (1997) *Influence and Autonomy in Psychoanalysis*. Hillsdale, NJ: Analytic Press.

Ogden, T.H. (1980) On the Nature of the Schizophrenic Conflict. *International Journal of Psychoanalysis* 61: 513–533.

—— (1990) *The Matrix of the Mind: Object Relations and the Psychoanalytic Dialogue*. Northvale, NJ: Jason Aronson.

Pruyser, P.W. (1974) *Between Belief and Unbelief*. New York: Harper and Row.

Rosenfeld, H. (1987) *Impasse and Interpretation: Therapeutic and Anti-Therapeutic Factors in the Psychoanalytic Treatment of Psychotic, Borderline, and Neurotic Patients*. New York: Routledge.

Schore, A.N. (2003) *Affect Regulation and the Repair of the Self*. New York: W.W. Norton.

Segal, H. (1988) Notes on Symbol Formation. In E.B. Spillius (ed.) *Melanie Klein Today. Developments in Theory and Practice. Volume I: Mainly Theory*. New York: Routledge.

Steiner, J. (1993) *Psychic Retreats: Pathological Organizations in Psychotic, Neurotic and Borderline Patients*. New York: Routledge.

Stern, Daniel N. (1985) *The Interpersonal World of the Infant: A View from Psychoanalysis and Developmental Psychology*. New York: Basic Books.

Symington, N. (1993) *Narcissism: A New Theory*. London: Karnac.

—— (1994) *Emotion and Spirit: Questioning the Claims of Psychoanalysis and Religion*. London: Karnac.

Symington, J. and Symington, N. (1996) *The Clinical Thinking of Wilfred Bion*. New York: Routledge.

Target, M. and Fonagy, P. (1996) Playing with Reality: II. The Development of Psychic Reality from a Theoretic Perspective. *International Journal of Psychoanalysis* 77: 459–479.

Chapter 10

Kleinian theory is natural law theory

C. Fred Alford

What could it mean to call Melanie Klein and those she influenced, such as Wilfred Bion, natural law theorists? Natural law is generally seen as at least loosely bound to a religious vision, and one could hardly call Klein and Bion religious thinkers. Perhaps the simplest thing to say is that the tradition of natural law, reaching back to Augustine and Aquinas, is one that binds nature and moral obligation: what is natural to do is what is right to do, a formulation that raises almost as many questions as it answers, for not everything natural is good.

Consider the preamble to the Declaration of Independence of the United States. "We hold these truths to be self-evident, that all men are created equal, that they are endowed by their Creator with certain unalienable Rights, that among these are Life, Liberty and the pursuit of Happiness." Though the link between Melanie Klein and the Declaration of Independence is hardly obvious, the Declaration exhibits the first quality of natural law. Self-evident truths are truths that most mature human beings know by virtue of living with other humans. This is the way in which nature is generally referred to in the natural law tradition. Nature refers not to some external entity or property, but to knowledge that already exists within every human being, even if for various reasons, such as a bad upbringing, particular human beings are incapable of gaining access to what they already know.

I argue that what Klein calls the depressive position, in which one comes to know how much one has hated as well as loved, and accordingly feels obligated to make reparation, has the quality of a self-evident truth. While the *content* of this self-evident truth varies greatly from the truths disclosed by Jefferson, author of the Declaration, the natural law status of these truths is similar. Both are self-evident in the sense that they come to be known to most humans in the course of normal development within a decent culture, one that does not idealize what Klein calls the paranoid-schizoid position.

The second quality of natural law, closely related to the first, is that human development is teleologically oriented. One may intelligibly talk about an ideal course of human development. The way in which this fits Klein is fairly obvious. As Michael Rustin puts it in *The Good Society and the Inner World: Psychoanalysis, Politics and Culture*

> A third aspect of Kleinian thinking, which, I shall argue, had significant social affinities was its teleological dimension. There is inherent in Kleinian theory the idea of a "normal" pathway of development . . . . The "depressive position" defined as a state of affairs that was normative . . . was held in some way to correspond to the potential of human nature.
>
> (Rustin 1991, 147–149)

The problem in this case is not to demonstrate that Klein's thinking is teleological, but that the sense in which Rustin uses the term "teleological" has anything to do with the way in which natural law uses the term. Many natural law theorists hold that the teleology in question must include the cosmos if teleology is going to join nature with moral obligation. As Kai Nielsen puts it,

> The natural moral law theory only makes sense in terms of an acceptance of medieval physics and cosmology. If we give up the view that the universe is purposive and that all motions are just so many attempts to reach the changeless, we must give up natural moral law theories. One might say, as a criticism of the Thomistic doctrine of natural moral law, that since medieval physics is false then it follows that natural moral law theory must be false.
>
> (Nielsen 1988, 212)

Recent years have seen a rethinking of teleology, however. Stimulated by the work of Alasdair MacIntyre (1981), many have argued that the teleology in question is narrative. As narratology, the study of narrative, has taught us, stories are defined by their end. Everything that happens before is reinterpreted in light of how it all turns out in the end. Without an ending there can be no plot, and hence no satisfactory meaning (Prince 1987, 26). And without narrative, there can be no meaning to life at all. Or as Barbara Hardy puts it, "we dream in narrative, daydream in narrative, remember, anticipate, hope, despair, believe, doubt, plan, revise, criticize, construct, gossip, learn, hate and love by narrative" (Hardy 1968, 5).

Understood as a narrative quest, human life too can be understood in teleological terms. A successful human life is a passage through threats and dangers that may be characterized in terms of what Klein calls the paranoid-schizoid position, to a particular constellation of feelings and experiences that constitute maturity, what Klein calls the depressive position. That the nature in question refers not to some human essence, but to the nature of a human life as pilgrimage, makes less difference than one might suppose in concluding that Klein is a natural law theorist.[1] Indeed, in *Narrative and the Natural Law: An Interpretation of Thomistic Ethics*, Pamela Hall (1994) interprets Aquinas' teleology as though it were a narrative, not a claim on the cosmos.

"Written in our hearts," and expressed in a combination of general principles and stories, natural law is more about feeling than reason, or rather it combines the two. As the Thomistic natural law theorist Jacques Maritain recognizes, the reason that knows natural law does not operate on its own, but under the impress of the inclinations of human nature in history.

> Knowledge by inclination or by connaturality is a kind of knowledge that is not clear, like that obtained through concepts and conceptual judgments. It is obscure, unsystematic, vital knowledge by means of instinct or sympathy, and in which the intellect, in order to make its judgments, consults the inner leanings of the subject – the experience that he has of himself – and listens to the melody produced by the vibration of deep-rooted tendencies made present in the subject.
>
> (Maritain 2001, 34–35)[2]

Vernon Bourke goes further, arguing that most men and women come to know the natural law by means of "ordinary grasping . . . a combination of low-grade cognitive and affective activity. Sometimes it is close to animal feeling" (Bourke 1988, 218).

I argue that this "ordinary grasping" is in fact quite extraordinary, occurring only when the natural impulse to make reparation (what Klein calls love) is joined to the act of thinking about what one is doing. This conjunction is about as rare as the conjunction of the planets, and not nearly as reliable. Nor is a strictly Kleinian account sufficient to achieve this conjunction. For that we need to draw on Wilfred Bion, in order to explain why thinking about what one is doing is so difficult and hence so rare.[3] Unless we think about what we are doing, reparation may be self-indulgent.

Do good, avoid evil

Let us begin with Thomas Aquinas (1225–1274), the paradigmatic natural law theorist. Everyone who studies natural law, and virtually every selection of readings on natural law, includes Aquinas as the clearest exemplar of the genre. Not because all agree with Aquinas. On the contrary, the most academically influential version of natural law today, that of John Finnis (1980), explicitly abandons the link between natural law and Eternal Law, a link that was taken for granted by Aquinas.

What makes Aquinas paradigmatic is his view that "since human nature is not so completely corrupted by sin as to be totally lacking in goodness," it is possible to talk about natural law in strictly human terms. (ST I–II, 109) Or as Hugo Grotius put it three centuries later,

What we have been saying [about natural law] would have a degree of validity even if we should concede that which cannot be conceded without the utmost wickedness, that there is no God, or that the affairs of men are of no concern to Him.

(Grotius 1964, Prolegomena, II)

Since Grotius was not an atheist, his insistence on this point is significant (Buckle 1991, 167). A recent commentator put the same point a little differently when he said "St. Thomas would disagree with Dostoyevski's saying 'If God does not exist, everything is permissible' " (Kreeft 1990, 505). If God does not exist, natural human goodness remains.

Good is to be done, and evil is to be avoided. This is how Aquinas defines the natural law (ST I–II, 94, 2). The most common objection, as might be imagined, is that Aquinas' definition is without content, a tautology, similar in structure to the statement "all bachelors are unmarried." Those familiar with the work of Klein will know that Aquinas' definition of the natural law is rich in content. For Aquinas, as for Augustine (whose encounter with evil is considered shortly), evil is the privation or absence of the good. "The good of the human being is being in accord with reason, and human evil is being outside the order of reasonableness" (ST I–II, 71, 2). Evil is where goodness is not. Klein, on the other hand, sees evil as an active force in the world. For Klein, "do good, avoid evil" means protecting the good from one's own desire to destroy the good because it is good, outside one's possession and control. Such malevolence Aquinas can hardly imagine.

Reading Aquinas, one is simply unprepared for the evil one finds in the world. Greed, selfishness, egoism, aggression, and self-aggrandizement – all are readily explained by Aquinas. Left unexplained is not only the sheer malevolence behind so much of what people do, but the sheer bloodiness of the last century, the bloodiest in world history: over 100 million killed in armed conflict, over 160 million if one includes "democide," such as the 40 million Russian deaths ordered by Stalin. One does not, of course, expect Aquinas to explain twentieth-century history, but if his view of natural law is to be fruitful, the events of this bloody century should not be alien to his thought. Klein allows us to take the natural law seriously (it exists), while more adequately explaining not just the absence of the natural law in the lives of millions, but the love of evil that sometimes seems to make a mockery of natural law. To natural law, Klein adds natural evil.[4]

If Klein's vision is more tragic than that of Aquinas, her view is also more morally problematic. Protecting and preserving one's good internal objects, as Klein calls our mental images of parents and others, making reparation for harming them in phantasy and reality, is not the same thing as *doing* good. Kleinian reparation needs to be drawn more fully into the moral world.

Klein as natural law theorist

Though Klein likely never thought of herself as a natural law theorist, others have come close to this conclusion, even if they don't use the language of natural law. Rustin's appreciative account of Klein and the Kleinians as theorists of social justice is exemplary (Rustin 1991).

"Melanie Klein's investigation of the mental states of infancy gave rise to an intensely *social* view of the origins of the self." The pleasure in being fed is less important than being held and cared for, or rather these pleasures are inseparable. Contra Freud, pleasure is not the infant's goal. Pleasure is a mere "signpost to the object," the human relationship. Even the infant is social.

There are, by the way, affinities between Klein's view of the infant and that of Augustine, though one should not make too much of them. "He could not yet speak and pale with jealousy and bitterness, glared at his brother sharing his mother's milk," says Augustine of a jealous baby (*Confessions* 1.10–11). While the grown up baby (aren't we all?) may one day feel guilt, there is little sense in Augustine of the love that from the beginning of life will contend with hate. For Augustine, love comes later.

Rustin continues, "a second characteristic of Kleinian analysis was its emphasis on the ethical. Kleinian theory makes the development of moral capacities in the infant a criterion of normal personality development. Moral feelings are held to be innate, arising from the primary intensity of feelings of love and hate for the object." From almost the beginning of life, and certainly by the age of 6 months, the infant feels not just satisfaction from being fed and cuddled, but gratitude, as well as hate and rage when these satisfactions are not forthcoming.

"A third aspect of Kleinian thinking, which, I shall argue, had significant social affinities was its teleological dimension." This aspect of Rustin's thinking about Klein was considered in the introduction. Teleological reasoning is definitive of natural law.

"One central theme of Kleinian theory, however, was ... difficult to assimilate into its social thought. This was the emphasis on destructiveness and aggression – the concept of an innate 'death instinct' " (Rustin 1991, 147–149, emphasis his). For Klein, as for Freud, the conflict between love and hate is primary. Our deepest fear, as we grow older, is that we shall confuse love and hate, and so destroy all we love and care about.

With the exception of the fourth theme, Rustin renders Klein a theorist in the tradition of Aquinas, for whom natural law is, in the words of Jacques Maritain (2001, 29), "the ideal formula of development of a given being." A human being who is bound to others through a variety of family, social and political relationships, a human being who naturally seeks the good, even if he or she doesn't always know it. Especially Thomistic is the view of natural law not as a set of principles, but as an account of humanity's essential sociability. Humanity, says Aquinas, has a natural inclination to live in society: and in this respect, whatever pertains to this inclination belongs to the natural law: for instance, to shun ignorance, to avoid offending those among whom one has to live, and other such things regarding the above inclination.

(ST I–II, 94)

Among these other such things Aquinas includes educating the young.

Rustin's account of Klein as a theorist of social justice in the tradition of Aristotle and the British socialists (quite a combination!) makes it easier to argue that Klein is a natural law theorist. This does not, however, automatically make Rustin's account of Klein correct. Contrast Rustin's reading of Klein with that of Julia Kristeva (2001, 237) who argues that "all that Melanie demands from the powers originating from the outside is that they exist as little as possible, that they do not encroach too much upon the adjustments made by internal objects bouncing between envy and gratitude." From Kristeva's perspective, people just want to be left alone so they can make reparation to their internal objects.

Who is right, Rustin or Kristeva? Does it depend on how seriously we take the death drive? To the second question the answer is "no." Rustin takes the death drive, humanity's pleasure in destruction, as seriously as anyone. How we draw on Klein as a social theorist in the tradition of natural law thinking will not depend on whether we can tame the death drive. It may, however, depend on how we interpret the *Todestrieb*, as Freud called it.

While both Freud and Klein set Eros against Thanatos, life against death, for Klein there is no nirvana principle, no connection between the hatred and aggression of Thanatos and the peace and absence of stimulation that Freud writes of in "Beyond the Pleasure Principle" (1920, 34–43). For Freud, the *Todestrieb* ultimately seeks to return to the origin of things, a state of oblivion. There is, in other words, a type of satisfaction inherent in the *Todestrieb*, a satisfaction from which life itself is a long detour. For Klein, on the other hand, the *Todestrieb* is sadism, envy, and destruction. Nothing in Klein's account of the *Todestrieb* suggests she shared Freud's idea that death is the telos of life (Alford 1989, 25).

This might make it seem as if Klein's account of the "death instinct" would be easier to assimilate into mainstream psychoanalytic thought than Freud's. That may not be the case, for the Kleinian account makes it clear that the infant and young child hates, envies, and would destroy its mother if it could, regardless of how responsive and loving the mother truly is. To be sure, Klein and Kleinians recognize that the mother's response to the child's aggression, how well she is able to contain the child's hatred and envy, will make an enormous difference in how well the child is able to integrate its experiences of loving and hating, and so enter into and remain within the depressive position (Klein 1975c). Nevertheless, the thesis that the child's hatred and destructiveness are innate, unrelated, at least at first, to the quality of the child's relationship with its mother and others, leaves even some sympathetic followers cold. In "Hate in the Counter-Transference," D.W. Winnicott writes that "the mother hates the baby before the baby hates the mother, and before the baby can know his mother hates him" (Winnicott 1978, 73). If this is so, then we must rethink the "death instinct," seeing it as a response to real relationships, including the relationship of being hated.

The difference between Klein and Winnicott matters, but it cannot be settled here. Suffice to say that from a Kleinian perspective, hate, envy, and the lust to destroy are primary, whether or not they originate in response to real relationships. It is these dreadful passions that constitute the death instinct for Klein, which is theoretically quite different from Freud's *Todestrieb*, even if the practical difference is not so great. For both, life is a conflict between love and hate. Or as Freud so famously put it,

> And now, I think, the meaning of the evolution of civilization is no longer obscure to us. It must present the struggle between Eros and Death, between the instinct of life and the instinct of destruction, as it works itself out in the human species. This struggle is what all life essentially consists of, and the evolution of civilization may therefore be simply described as the struggle for life of the human species. And it is this battle of the giants that our nurse-maids try to appease with their lullaby about Heaven.
>
> (1930, 121–122)

Let us not let natural law become one more lullaby.

For all her intercourse with death and destruction, Klein is in the end a more optimistic thinker than Freud. In the fully developed self, love is stronger than death. As the individual matures, the destructive elements of the self are split off and regained, over and over, until greater integration comes about.

> As a result, the feeling of responsibility becomes stronger, and guilt and depression are more fully experienced. When this happens, the ego is strengthened, omnipotence of destructive impulses is diminished, together with envy, and the capacity for love and gratitude, stifled in the course of the splitting processes, is released.
>
> (Klein 1975c, 225)

This is the telos of development, and it is dependent on the integration of destructive, hateful, sadistic, and envious aspects of the self. Neither individuals nor societies do it very well, but analysis can help. Maritain expresses a related idea in the language of natural law, knowledge of which "develops in proportion to the degree of moral experience and self-reflection, and of social experience also, of which man is capable in the various ages of his history" (Maritain 2001, 38). Though Maritain is evidently referring to human history, it would not be misleading to read him as referring to individual history as well, what is called moral development.

In Klein's original account, analysis fosters integration by interpreting the anxiety over aggression that splits the ego, alienating the loving from the hating self. Post-Kleinians tend to stress the analyst's containing function, his or her ability to contain the analysand's projections, particularly the terrified sadism, so that the projection can be reintrojected without scaring the self to death (Hinshelwood 1989, 244–250).

Not only does Klein allow us to see more deeply into the horrors of human history than other natural law theorists, but she gives Thomistic natural law a new twist. Do good and avoid evil means, from a Kleinian perspective, that our task is to protect the good from our own evil, which Klein equates with envy. Evil is not just the privation (absence) of good, but the wilful destruction of good because it is good. Envy is the leading expression of the death drive. Or as Klein (1975c, 189) puts it, quoting Chaucer, envy is the worst sin because it opposes life and creativity itself. "It is certain that envy is the worst sin that is; for all other sins are sins only against one virtue, whereas envy is against all virtue and against all goodness." Klein might have continued to quote Chaucer, who goes on to say that envy "is sorry for all the goodness of one's neighbor, making it different from all other sins. There is scarcely any sin that doesn't have within it some delight, but Envy has within it only anguish and sorrow" (*Canterbury Tales*, "The Parson's Tale," 485–490).[5]

Foster life in all its aspects, from bearing children to building community, is the practical implication of "do good, avoid evil," according to Aquinas (ST I–II, 91–96; II–II, 66). This is the leading implication of Kleinian natural law as well. Or as Kristeva (2001, 84) puts it, "it is for Eros's sake that our anxiety about the annihilation of life penetrates the deepest layers of the psyche." We long to foster life in the face of death, but fear we are too hateful, envious, and weak. Fostering community in all its guises, from raising children to caring for the elderly, helps to gradually convince us that our love is stronger than our hate.

The death of thought

If Melanie Klein is a theorist of endangered love, Wilfred Bion is the theorist of endangered thought: our inability to think about what we are doing. The first step in morality is to say (at least to oneself) what one is doing. Bion, even better than Klein, tells us why this is so rare. Klein, says Donald Meltzer, constructed a theological model of the mind, in which our internal objects are our gods. For Bion, the problem is how to get outside the theater of the mind (one thinks of Plato's cave), and make contact with the world (Meltzer 1978, pt 3, 2; 1981, 170).

Especially Platonic is Klein's vision of the good as that which makes everything else worthwhile. Plato made an almost identical argument about what he called the Form of the Good. Even more than knowledge, Plato valued goodness, or at least that is the implication of the Form of the Good, set above even knowledge and justice. For if we don't know why knowledge and justice are good, then we don't really know anything at all. So runs Plato's argument in *The Republic* (507a–509d). What Klein adds is an appreciation of how much we want to spoil what we most value, precisely because it is so valuable, representing goodness beyond our possession and control.

For Klein, the leading result of splitting, projection, introjection, and all the other things we do to protect the good object from our wrath is confusion over good and bad itself. One sees this in Klein's (1975b) account of Richard in her *Narrative of a Child Analysis*, about a little boy who could not keep clear in his own mind whether the cook and the maid were good or bad, to say nothing of his mommy and daddy. He could not do so because of inadequate splitting-and-idealization (Meltzer runs these terms together with hyphens as though they were one process), which fails to protect the good object from the split-off bad parts of the self. The result was confusion and emotional immaturity, as Richard "could not keep the destructive and Hitleresque part of himself from crowding in on and taking over the good part." The result (though the judgment seems harsh about a 10-year-old boy) was "consequent hypocrisy in his character" (Meltzer 1978, pt 2, 64).

Richard is not just a disturbed little boy. He represents the threat faced by us all, that we shall mistake good and bad, and so destroy all we love and care about. Culture, institutions, and leaders are generally eager to tell us which is which, and so reinforce paranoid-schizoid defenses against anxiety.[6] From confusion to clarity, but at the cost of dividing the world in two, alienating one's own hatred and aggression in others and fighting it there. Here is a defense that almost guarantees that we shall never arrive at a more complex resolution of our angst, one that sees the good and bad mixed together in ourselves as well as others.

Bion's (1970) account is somewhat different, focusing less on splitting and reification, more on what he calls attacks on linking, by which he means the connection between thoughts. It is easy to have thoughts. The trick is to know how to put them together, what is called thinking, without being overwhelmed with terror or despair. One wants to say that attacks on linking stem from the hatred of thought itself, a hatred of knowing what one is doing and feeling, a hatred of connecting thought, word, and deed with their consequences. Consequences that include not just the effect on others, but the feelings evoked in oneself. For Bion, much of mental life is devoted to the destruction of thought. In other words, the death instinct operates at the level of thought itself. The result is utter irresponsibility, as we destroy the possibility of knowing what we are doing. For Bion, the defense mechanisms are really defenses against knowing reality.

Bion calls the desire not to know the minus-K (minus-Knowledge) link, which must eventually empty experience of meaning, leading to a barren existence that gives rise to terror, what Bion calls nameless dread. Antoine Roquentin's nausea in Jean-Paul Sartre's novel *Nausea* is a good literary example of this dread, including its origin in minus-K, the desire not to know the insistent particularity of the world. "I would have liked [it] to exist less strongly, more dryly, in a more abstract way," says Roquentin (Sartre 1964, 127).

Reality is a suspect word these days, almost as suspect as the term nature. More useful is to focus on the lie, characterized not so much by its content as the motivation behind it. Lies are not just attacks on linking. Lies stem from the inability to tolerate the distance between container and contained. In order to think and to know, our minds must be able to hold our experiences, letting new experiences in without being overwhelmed and reduced to chaos. For a brief moment we must know nothing at all (what Bion calls living without memory or desire), so that the container that is our mind is open to new experience. The trouble is, this synapse between container and contained, this gap in time and space, can feel like an eternity – that is, like death. We must experience a little death in order to think and to know. For many this experience is unbearable, for it recalls all too many little deaths (failures of containment) in our lives.

Lies are like Milton's Satan in *Paradise Lost*, living in exile in Pandemonium. Busy, busy, busy, always building, marching, celebrating, and preparing for war (I.717–719). All in the service of not stopping long enough to know what one is feeling and doing, as it is this knowledge itself that is unbearable. Put this passionate ignorance together with a Kleinian account of what one is really doing deep inside the cave of one's mind, enviously destroying the good not just because one has confused it with the bad, but because it is good (goodness existing outside oneself, beyond one's appropriation and control), and one has a view of human history that aspires to tragedy. The tragedy of not knowing one's own destructiveness, even as one is living it out.

From Plato to Aquinas, no one came close to this understanding of evil. Writing four centuries after Aquinas, Milton did, writing about a Satan who would rather rule in hell than serve in heaven. Not just because he wanted to rule, but because he could not abide God's goodness.

> I . . . thought one step higher
> Would set me highest, and in a moment quit
> The debt immense of endless gratitude,
> So burdensome still paying, still to owe;
> Forgetful what from Him I still received.
> (IV.50–55)

In old English "quit" means requite, or to take revenge.

Satan would take revenge on God *because* He is good, because His rule was mild and loving (IV.43). Satan does not just envy God's power; he envies His goodness. And envy, Klein tells us, is the leading expression of the death drive: the hatred of goodness because it is good and not me, outside my possession and control. Aquinas never came close to such an understanding of evil. For just a moment Augustine did when he came to wonder why he stole some pears.

Augustine was about 16 when he pilfered the pears. Earlier, when still a child, he tells us, he stole food from the family larder. He knew it was wrong, but he understood the motive. The food was a bribe, used to get other children to play with him. Later he would commit what he came to regard as sexual sin. But it was the theft of the pears that disturbed him most.

Coming home one day with some friends, they stole into a farmer's orchard and carted off a load of pears. Augustine didn't want the pears. He had better pears at home. Eventually he and his friends dumped the pears before swine. Why did they do it? Augustine wonders if he stole the pears out of the pleasure of transgression itself. Was it an *acte gratuit*? "Simply what was not allowed allured us" (*Confessions* 2.9).

In his *Confessions*, Augustine writes in the same vein as Aquinas (ST I, 49), arguing that people do bad things in the pursuit of an apparent good. But stealing the pears pursued no good at all. Could that be in some way worse than murder?

> A murder is committed. Why? To get another's wife or wealth, or to get the necessities of life. Or for fear another would deprive the murderer of such things. Or from a sense of wrong burning for redress. Who murders with no cause but to enjoy the mere murdering? Who would credit such a motive?
>
> (*Confessions* 2.10)

Stealing pears isn't murder, but Augustine is as troubled over his motive as if it were. As he rejects the possibility of pleasure in murder for its own sake, for the pleasure of the destruction of life, Augustine finally rejects the possibility of pleasure in theft, done for its own sake. Even the brutal and cruel Catiline, of whom it was said that he was evil and savage without reason, had a rational motive: to keep in practice, lest he be slow to react when attacked. Augustine concludes, "No, not even Catiline himself loved his crimes; something else motivated him to commit them" (*Confessions* 2.10). Is not Augustine working a little too hard to make Catiline's savagery a rational act, perverse but nonetheless based on reason?

Augustine's view of evil as privation is neither shallow nor banal. Evil as the privation of good implies not merely the absence of good, but an absence stemming from an act of self-assertion in which one makes one's own will absolute, so that the good begins and ends with me. Or as Alasdair MacIntyre puts it about Augustine's concept of evil, "Augustine sees the evil of human nature in the consent which the will gives to evil . . . . Evil is somehow or other such and the human will is somehow or other such that the will can delight in evil" (MacIntyre 1981, 163).

Evil as privation is a serious concept; it is by no means merely an absence or lack of goodness. Privation involves a willing identification with evil.[7] Nevertheless, Augustine's view lacks the distinctly Kleinian sense of evil: the spoiling and destruction of the good because it is good and not me, the hatred of goodness itself. Not even in Catiline can Augustine find that. Augustine sets *caritas* against *cupiditas*, brotherly and sisterly love against cupidity. Freud and Klein set Eros against Thanatos, and that is really the difference. When he says "Evil be thou my Good," Milton's Satan comes closer to Freud and Klein than Augustine (IV.105–110).

Could one argue that the envious spoiling of the good about which Klein writes is similar to Augustine's precept of privation? Both would render the good less than wholly good without putting anything substantial in its place. In that way their views are similar. Nevertheless, a will to destruction of the good exists in Klein's account, an active hatred of goodness for its own sake that is absent in Augustine, even if it is hinted at in the story of the pears. The will to evil that Augustine discovers in himself is the will to transgression for its own sake, and the perverse pleasure in being wicked that goes with it (*Confessions* 2.9–10). Taking pleasure in the powerfulness of being bad may sound evil, and perhaps it is. Still, there is something adolescent in the way being bad thrills Augustine (as one might expect of a 16-year-old), revealing a different, and lesser, order of evil than the envious hatred of goodness just because it is good and not wholly mine.

As he rejects the possibility of pleasure in murder for its own sake, for the pleasure of the destruction of life, Augustine finally rejects the possibility of pleasure in theft, done for its own sake. Puzzling long and hard over his larceny, Augustine concludes that it had something to do with his friends, that he wouldn't have done it alone. Could "bonding" with his friends, as it is called today, have been the reason, the apparent good that justifies the bad (*Confessions* 2.16)?[8] Augustine appears content with this answer. He reflects no further, even as he seems to sense that his answer is inadequate, that he has crossed a threshold of moral possibility (the love of evil for its own sake) but is unable to go further. Aquinas does not go as far (ST I–II, 71, 2).

My interpretation of Augustine's theft is not the only possible one. Peter Rudnytsky sees Augustine's recollection of the theft of the pears as a "screen memory," as Freud called it, in which "everyday and indifferent events" take the place of "serious and tragic ones" (Rudnytsky 1994; Freud 1889, 305). And what does the theft screen? Augustine's Oedipal desires for his mother, Monica, with whom he had an intensely close relationship. Rudnytsky's strongest argument is "the disproportion between the triviality of Augustine's offense and the extreme importance he attaches to it." This disproportion may thus be explained psychoanalytically as a displacement of the sense of guilt attaching itself to the former events [his desire for his mother] onto the latter. It is this displacement of affect from something serious onto something trivial that makes the theft of the pears truly a "screen memory."

(Rudnytsky 1994, 140)

Rudnytsky could be correct. This is one of those questions whose answer is impossible to know. What we are talking about, in any case, is not simply how close an interpretation comes to reality, but what the interpretation allows us to do. Rudnytsky's allows us to see the theft of the pears not just as an Oedipal displacement, but as a trope that connects two primordial sins: the Original Sin that led to the Fall with Oedipal guilt. As Augustine remarks in the *City of God*, the lure of the forbidden fruit for Adam (as for Augustine) was that it was forbidden (XIV.12). Indeed, Augustine refers to the pears as *poma*, the same term used in the Latin Vulgate Bible to refer to the fruit in the Garden of Eden (Rudnytsky 1994, 138–139).

My interpretation, on the other hand, allows us to take Augustine at his word: that he really is troubled and puzzled by the thrill of transgression for its own sake. It is this, and the problem of evil that it represents, that so vexes Augustine. When in doubt about a person's motives, it is not the worst principle to take him at his word. Not perhaps, as the last word, but the first, in this case that Augustine is truly puzzled about what he claims to be puzzled about, his pleasure in destruction for its own sake. In any case, Augustine's reference to the brutality of Catiline, his desperate attempt to make Catiline's savagery rational, fits only my account. (One could make something of the fact that it was the mistress of Lucius Sergius Catilina who betrayed him to Cicero, but to make this the unconscious significance of Augustine's reference to Catiline seems a stretch.)

One is tempted to let Rudnytsky have the last word here. "Just as the oedipal patterns in Augustine's life as a whole are superimposed upon preoedipal ones, so his theft of the pears is open to interpretations on multiple psychological levels" (Rudnytsky 1994, 140). Klein always understood that Oedipal desire begins in the savage desire to possess the contents of mother's body, and so perhaps there is not so much difference between Klein and Freud here, a point I think Rudnytsky is getting at when he quotes Edward Glover to the effect that Klein's view of the infant's relationship to its mother is a version of Original Sin (1994, 46). Since Rudnytsky has already linked Freud's account of the Oedipal conflict with Original Sin, the connection to Klein is transitive, so to speak.

While one is tempted to give Rudnytsky the last word, there is one more possibility to consider, one that fits neither Rudnytsky's categories nor my own, at least not neatly. An Old Testament term often translated as evil, *raᶜ*, refers to anything bad, displeasing, or harmful to man. Evil is not just what man does, but what one suffers (Isa. 45: 7; Jer. 4: 6; Amos 3: 6; Mic. 2: 3; Eccles. 1: 13; Job 2: 10) (Alford 1997, 62–63). The saying that one has "fallen on evil days," captures something of this original meaning.

If this is so, then another way of thinking about Augustine's view of evil as privation suggests itself. Evil as de-privation, the loss of all one cares about, all that makes life worth living. Augustine was remarkably sensitive to this experience, writing of the death of his friend.

> My eyes look for him everywhere, and he was not there. I hated everything because they did not have him, nor could they now tell me "look, he is on the way," as used to be the case when he was alive and absent from me . . . . I was surprised that any other mortals were alive . . . . I was even more surprised that when he was dead I was alive.
>
> (*Confessions* 4.9)

Seen from this perspective, evil as privation is not simply the absence of the good. It is the loss of one who seems to embody all goodness. Elaine Pagels, author of *The Origin of Satan*, writes that the book was composed under the impress of the loss of her husband, and shortly thereafter her son (Pagels 1995, 184). If we see evil as privation as a way of talking about human loss, then evil itself begins to make more sense. Evil is the loss of everything that makes life worth living, an experience so awesome and awful that it must be attributed to malevolent forces, lest life itself be emptied of meaning, and goodness rendered void. What Klein adds is the fear that this malevolent force might be located inside oneself, the hate we harbor for those we love. Evil is, in other words, the experience of loss in the paranoid-schizoid dimension. With this too natural law must deal.

What difference does it make?

What difference does it make, the reader may be wondering? Augustine's account of evil as privation of the good is surely powerful enough to explain the horrors of this world. Perhaps, but consider that it is Augustine's vision of evil as privation that the political philosopher Hannah Arendt draws upon to explain the evil of Adolph Eichmann, the Nazi bureaucrat who organized the Holocaust. (Arendt was no stranger to Augustine; her dissertation was titled *Der Liebesbegriff bei Augustin*.) Both the insight and the insufficiency of her account are related to Augustine's vision of evil.

Arendt's report on the trial of Eichmann, which originally ran as a series of articles in *The New Yorker* in 1963, remains controversial to this day, as Arendt seemed to say that Eichmann was such a banal bureaucrat that he never truly thought about what he was doing, murdering millions of Jews. Indeed, this is what puzzles Arendt so. How could pale little men do such awful deeds, the murder of millions? In coming to terms with this fact, Arendt says that she had to give up her belief in radical evil.

> It is indeed my opinion now that evil is never "radical," that it is only extreme, and that it possesses neither depth nor any demonic dimension. It can overgrow and lay waste the whole world precisely because it spreads like a fungus on the surface. It [evil] is "thought-defying," as I said, because thought tries to reach some depth, to go to the roots, and the moment it concerns itself with evil, it is frustrated because there is nothing. That is its "banality." Only the good has depth and can be radical.
>
> (Elshtain 1995, 76)[9]

Earlier, in *The Origins of Totalitarianism* (originally published in 1951), Arendt characterized the last stages of totalitarianism as "absolute evil."

> If it is true that in the final stages of totalitarianism an absolute evil appears (absolute because it can no longer be deduced from comprehensively human motives), it is also true that without it we might never have known the truly radical nature of evil.
>
> (Arendt 1973, ix)

In *Eichmann in Jerusalem*, Arendt (1965) does not change what she thinks about evil. Evil is still defined in terms of its incomprehensibility, what she now calls "thought defying." What changes is her judgment about what makes evil thought defying – that it possesses no qualities to think about. Indeed, one might argue that not even this changed, just the location of evil, so to speak, from deeply rooted to on the surface.

Behind Arendt's reformulation of evil was her determination not to permit Eichmann or any of his fellow Nazis to attain the status of dramatic or romantic demiurges. They must be shown to be who they really were: limited, hollowed-out, pale and empty men. This is the banality of evil. Especially important for Arendt was to strip evil of its generative power. Above all, evil cannot be creative; evil cannot be allowed to bring anything new into the world (Elshtain 1995, 84–85).

Surely Arendt grasps an important point? William Blake's *bon mot*, that Satan gets all the best lines in *Paradise Lost*, should remind us that there is something attractive about evil, and that should worry us. Something like this way of thinking certainly lies behind Augustine's concerns as well: only God is great; only God is creative and fruitful. Evil just is, the absence of goodness and fecundity. Not only that, but whereas for Augustine God is abstract, everywhere, and not diluted, evil is concrete, and tied to bodies. In a related fashion, Klein characterizes the nadir of the paranoid-schizoid position in terms of the inability to abstract symbols from the bodies that they represent (Klein 1975f). Or as Janine Chasseguet-Smirgel (1994, 235) puts it, "symbol formation derives from the need of the child to protect his object, or parts of the object, from the effects of his attacks." Perhaps one reason we do philosophy is to protect those we love from our unutterable wrath.

Missing from Arendt's account but found in Augustine's is a vision of evil as confusion, fog, and lack of clarity. For Augustine, the tangled knot is a leading symbol of evil (*Confessions* 2.18, 6.4–5; Evans 1982, 4). Klein too writes about the importance of confusion, as we become terrified that we might confuse good and bad, and so destroy all we care about, which is the reason Richard is so troubled. A fine literary example of the connection between confusion and evil is the family of Satan in *Paradise Lost*. Having intercourse with his daughter Sin after she springs from his head, Satan fathers Death, who goes on to rape his mother, who subsequently gives birth to the hounds of hell, who will gnaw forever at the womb of Sin (II.746–870).

Rudnytsky stresses the Oedipal quality of the confusion of generations (Satan's son is also his grandson), as they finally meet at a point between earth, heaven, and hell, characterized by Milton as the place where three roads meet ("three sev'ral ways," X.323), the same place that Oedipus killed his father (Rudnytsky 1988, 170–171). A Kleinian reading seems at least as plausible, emphasizing not just confusion, but the primitive persecutory anxiety that is confusion's result, and cause. In any case, these readings are not mutually exclusive. Important is the insight that evil is both confused and confusing, partly because we do not want to know, partly because confusion is itself experienced as threatening the watertight distinction between good and bad that marks the paranoid-schizoid position.

Confusion is not a leading category of evil in Arendt. One speculates that making evil superficial and banal is an attempt by Arendt to eliminate confusion, as though there were no depth to be confused about. This, though, comes too close to not thinking.

If we understand evil as an attack on linking, destroying thinking and understanding as well as feeling, then the banality of evil begins to look intentional, as though one could give oneself over to the *Todestrieb* without knowing it. As though this were half the pleasure, doing evil without having to recognize it. The contribution of psychoanalysis to an understanding of the evil of men like Eichmann, says Emilia Steuerman, "is the recognition that our capacity for thinking and tolerating separateness and difference has to acknowledge an unconscious world that can attack the most basic links that make understanding possible" (Steuerman 2000, 35–36).

Though Arendt understands something important about evil, aspects of her project are troubling. It is as if the goal of showing that evil cannot be great (even greatly evil and terrible) is so important that something of the horror of the evil gets lost: that behind evil lies the will to destroy the pure, the innocent, and the good because the other is pure, innocent, and good, and the evil doer is not. It is this that Milton's Satan grasps, the same point that Augustine comes so close to seeing before turning away.

Let me suggest another way of thinking about evil and evil doers, along the lines of the cliché "way down deep he's shallow." Admittedly, the Nazis were shallow men, but that does not mean their evil was shallow. On the contrary, it is because they were shallow men that their evil ran so deep. Evil may be deep even as evil doers are generally (always?) shallow. To make evil deep is not to glorify it, only to suggest that evil is a force that transcends (as the unconscious transcends) the awareness of those who practice it.

At about this point the thoughtful reader may be asking, "what is this deep and shallow business anyway? What sort of intuitive but vague distinction does it represent?" One result of the Freudian revolution was to see that even the most ordinary man has a creative unconscious, expressed for example in dreams. Even the most boring bureaucrat may have fantastic fantasies. Philip Rieff makes this same point when he says, "Freud democratized genius by giving everyone a creative unconscious" (Rieff 1961, 36). Banal Nazi bureaucrats likely possessed an extraordinary unconscious, filled with fantasies of hate and destruction, as well as perverse urges to purify the world. That these men and women, like Eichmann, may not have been aware of their destructive fantasies, that they may have deeply repressed them, does not mean that these fantasies were absent. On the contrary, the more repressed the fantasy, the greater (not the lesser) power it has over its possessor, as the possessor has no opportunity to exercise rational control over that about which he knows nothing. It is incorrect to say that the motivation of someone like Eichmann is shallow. Eichmann may be shallow, but his motivation is deep, as deep as the hating human heart, and the most destructive human fantasy.

Evil may run deep, even as those in whom it runs deep are shallow and banal, unaware of the world of death and destruction that lies within. Perhaps it is the very shallowness of their understanding that makes them more vulnerable to the acting-out of these fantasies when they become socially sanctioned, as was the case under the Nazis. Indeed, in these circumstances we might even be justified in talking about a collective destructive unconscious, though precisely what that might mean remains obscure. Perhaps just that the ideology of the times encouraged and channeled the destructive fantasies of millions in a similar direction, as though to socialize fantasy itself.

While it may be correct to argue that evil is not creative, reducing the world to the dimensions of pain, suffering, and destruction, one wants to be careful about applying aesthetic categories, such as creativity, to moral debate. Is the good always creative? Sometimes the good itself is boring, and mundane, the tedious work of feeding the hungry, and curing the sick, including victims who are not always ennobled by their victimhood. Why make creativity the issue one way or the other? Is it not enough to say that evil is bad and should be avoided, whereas goodness is good and should be pursued?

The confusion of art and morals has a long history, and while art has certainly portrayed suffering so as to move its audience, the Frankfurt School of Critical Theory is neither the first nor the last group of thinkers to be deeply suspicious about the creative, artistic rendering of suffering, as though this somehow made the suffering meaningful or worthwhile. To make beauty out of suffering always risks ignoring or devaluing the reality of those individuals who have suffered (Marcuse 1978). This is the context of Theodor Adorno's (1983, 34) famous saying that to write (lyric) poetry after Auschwitz is barbaric. Adorno exaggerates, but he is not completely wrong. To transform suffering into beautiful form always runs the risk of making the suffering somehow less horrifying, more meaningful, even worth it. Klein's account of reparation runs this risk.

Making reparation moral

Not the death drive, but the puzzling and mysterious quality of reparation in Klein's account is the biggest barrier to transforming Klein into a decent natural law theorist. For while it often seems that Klein is writing about making reparation to other people, in many cases she is not. She is writing about making reparation to one's injured internal objects. This risks rendering reparation morally irresponsible – that is, all about me. Klein risks, in other words, turning reparation into art.

That this aesthetic interpretation of Kleinian reparation is correct is seen in the work of Klein's followers, such as Hanna Segal, who write about art in the language of reparation, as though they were virtually the same. In "A Psycho-Analytical Approach to Aesthetics," Segal (1955, 397) writes that artistic creation requires that we mourn our lost objects; only when we do so can we fully distinguish symbolic reality from its external counterpart. Only then can we get to work on internal reality, giving it beautiful form so as to compensate us for the loss of an external world, a loss that occurs not only through death, but through the separation of symbol and reality itself, a loss of identification with the object.

For Klein, the goal is to transform into symbols our phantasies of love and hate that otherwise remain so terribly embodied and reified. If Jesus Christ is the word (*logos*) made flesh (John 1: 14), then Klein's goal is the opposite: to transform the phantasies of the flesh into the word, so that we might finally hear ourselves and be healed. Not only is this good therapy, but it is good natural law, promoting the ascendance of life over death, love over hate, good over evil. Rather than denying our pleasure in destruction, lest we destroy those we truly care for, we can acknowledge our sadism, and make reparation for it.

Only one thing gets lost in this scheme, the obligation to think about and make reparation to the ones truly harmed by our own and others' aggression. In the end, reparation is so inward-directed, so symbolically oriented, that this hardly matters to Klein. Reparation is symbolically oriented because the goal is to separate the body from the symbol, so that thought becomes freer, less reified (Klein 1975f). While it would be contrary to the telos of normal development to say that the ultimate goal should be to reconnect body and symbol, the goal should be to keep symbol and reality in constant conversation.

In what is probably her most well-known account of reparation, Klein writes of the painter Ruth Kjär, who had been in a state of anguish since someone removed a painting from her wall. The empty space tormented her, as though it were her own empty body, robbed of its babies. Never having painted before, Kjär painted a "life size figure of a naked negress," as Klein puts it, demonstrating an extraordinary talent that she had never known she possessed. It is obvious, says Klein, "that the desire to make reparation, to make good the injury psychologically done to the mother, and also to restore herself was at the bottom of the compelling urge to paint" (Klein 1975e, 215–218). That the first image Kjär painted was of a naked negress is not addressed by Klein. Presumably it was easier for Kjär to get in touch with her own feelings by projecting them into the sensual "primitive" other. Why this might not always be such a good thing is not addressed by Klein either.

In another account of reparation, Klein writes of reparation as an act of social contrition, as when "in former times . . . ruthless cruelty against native populations was displayed by people who not only explored, but conquered and colonized." And how might the colonists or their descendants make reparation? By "repopulating the country with people of their own nationality."

> We can see that through the interest in exploring (whether or not aggression is openly shown) various impulses and emotions – aggression, feelings of guilt, love and the drive to reparation – can be transferred to another sphere, far away from the original person.
>
> (Klein 1964, 104–105)

Including far away from the original victims.

Why is Klein so dense? One might argue that she wrote in less politically correct times, but that is hardly the whole reason. Consider Rustin's (1991, 35) comment that "good object relations and reparation for past damage, in phantasy or reality, constitute a natural and desired condition of individuals." Rustin makes this statement in an essay titled "A Socialist Consideration of Kleinian Psychoanalysis," in which he is concerned to demonstrate that Kleinian thought provides a resource for social democracy. But social democracy requires that people make reparation in reality, not just phantasy, and that they know the difference. With enough amendments, Klein's account can be made to support Rustin's good society, but it should be clear that for Klein it makes little difference whether the harm or the reparation stems from acts of phantasy or reality. It might, however, matter to the victims. (I never quite understood the desire of some African-Americans in the United States for reparations until I thought about it in the Kleinian sense of the term; now it makes perfect sense.)

Dozens of similar comments by Klein and her interpreters are readily found, all illustrating the way in which reparation in phantasy and reality are interchangeable. Consider Meltzer's comment that Richard was able to repair "in phantasy, not in psychic reality," his good objects (Meltzer 1978, pt 2, 115). This is fine, as long as it is Richard as a 10-year-old boy in analysis we are concerned with, not Richard as a man sharing the world with others.

To be sure, Klein (1975d) distinguishes between genuine and manic or mock reparation, and one might be inclined to argue that only mock reparation substitutes reparation in phantasy for reparation in reality. But this is not what Klein says. Mock reparation is distinguished by its manic character, the way it denies the harm inflicted, and the sadism behind it. Absent too is a genuine concern for the object. The thinking behind mock reparation is more akin to "poor me, if I hurt mommy, I won't have her to care for me any more." The trouble is, mock reparation is a way of characterizing the quality of the reparative phantasy, not the quality of the act. The distinction between mock and real reparation has little to do with whether I make reparation to a person whom I have harmed, or whether I simply go home and write a poem about it. Whether one authentically cares about the reality of the other distinguishes mock from real reparation, but because care is measured by phantasy and feeling, not action, the distinction is not morally useful.

In fact, the problem with Klein's account of reparation is a little more complex than this. Klein understands that getting reparation out into the world can create a good feedback loop, in which fostering life strengthens one's beliefs in one's own reparative powers. But, as with the colonialists, Klein gives us no reason to think that the world we make reparation to is the world we have harmed. The Kleinian category of mock reparation, important as a warning against the tendency to deny the harm we have done with our hatred, is not very helpful here. Why? Why can't we say that repopulating a land decimated by explorers with the descendants of the explorers is mock reparation and manic denial? First, because Klein in no way suggests it is. Second, and more importantly, what makes mock reparation mock is the denial of the hurt and pain inflicted, and especially the denial of the sadism behind it. Admit that, do something life-enhancing about it, and all is for-given, at least as far as one's internal world is concerned. Reparation recognizes pain and serves life, but it need not be the pain and life of the original victims.

To end on this note would not be entirely fair to Klein, however. Nowhere in her work does Klein suggest that people think or feel about reparation the way I have just described. Never do they say to themselves, even unconsciously, "I'll paint a beautiful picture, and so feel less guilty about my rapacious greed." People do not, in other words, think like the popular media, which tell us that it is good to pray because it lowers one's blood pressure and strengthens the immune system. On the contrary, Klein tells us over and over, nowhere more than in *Love, Hate and Reparation*, written for a popular audience, but in dozens of her works, that we love and make reparation to people because we care about them as people. When we are successful in doing so, we feel strengthened in the power of our love. Hope is reborn, the hope behind all hope: that love is stronger than hate, life stronger than death.

The tendency to aestheticize reparation is a quality of Klein's theoretical account of the world of internal objects. It is not reflected in her writings about the lives of real people. It is as though the internal world of object relations lives a life parallel to that of the real world of human relations. They interact, but each is only intermittently in contact with the other. Or as Meltzer (1978, pt 2, 44–46) puts it, "reparation began to take on a more mysterious meaning" in Klein's later work. "The true reparation is something that happens when the mental condition, the mental atmosphere is conducive to the objects repairing one another." This seems about right.

How to think about this aspect of Klein's work, the tendency to make reparation primarily an internal drama, in which objects destroy and repair each other according to their own script, one that only loosely glosses the real world?[10] I suggest we think about this aspect as Aquinas did about the German robbers, among whom according to Julius Caesar theft was considered good. When people don't know or observe natural law, says Aquinas, it is usually because "reason is perverted by passion, or evil habit, or an evil disposition of nature" (ST I–II, 94, 4, 6). Brought up to admire theft as noble self-assertion, the German robbers never learned any differently. Similarly, those who would make reparation for the native peoples they have destroyed by colonizing the new land with their own kind have never truly learned the difference between self and other, between reparation as mere feeling and reparation as an ethic that asks us to think about what we have done and to whom we have done it.

The result is immorality, but the failure is as much intellectual as moral. If, that is, we understand intellectual as Bion does, as a failure of thinking and linking. The reparative impulse is present. It requires education and cultivation so that it is directed toward the right people. Or, to paraphrase Aristotle (N. Ethics 1109a20–30) on virtue, it is easy to make reparation. What is difficult is to make the right amount of reparation to the right people in the right circumstances. Because it is difficult, doing so is a rare, fine and laudable achievement, one fostered by education in all its aspects, from good parents to a good society. If it is properly cultivated, we may say that the passion of reparation becomes a virtue – that is, a civilized human excellence.

A decent society, roughly like that characterized by Rustin in *The Good Society and the Inner World*, will direct reparation outward, toward the real victims of one's own and society's greed and aggression. To be sure, there is a distinction to be made here. Society's greed and aggression is not necessarily my own. Nevertheless, I live in this society, and share its benefits. Conversely,

I cannot always make reparation to the victims of my own aggression. Some have died, moved on, and so forth. It is the task of an ethical culture to direct our reparation toward those most deserving, some combination of those whom I have actually harmed and their symbolic stand-ins, the widow, the orphan, the afflicted, and the destitute (Psalms 82: 3–4; II Esdras 2: 20–22). This is the leading task of any ethical culture: to contain our fear while directing our reparation toward those most deserving. Such a culture makes it possible for us to think about what we are doing, and to act on this basis.

The novelist and philosopher Iris Murdoch (1998, 70) characterizes natural law morality as one in which "the individual is seen as held in a framework which transcends him." With the term "transcend" Murdoch refers not to a cosmological design, but a framework as big as the human world. Those familiar with the work of Donald Winnicott (1971) will know that one can read the term "held in a framework which transcends him" in a different way. For Winnicott, holding is the condition of transitional experience, as he calls it, in which we let ourselves belong to the experience. If we are securely held, we do not have to worry about falling out of the world, as Freud (1930, 68–73) once put it. We don't even have to think about it. We can just be. Mothers are generally the first ones to hold us, but holding isn't just for babies. Culture and the meanings it provides are leading ways adults are held. Culture would mean nothing if it were merely outside of me, an alien thing. But only crazy people live entirely in their own private cultures. Culture is what Winnicott calls a transitional object, me and not me at the same time.

Those narratives known as natural law should be judged not just by whether they are true or false (if we are truly being held, we do not always need to ask), but by whether they avoid crushing us with their rigidity, or dropping us in their vacuity. Jacques Maritain writes of our knowledge of the natural law as developing "within the double protecting tissue of human inclinations and human society" (Maritain 2001, 35–36). Though it is unlikely he ever read Winnicott, Maritain understands the way in which culture is not just second nature, but a second skin, woven together with our own. It is this that makes culture the transitional object *par excellence*.

Why is holding so important? Only if we are properly held can we think about what we are doing, and to whom we are doing it. This, as Wilfred Bion reveals, is key to making reparation moral. When I refer to Kleinian natural law, it is really Klein as developed and interpreted by Bion as a theorist of thinking that I have in mind.

Reparation and obligation

If one were to put Klein's teaching in the form of a natural law, it might read like this. "You ought to make reparation to those you have harmed in reality, as well as to their real-world stand-ins, the needy, the desperate, and the despised. You should not just paint a picture or write a poem about your feelings, though you may do that too."

If we are morally fortunate, which means morally well-educated, these two dimensions of reparation will reinforce each other. As you paint a beautiful picture of a naked negress, you may be reminded not only of your white relatives whom you have hated as well as loved, but of African-Americans and others whom many of us have used to hold alienated parts of ourselves. This is more likely when society and culture encourage us to think about what we are doing, rather than being organized around denial and projective identification, as societies and cultures usually are.

Why can't I just stay home and make reparation to my internal objects? Rustin has given part of the answer. As the self is inherently social and relational, so is reparation. The other, and more important, part of the answer is that doing so is a lie. Thinking means linking. Thinking means saying what we are doing, with some sense of the feeling and phantasy behind it, such as sadism, envy, love and hate. Thinking as linking is a developmental telos that is constantly endangered by all the enemies of good development, above all failed containment, what Winnicott calls holding. Containment begins with mother, and comes to include all of a decent society, from its art and literature to its police and welfare programs, to its retirement security. Containment is what keeps our natural paranoid-schizoid impulses from concluding that the world is out to destroy us. The adult version of containment is a combination of loving personal relationships and a decent social compact.

Hannah Arendt argues that Socrates' morality stemmed from his inability not to think about what he was doing. Indeed, this is how Arendt defines rationality: talking with oneself about what one is doing in a spirit serious enough that it might make a difference in what one does. Thinking for Arendt is similar to what Bion calls linking, making the connection between thoughts by becoming interlocutor to oneself. The two-in-one is how Arendt refers to this aspect of the self, divided but not split, the parts in constant contact. "The Socratic two-in-one heals the solitariness of thought," says Arendt (1978, pt 1, 187). Such a dialogue is not an alternative to friendship, but a part of it: friendship with oneself modeled on friendship with others, and vice versa.

> What Socrates discovered was that we can have intercourse with ourselves, as well as with others, and that the two kinds of intercourse are somehow related. Aristotle, speaking about friendship, remarked: "The friend is another self" – meaning that you can carry on the dialogue of thought with him just as well as with yourself. This is still in the Socratic tradition, except that Socrates would have said: The self, too, is a kind of friend.
>
> (Arendt 1978, pt 1, 188–189)

Arendt has her own agenda: to demonstrate that there is something in thinking itself that can prevent men from doing evil (Arendt 1978, pt 1, 180, 5).

Why? So thought can reclaim a little something of the great spirit of Enlightened Reason? That seems to be Arendt's motive. But while there is nothing in thought itself that can prevent evil, the combination of reparation and thought may be sufficient. Cultural containment is provision of the support necessary for reparation and thought to talk with each other, and with the world.

Still missing in such an account is any sense of obligation. Natural law is not just what we naturally want to do, including making reparation. Natural law is about what we should do, what we ought to do. How best to think about the obligation inherent in natural law? Imagine that Peter is the most important person in the world for Joan. You know this because she has told you this many times over lunch. Suddenly Peter dies, and Joan just goes on with her life, hardly pausing to go the funeral. You would have to say (unless you think Joan was lying) that Joan does not yet really know that Peter has died, and that it will take a while for the knowledge to sink in. When it does she will be devastated. Certain types of knowledge, it appears, are inseparable from our emotional response. Or rather, our emotional response *is* knowledge (Nussbaum 1990, 41).

One may say much the same thing about thinking about what one is doing. Truly thinking about what one is doing, thinking as linking, means that one feels not just the need to make reparation, not just the desire to make reparation, but the obligation to do so. One is obligated because the conjunction of thinking about what one is doing and reparation means that one cannot understand one's envy, hatred, and sadism (that is, the presence of the death instinct in so much of what one does) without feeling an overwhelming responsibility to make reparation. Experienced fully only in what Klein calls the depressive position, in which one knows how much one has hated as well as loved, reparation feels obligatory, the only conceivable response to such grave and dreadful passions directed not just at the world in general, but toward those we love and care for. That such grave and dreadful passions are merely human, all too human, may make them less grave and dreadful when we stand back from ourselves, seeing these same passions in others whom we believe to be basically good souls.

Experiencing these emotions in oneself, a version of thinking as linking, offers no such consolation, only the obligation of reparation. In a word, the experience of reparation is inseparable from the obligation to act. The problem, I have argued, is not that we experience reparation in the absence of obligation to act, but that this obligation may be turned inward and become art. This has its place, but a decent culture will constantly draw us back into the real world, even as it uses the artistic impulse to do so. Kleinian natural law quite rightly contains the word ought, as in "You ought to make reparation to those you have harmed in reality, and to those most deserving; you should not just retire to your room (or studio) in order to let your internal objects repair themselves. In other words, you ought to mend others, not just yourself. As a member of society, you are involved in the suffering of others."

Aren't you committing the "naturalistic fallacy" (the derivation of ought from is, jumping from statements of fact to conclusions about value), a thoughtful reader might ask. No. Sentences such as "you ought to make reparation to those you have harmed and to those most deserving" do not stand alone. They are what it means to experience the reparative impulse, an expression of human nature, while thinking about it in a culture of containment. Or as John Hittinger puts it following Maritain, "the political task, therefore, is 'essentially the task of civilization and culture' " (Hittinger 2002, 12). The political task is to create a regime of sufficient security and stability where a culture of containment might flourish.

Facts are discovered in nature; values are created by the human decision to observe them. This is the distinction the naturalistic fallacy asks us to remember. It is, however, only a logical distinction, not a metaphysical one. There is no reason to transform a piece of practical advice for clear thinking in many circumstances into a fundamental property of reality. What is a fundamental property of reality is that from the day of our birth we experience the world in terms of the values of good and bad: good is what soothes and satisfies, bad is what frustrates and agitates. It is the task of a decent culture to make sure that this original experience of natural value corresponds to our highest values. A decent culture fosters the ability to think about what one is doing, and so directs the reparative impulse toward those most deserving. Within a decent culture it makes perfect sense to say that the obligation to make reparation is a fact, not just a value. Or rather, there is no meaningful distinction to be made. Alasdair MacIntyre (2000) and John Searle (1969, 175–198) have made this argument at length, so there is no need to pursue it further here.

I believe that this is what Anthony Lisska (1996) means when he says that Aquinas' natural law ethics avoids the naturalistic fallacy because the developmental aspects of human nature already implant an ought within the is. We experience the world as a world of oughts from the beginning of life. Properly cultivated, the result is not the derivation of ought from is, but the education of this primordially ought-driven experience of the world so that it becomes more refined, more moral. I am making precisely the same argument about a Kleinian account of the natural law of reparation.

Thinking about what one is doing functions as the education in virtue that Aquinas tells us is necessary is we are to truly know and obey the natural law. Reparation, on the other hand, functions more like the grace of God that Aquinas writes about, leading us to love the natural law, and to want to follow it. (ST I–II, 105). Comparing Klein with Augustine would be less apt, even though it is tempting, both for what Augustine says about evil, as well as what he says about the frustrations of infancy. For Augustine, grace does not perfect nature, but replaces a fallen nature.

Kleinian natural law believes in nature, but does not fully trust it. Reparation, nature's gift of grace, becomes moral when it is fostered by a decent culture, one that encourages us to think about what we are doing, and to whom. Aquinas made a similar argument, explaining the existence of generations of German robbers, among whom theft was considered good, in terms of their bad fortune in never having been taught the natural law (ST I–II, 94, 4, 6). Kleinian natural law exists neither in a vacuum, nor in some abstract realm akin to Plato's forms. Natural law exists in each one of us, but it exists more precariously than Aquinas knew, more deeply and permanently threatened by the death instinct than any of the natural law theorists ever imagined.

Notes

1 It is only fair to note that two recent and influential works in natural law, that of John Finnis (1980) and that of Larry Arnhart (1998), fulfill neither of these conditions. Finnis argues from the givenness of natural goods (they are simply what people say they want); Arnhart from the adaptive functions of social cooperation. Neither brings nature and moral obligation onto the same page, which is why scholars such as Hittinger do not regard them as natural law theorists at all. Natural law, says Hittinger, is not just a list of what people, or even groups of people, say they want. Natural law is what people who have properly cultivated their lives know they have an obligation to do (Hittinger 2002, 12, 140).

2 Some contemporary natural law theorists, including Kai Nielsen (1988), would disagree with Maritain's insistence that natural law is known not just by reason reflecting upon nature, a standard definition, but by inclination, an almost ineffable knowledge. Maritain was a student of Henri Bergson (1935) and the concept of inclination seems to be a (valuable) holdover from the phenomenological tradition, which knows that knowledge isn't equivalent to reason.

3 It would be incorrect to suggest that Klein is not a theorist of thought. Klein first saw psychoanalysis as an account of failed thought and failed symbolism, both the result of the intense aggression associated with the desire to know, the epistemophilic impulse as Klein calls it (1975a). Bion developed what was begun in Klein.

4 In *What Evil Means to Us*, I define evil as pleasure in hurting and lack of remorse. Or rather, I report that this is how most subjects interviewed define evil. (Alford 1997). It is, however, the definition of evil expressed by Milton's Satan in *Paradise Lost*, which is employed in this chapter.

5 Klein (1975c, 189) does not give the source for her translation into modern English. Mine is Chaucer 1993, 536.

6 The two most famous applications of Kleinian thought to institutions, Isabel Menzies Lyth's (1992) study of student nurses, and Elliott Jaques (1975) study of Glacier Metal, attribute precisely this paranoid-schizoid defensive function to the institutions they studied. Which is why these institutions were so dysfunctional. They were organized to defend their members against making contact with emotional reality.

7 Toward the end of his life, Augustine became less interested in evil. His teachings on predestination have the effect of making even good will a gift of God. From this perspective, human evil is insignificant, no more than a gnat-bite, when measured against God's grace (Evans 1982, xi, 149). My concern is with Augustine's earlier, but post-Manichean, thinking about evil.

8 Kenneth Burke suggests that the band of boys who stole the pears "form a blasphemous counterpart to the fellowship of the Christian Church, in that the *gratuitousness* of the sin that binds them together is balanced and redeemed by Christ's gift of *grace* to all who accept the offer of salvation through H is blood" (Rudnytsky 1994, 138, author's emphasis; I am quoting Rudnytsky).

9 The passage is from an "acrimonious exchange" between Arendt and Gershom Scholem (Elshtain 1995, 76). Elshtain's account of Arendt's reliance on Augustine's concept of privation in explaining Eichmann's evil is helpful, and I draw upon it in this section.

10 Richard Wollheim (1984, 216–218) suggests that the tendency to confuse the impulse with the act is a flaw that seems inherent in any psychoanalytic account of ethics. If so, it is a tendency that may be corrected by awareness.

References

Classical citations given in the text in the form that is usual in classical studies are not repeated here. Aquinas' *Summa of Theology* is abbreviated as ST in the text.

Adorno, Theodor. 1983. *Prisms*, trans. Shierry Weber Nicholsen and Samuel Weber. Cambridge, Mass.: MIT Press (reprint edition).

Alford, C. Fred. 1989. *Melanie Klein and Critical Social Theory*. New Haven: Yale University Press.

—— 1997. *What Evil Means to Us*. Ithaca, NY: Cornell University Press.

Arendt, Hannah. 1965. *Eichmann in Jerusalem: A Report on the Banality of Evil*, revised and enlarged edition. New York: Viking Press.

—— 1973. *The Origins of Totalitarianism*, new edition with added prefaces. New York: Harvest Books.

—— 1978. *The Life of the Mind*. New York: Harcourt Brace (one-volume edition).

Arnhart, Larry. 1998. *Darwinian Natural Right: The Biological Ethics of Human Nature*. Albany: State University of New York Press.

Bergson, Henri. 1935. *The Two Sources of Religion and Morality*. New York: Holt.

Bion, Wilfred R. 1970. *Attention and Interpretation*. New York: Basic Books.

Bourke, Vernon, 1988. "Natural Law, Thomism – and Professor Nielsen," in *Saint Thomas Aquinas on Politics and Ethics*, ed. Paul Sigmund. New York: W.W. Norton.

Buckle, Stephen. 1991. "Natural Law," in *A Companion to Ethics*, ed. Peter Singer. Oxford: Blackwell.

Chasseguet-Smirgel, Janine. 1994. "Brief Reflections on the Disappearance in Nazi Racial Theory of the Capacity to Create Symbols," in *The Spectrum of Psycho-analysis*, ed. A.K. Richard and A. Richards. Madison, Conn.: International Universities Press.

Chaucer, Geoffrey. 1993. *The Canterbury Tales: A Complete Translation into Modern English*, trans. Ronald L. Ecker and Eugene J. Crook. Palatka, Fla.: Hodge and Braddock.

Elshtain, Jean Bethke. 1995. *Augustine and the Limits of Politics*. Notre Dame, Ind.: University of Notre Dame Press.

Evans, G.R. 1982. *Augustine on Evil*. Cambridge: Cambridge University Press.

Finnis, John. 1980. *Natural Law and Natural Rights*. Oxford: Clarendon Press.

Freud, Sigmund. 1889. "Screen Memories," in *The Standard Edition of the Complete*

Psychological Works of Sigmund Freud, ed. and trans. James Strachey *et al.*, 24 vols. London: Hogarth Press, 1953–1974, vol. 3: 303–332. (Hereafter cited as *The Standard Edition*.)

—— 1920. "Beyond the Pleasure Principle," in *The Standard Edition*, vol. 18: 3–66.

—— 1930. "Civilization and its Discontents," in *The Standard Edition*, vol. 21: 59–148.

Grotius, Hugo. 1964. *On the Law of War and Peace*. New York: Wiley and Sons (original *De Jure Belli ac Pacis*, 1625).

Hall, Pamela. 1994. *Narrative and the Natural Law: An Interpretation of Thomistic Ethics*. Notre Dame, Ind.: University of Notre Dame Press.

Hardy, Barbara. 1968. "Towards a Poetics of Fiction: An Approach through Narrative," in *Novel*, 2: 5–14.

Hinshelwood, R.D. 1989. *A Dictionary of Kleinian Thought*. London: Free Association Books.

Hittinger, John. 2002. *Liberty, Wisdom, and Grace: Thomism and Democratic Political Theory*. Lanham, Md.: Lexington Books.

Jaques, Elliott. 1975. "Social Systems as Defence Against Persecutory and Depressive Anxiety," in *New Directions in Psycho-Analysis*, ed. Melanie Klein, Paula Heimann and R.E. Money-Kyrle. London: Maresfield Library (reprint edition).

Klein, Melanie. 1964. "Love, Guilt and Reparation," in Melanie Klein and Joan Riviere. *Love, Hate and Reparation*, New York: W.W. Norton.

—— 1975a. "Early Stages of the Oedipus Conflict," in *Love, Guilt and Reparation and Other Works 1921–1945*, 186–198. New York: The Free Press (Volume 1 of *The Writings of Melanie Klein*).

—— 1975b. *Narrative of a Child Analysis*. New York: The Free Press (Volume 4 of *The Writings of Melanie Klein*).

—— 1975c. "Envy and Gratitude," in *Envy and Gratitude and Other Works 1946–1963*, 176–235. New York: The Free Press (Volume 3 of *The Writings of Melanie Klein*).

—— 1975d. "Mourning and its Relation to Manic-Depressive States," in *Love, Guilt and Reparation and Other Works 1921–1945*, 344–369. New York: The Free Press (Volume 1 of *The Writings of Melanie Klein*).

—— 1975e. "Infantile Anxiety-Situations Reflected in a Work of Art and in The Creative Impulse," in *Love, Guilt and Reparation and Other Works 1921–1945*, 210–218. New York: The Free Press (Volume 1 of *The Writings of Melanie Klein*).

—— 1975f. "The Importance of Symbol-Formation in the Development of the Ego," in *Love, Guilt and Reparation and Other Works 1921–1945*, 219–232. New York: The Free Press (Volume 1 of *The Writings of Melanie Klein*).

Kreeft, Peter. 1990. *A Summa of the Summa*. San Francisco: Ignatius Press.

Kristeva, Julia. 2001. *Melanie Klein*, trans. Ross Guberman. New York: Columbia University Press.

Lisska, Anthony. 1996. *Aquinas's Theory of Natural Law: An Analytical Reconstruction*. Oxford: Oxford University Press (reprint edition).

Lyth, Isabel Menzies. 1992. *Containing Anxiety in Institutions: Selected Essays*. London: Free Association Books.

MacIntyre, Alasdair. 1981. *After Virtue*. Notre Dame, Ind.: Notre Dame University Press.

—— 2000. "Theories of Natural Law in the Culture of Advanced Modernity," in

Common Truths: New Perspectives on Natural Law, ed. Edward McLean. Wilmington, Del.: ISI Books.

Marcuse, Herbert. 1978. *The Aesthetic Dimension: Toward a Critique of Marxist Aesthetics*. Boston: Beacon Press.

Maritain, Jacques. 2001. *Natural Law: Reflections on Theory and Practice*, ed. William Sweet. South Bend, Ind.: St. Augustine's Press.

Meltzer, Donald. 1978. *The Kleinian Development*. Strath Tay, Perthshire: Clunie Press (3 parts in 1 volume).

—— 1981. "The Kleinian Expansion of Freud's Metapsychology," in *International Journal of Psycho-Analysis*, 62: 177–184.

Murdoch, Iris. 1998. "Metaphysics and Ethics," in *Existentialists and Mystics: Writings on Philosophy and Literature*, ed. Peter Conradi. New York: Penguin Books.

Nielsen, Kai. 1988. "An Examination of the Thomistic Theory of Natural Law," in *Saint Thomas Aquinas on Politics and Ethics*, ed. Paul Sigmund. New York: W.W. Norton.

Nussbaum, Martha. 1990. *Love's Knowledge: Essays on Philosophy and Literature*. Oxford: Oxford University Press.

Pagels, Elaine. 1995. *The Origin of Satan*. New York: Random House.

Prince, Gerald. 1987. *Dictionary of Narratology*. Lincoln: University of Nebraska Press.

Rieff, Philip. 1961. *Freud: The Mind of the Moralist*. New York: Harper & Row.

Rudnytsky, Peter. 1988. " 'Here Only Weak': Sexuality and the Structure of Trauma in *Paradise Lost*," in *The Persistence of Myth: Psychoanalytic and Structuralist Perspectives*, ed. Peter Rudnytsky. New York: Guilford Press.

—— 1994. "Freud and Augustine," in *Freud and Forbidden Knowledge*, ed. Peter Rudnytsky and Ellen Handler Spitz. New York: New York University Press.

Rustin, Michael. 1991. *The Good Society and the Inner World: Psychoanalysis, Politics and Culture*. London: Verso.

Sartre, Jean-Paul. 1964. *Nausea*, trans. Lloyd Alexander. New York: New Directions.

Searle, John. 1969. *Speech Acts: An Essay in the Philosophy of Language*. Cambridge: Cambridge University Press.

Segal, Hanna. 1955. "A Psycho-Analytical Approach to Aesthetics," in *New Directions in Psycho-Analysis*, ed. Melanie Klein, Paula Heimann and R.E. Money-Kyrle. London: Maresfield Library (reprint edition).

Steuerman, Emilia. 2000. *The Bounds of Reason: Habermas, Lyotard and Melanie Klein on Rationality*. London and New York: Routledge.

Winnicott, D.W. 1971. "The Location of Cultural Experience," in *Playing and Reality*. London and New York: Routledge.

—— 1978. "Hate in the Counter-Transference," in *Through Paediatrics to Psycho-Analysis*. London: Hogarth Press.

Wollheim, Richard. 1984. *The Thread of Life*. Cambridge, Mass.: Harvard University Press.

Index